Praise for

TWELVE TREES

"A modest title for an extraordinary book, *Twelve Trees* reexamines the arboreal world from roots to canopy and makes you see trees as you've never seen them before. Taking twelve species (in reality many more), Daniel Lewis exults in their sheer individuality and majesty and tells their tenacious stories with passion, humor, and deep understanding. Despite real ecological threats, there's optimism in his account—all trees are good and with care and conservation, they're bound to succeed!"

—2024 Banff Centre Mountain Book Competition,
Special Jury Mention

"Enchanting . . . The plentiful trivia fascinates, and Lewis has a talent for complicating conventional wisdom. . . . The result is a loving paean to all things arboreal."

—*Publishers Weekly*

"The environmental historian offers vivid portraits of 12 trees from around the world—including ebony, olive, and sandalwood—scoping out the threats they face and the extraordinary ways they are able to adapt."

—*The Guardian*, "The Books to Look Out for in 2024"

"This engaging heart-and-mind approach to educating readers about trees reveals that they too have lessons to offer to the world. . . . Lewis exhorts readers to try to see the world from a tree's perspective and to practice empathy. Nyquist's exquisite illustrations complement and enhance the book's gorgeous world."

—*Library Journal* (starred review)

"Daniel Lewis, author of *The Feathery Tribe*, could not have chosen a group of trees more biologically and culturally fascinating than this variously endangered dozen. . . . He offers a meticulous survey of these species, as well as their personal histories and importance. . . . He deals with the complexities of conservation efforts (and resistance to them) with an even hand, and the book is as rigorous as it is readable. . . . A well-informed, staunch defense of trees' capacity to multiply biodiversity and support life on Earth."

—*Kirkus Reviews*

"This captivating exploration of nature and survival through the lens of twelve remarkable tree species takes readers on a global journey, delving into the science, history, and cultural significance of each tree. From the majestic redwoods of California to the ancient bristlecone pines of the Great Basin, engaging prose and thorough research show the vital role trees play in our world and the urgent need to protect them. A compelling and enlightening read for anyone passionate about nature and conservation."

—*Arlington Magazine*

"*Twelve Trees* is a remarkable adventure that takes us from the heights of the redwood canopy to the craters of Easter Island and the depths of the Congo Basin, using cutting-edge science and personal stories to explain the ways these incredible trees shape our world."

—Eric Rutkow, author of *American Canopy*

"Daniel Lewis channels the wisdom of twelve of the planet's most eloquent teachers—the oldest, the tallest, and even the extinct—to share their deep-time lessons with us. With the precision of a scientist, the skill of a historian, and the voice of a poet, Lewis speaks for the trees. If we listen, we will grow to love these twelve trees deeply, and come to recognize how closely our own lives and fates are linked to theirs."

—Melanie Choukas-Bradley, author of *City of Trees* and *A Year in Rock Creek Park*

ALSO BY DANIEL LEWIS

*Belonging on an Island: Birds, Extinction,
and Evolution in Hawai'i*

*The Feathery Tribe: Robert Ridgway and
the Modern Study of Birds*

TWELVE TREES

The Deep Roots of Our Future

DANIEL LEWIS

Avid Reader Press

NEW YORK   AMSTERDAM/ANTWERP   LONDON
TORONTO   SYDNEY   NEW DELHI

Avid Reader Press

An Imprint of Simon & Schuster, LLC

1230 Avenue of the Americas

New York, NY 10020

First Avid Reader Press trade paperback edition March 2025

AVID READER PRESS and colophon are trademarks of Simon & Schuster, LLC

For information about special discounts for bulk purchases, please contact Simon & Schuster Special Sales at 1-866-506-1949 or business@simonandschuster.com.

The Simon & Schuster Speakers Bureau can bring authors to your live event. For more information or to book an event, contact the Simon & Schuster Speakers Bureau at 1-866-248-3049 or visit our website at www.simonspeakers.com.

Illustrations by Eric Nyquist

Manufactured in the United States of America

1   3   5   7   9   10   8   6   4   2

Library of Congress Cataloging-in-Publication Data

Names: Lewis, Daniel, 1959– author.
Title: Twelve trees : the deep roots of our future / Daniel Lewis.
Identifiers: LCCN 2023040314 (print) | LCCN 2023040315 (ebook) | ISBN 9781982164058 (hardcover) | ISBN 9781982164065 (paperback) | ISBN 9781982164072 (ebook)
Subjects: LCSH: Trees—Climatic factors. | Trees—Ecophysiology. | BISAC: NATURE / Plants / Trees | NATURE / Ecosystems & Habitats / Forests & Rainforests
Classification: LCC SD395.L49 2024 (print) | LCC SD395 (ebook) | DDC 582.16—dc23/eng/20231108
LC record available at https://lccn.loc.gov/2023040314
LC ebook record available at https://lccn.loc.gov/2023040315

ISBN 978-1-9821-6405-8
ISBN 978-1-9821-6406-5 (pbk)
ISBN 978-1-9821-6407-2 (ebook)

For Pam

My rooting force

My pocketful of joy

My dazzling, gathering light

CONTENTS

PREFACE

A few years ago in Melbourne, Australia, nearly half of the city's seventy-seven thousand trees were struggling, plagued by drought and other difficulties. City planners mapped all of the trees, gave them individual IDs, and assigned email addresses to each tree so citizens could report problems. This plan was a practical attempt designed to rehabilitate an urban forest. But along with reporting problems, people wrote thousands of love letters—treemail—to their favorites. One fan wrote to an elm, "As I was leaving St. Mary's College today I was struck, not by a branch, but by your radiant beauty. You must get these messages all the time. You're such an attractive tree." Other responses by the thousands ranged from bad tree jokes to love letters to expressions of concern—not only from Melburnians but from all over the world, often from expats who once lived in the city, or people who'd never visited. A New Yorker wrote to say, "You are loved and deserve the world." People asked for advice. "I write about a friend of mine . . . someone who has reached an intersection in life. To the outside world he has control, but within it can feel like a labyrinth with too many possible pathways, all without much clarity or light. How can I help him during this time of decision and indecision?"

Every tree has a life, both individually and as part of a collective. I've chosen twelve trees that have been on long journeys, have many accomplices as well as enemies, and need our help to survive. They are our instructions, our instruments, and our futures. I've picked these trees in the ways that people find friends. In significant ways, they have found me. Some were flashy and omnipresent. A few arrived quietly in unexpected corners of my life, and some were introduced by others—but all started as relative strangers and became comrades. Each has crucial stories to tell.

Trees continue to populate our daily lives. They've been part of our sight lines and metaphors, our byways, our contexts. We all know them in one way or another, as consumers and users of their wood and by-products, or through closer associations with individual trees. We all know trees that grew up with us as children. Trees in parking lots, bristling with tiny unseen life, or ones that we witnessed falling, or helped to fell. Trees we hid under for shelter in the rain, or in baking heat. Trees whose smells and sounds and sights trigger deep memories. Trees that sat outside our houses and marked the seasons, losing foliage and growing back, or extending a limb to the windowsill so we could risk climbing down, to a wider, freer world.

Trees are symbionts, working in conjunction with an army of other organisms that build biodiversity and buttress life on the planet. They are ecosystems that sustain life in and among their roots, trunks, branches, and crowns. Forests also regulate our food security, feeding the planet through a profusion of fruits, vegetables, nuts, spices, and other edibles, as well as our medical needs. Trees provide urban identity, splendor, cooling, and coherence. They need to have their own rights, and be accorded their own dignity. They are essential to all of our lives, and they need our help. The salvation of trees can be the salvation of humans.

The Quran has its Tree of Immortality. Besides people and God, trees are the living beings most frequently mentioned in the Bible. Buddhism has dozens of words for trees. They are everywhere in the close and far corners of the world's languages. We borrow their metaphors (we go out on a limb; we knock on wood; we can't see the forest for the trees; we branch out; we find root causes; we're stumped; and we leaf through books). Every language has its tree idioms. The Japanese say, "Even monkeys fall from trees"; that is, everyone makes mistakes. In Germany, when someone says something embarrassing and no one dares to respond, they say, "There is silence in the forest." We have written about, scrutinized, illustrated, photographed, climbed, contemplated, and cared a great deal about trees for a very long time. They serve as sentinels to our lives, deaths, and rebirths. They live in deep literary contexts, their roots everywhere. The poet Wendell Berry described his writing house, built up on wooden posts, as having "a peering, aerial look, as though built under the influence of trees."[2]

The sheer ubiquity of arboreal names also speaks to our cultural desire to signify their importance and to impart some essence of the tranquility and stability inherent in trees. Of the twenty most common street names in the United States, five are trees: Oak, Pine, Maple, Cedar, and Elm. We record them like scribes copying manuscripts, over and over again: holiday cards and directions and job applications and passwords. Larch and birch and oak and arbor. In my adopted state of California, the word "wood" shows up on the signs of fourteen thousand different streets. They are the nomenclatural currency of our lives, these tree words, and we find our way home through them.

Trees are also our custodians, forecasters, and predictors in an era of changing climates. They protect the ground beneath us through their stabilizing and biodiversifying effects. They lower our pulses and deepen our breath. These twelve species of trees are powerful actors on our environment. In their total biomass they provide nearly bottomless carbon sinks, annually sequestering millions of tons of carbon dioxide—a greenhouse gas that would otherwise remain in the atmosphere or leach into the Earth's oceans, heating the planet more rapidly. Their work with CO_2 is also easy to misunderstand: although it's often spoken of as a global evil, trees need it to live. Trees don't just house CO_2; they *use* it as they take it in, appropriate it for photosynthesis, and produce oxygen.

These twelve trees have an army of assistance from other species of trees, too. Some three trillion trees grow on the planet, about four hundred for each of us. Despite their declines, forests still occupy more than 30 percent of Earth's dry land. Around the world, trees absorb approximately 7.6 billion metric tons of carbon and sequester it in their leaves, stems, roots, and other parts for long stretches. But young trees don't do this very well, or at all, depending on the species of tree. To sequester a lot of carbon, trees have to live long and healthy lives: at a minimum, ten to twenty years. It takes that long for sufficient foliage to grow into a sizeable reservoir for carbon. And the longer a tree lives, the more carbon it sequesters, as a promise for the future: trees get bigger as they grow, so every year they sequester a bit more carbon than the year before.

The planet's three trillion trees constitute around seventy-five thousand species.[3] The great diversity among trees speaks to the diversity of life on Earth, and not just biological diversity but the cultural and social diversity they foster. Out of some, many and much. Our intersections with these twelve trees' lives are far more interesting—and more complicated—than people would ever expect. In the course of understanding their role in our futures, I hope you'll gain a fuller understanding of not just these specific trees, but the *classes* of trees in which they're contained: their cousins and aunts and uncles, as it were; the species with which they share a genus or a family or are otherwise allied, through genetics or morphology or destiny.

The ways their characteristics converge or diverge also tell us something significant about the tumbling, messy nature of evolution, including strategies to survive. Evolution has consequences: every tree came from an earlier plant form. To study the science of trees is thus also to study not just the present. It's a story of the world and its past, a biohistorical novel. Landscapes from deep time can be restored from pollen data; tree rings can tell us about weather and water and climate from both recent and ancient eras; fossil trees can tell us about the long arc of evolution; and all of this information points to the future.

Across all of these lessons, dangers lurk. Without trees, we would be stripped of a key layer of living tissue, on our way to being Mars or Venus. There are only half as many trees as there were at the dawn of agriculture twelve thousand years ago. Forests burn at the rate of twenty-two thousand square feet a minute in the Amazon; in Central Africa, ten million acres a year disappear. We're the sharpest predators on the planet, and we have done damage. Trees are at risk from many threats: insect and fungal infestations driven by a warming planet have brought down billions of individual trees, airborne poisons drift into forests, and tides are rising while freshwater tables are dropping. The story of decline is voluminous and complex.

The popular press frequently presents climate change as a monolithic threat, but the science is full of entanglements, time frames, geographies, and contradictions. Almost none of these trees overlap in their ranges—and because every species has different talents, and climate change varies greatly across regions, each of these dozen trees has a different relationship with our planet's warming and changing weather. Climate change is a part of our past, and our present, and, certainly, our human future, and its urgency has been reinforced countless times in recent years from intersecting disciplines. As the climate scientist Richard Alley noted, the more stately and older view was that climate change moved slowly, like a dial; in today's reckoning, it's a switch, almost instantaneous in its effects, especially against the background of deeper time.

Time changes everything, and it's a partner for all of these trees. Their time frames are largely rendered as a vast evolutionary sweep across the face of the planet's clock. But eons are made up of days and nights—infinitesimal slices of time in the larger march of life, and trees matter on tiny timescales, too. My father—a quiet man, stormy, unhappy, and dogged—spent some of his most satisfying moments on the sprawling grounds of our house, which stood on a cliff overlooking the Pacific Ocean in Hawai'i, where he planted ironwood saplings he hoped would grow large enough to stanch the constant erosion of our property into the sea eighty feet below. Many are still there, risen huge. One of my strongest childhood memories was of a tree I helped to remove—a large pandanus in our yard, with tall prop roots that emerged out of the ground, so the tree was on stilts. It was hot, sweaty work, but my dad offered to buy me anything I wanted (within reason) if I helped with the job. It took weeks. He had never offered up this kind of prize, so I was committed to the task. I was eleven or twelve, and I had been pining for a crossbow, and true to his word, my dad ordered one for me that soon arrived at our doorstep. I was thrilled, and then proceeded to fire this weapon high into the trunks of gigantic banyan trees on neighboring properties. The arrows are still there, a half century later. Humans are the tip of the arrow. We have paved the way to decline. Now it's our chance to pioneer a path to rejuvenation.

TWELVE TREES

CHAPTER 1

A Book Older Than God: The Great Basin Bristlecone Pine

"The tree is a slow, enduring force straining to win the sky."
—Antoine de Saint-Exupéry, *The Wisdom of the Sands*

The Great Basin bristlecone pine is not especially imposing in its height, greenery, or bulk. The tallest known individual is just fifty-two feet high, much shorter than many other mature tree species. It produces no oil, no fruits, no usable wood or other products humans covet or monetize. It needs little water. It's a twisted refugee, growing only at high altitude in cold, windy, and often icy conditions, and in poor soil. But the bristlecone is a beautiful survivor, and its most ancient individuals, the oldest of all trees, are full of instructions and fascinations.

No one knows how old the oldest bristlecone pine might be. One tree clocks in at more than five thousand years—fifty centuries, validated by careful counting of the rings on cores extracted from the living tree. There may well be older individuals. The bristlecone pine's longevity is baked into its scientific name: *Pinus longaeva*. Even its leaves can remain green for nearly a half century before dying. It serves as a crucial witness to the extended arc of the past. Many trees are like old books: they mark the passage of our years, including epochs of turbulence and calm. We can find evidence of these changes in numerous ways, but one key technique to understand their lives, and the planet's lives, year over year, is to study those annual rings. The seasons' variations in temperatures between winter and spring show up in the tree's wood: colder weather means slower growth, and warmer means faster development. When a tree begins this rapid growth, it lays down what is known as earlywood, a pale band in its annual rings. As summer slides into fall, wood growth slows and leaves a darker annual ring called latewood. These and other changes in color and cell density mean tree rings are usually highly visible, and thus countable.

The innards of bristlecone pines, in the form of these growth rings, describe a regular turn from the start of the tree's story to the present. They tell us not just about their lives but about the life around them. These trees record details to be deciphered by those with eyes and tools to see: changes in wind, weather, precipitation, and temperature, studied by attentive scientists who have the background to make sense of minute and subtle distinctions. There is inference, evidence, speculation, speciation—all visible in the rings of the trees, pages in life's book.

I work with a fellow rare book curator at the Huntington named Steve Tabor, whom I admire. He's thin, with a white mustache. He likes birds, and bicycles. Tabor is an authority on early printed books who, with no artifice or arrogance, will drop an obscure Latin phrase into a conversation or an email. He is utterly unselfconscious, often with his foot up on his desk through his open door, stretching. A book scientist, Tabor is deeply involved in the minute changes shown by paper, type, ink, and binding: forensic analysis of the fluctuating ways we've produced knowledge over the last five hundred years. He pointed out to me that the Latin word *liber*—the old common term for a book—means the inner bark or rind of a tree. He also explained a number of the deeper etymological ties between books and trees. The Germanic word for "book" and its cognates derive from the Indo-European word for "beech tree." The etymology and physical presence of books is saturated with trees, and with the ghosts of trees and their remains.[1]

The book world offers still other cognates. Paper, bindings, sewing, and leather are all part of the stream of testimony. In the same way that dendrochronologists—scientists who study the rings of trees—can tease out evidence you'd not anticipate, the same applies to old books, where papermakers crafted their products from remnants of cotton clothing, and printers and bookbinders created and assembled their products by hand. Old books are simply teeming with evidence if you have the right context and experience, and this applies to tree rings as well as to old books.

Occasionally, in looking at pages in an antiquarian book, you'll see a small, splattery dot, as if something wet had once landed on the page. Hundreds of years ago, artisans made paper by macerating cotton rags into a watery slurry, and then dipping a mold made of closely spaced wires into the pulpy mix, and draining out the liquid. But what causes that dot? They're common enough that these splashy marks have a name: vatman's tears. A vatman was the person responsible for dipping the mold into the heated slurry of water and pulped cotton rags. It was hot work, and the splash mark most likely came from a wet arm or sleeve, or possibly a bead or two of sweat from the vatman's forehead.

So paper is not just paper. It tells stories. And trees are not just trees, because their lives are marked by events that occur in the strata of formation. Some of this evidence about the past comes from immediate moments, such as a lightning strike. Other marks stem from longer intervals: a beetle boring through a layer of cambium, an ancient piece of barbed wire from a long-gone fence, or an old bullet buried in an even older tree. But more ubiquitously, trees reveal past details about matters of global interest and significance: changes in the climate; in the constitution of the air, water, and soil; and other

environmental variations. Climate hovers in and around the tree, literally and metaphorically, because the changing climate and its effects
on all lives on the planet is the existential issue of our time.

If a giant standing in the center of what is now California had
cupped some seeds of bristlecone pines in his hands and flung them
messily eastward, dropping a few and tossing the rest, you'd have
the approximate distribution of the bristlecone pine. Its distribution spills across a strap of higher-elevation land that reaches from
eastern California across Nevada and into Utah. The tree grows
very slowly, sometimes increasing its diameter a mere inch over
a century. It doesn't like shade, and tends to grow fairly widely
spaced, and only at high altitudes, typically above fifty-five hundred feet. This distribution reduces competition with other plants.
The extreme environment also slackens other predators' activities.
Wood-rotting fungi have a difficult time getting purchase in the
cold, dry, and windy climate. The tree lives in challenging soil, too:
rocky dolomitic and limestone-based ground, all of which keeps life
inching along.

Just as photographs of Charles Darwin invariably show the old,
infirm naturalist with his big white beard, though he was once a young
man, so too does the bristlecone pine appear in the public imagination
as an oldster, which of course it can become. But it starts as a sapling,
then fills out, adding many branches and cones. The tree's height is
limited by moisture stresses at its top; it can pump water up only so
high. And the taller it gets, the more exposed it is to drying winds.
Some old pines on windy summits are shaped into spectacular posi-
tions by relentless winds, which sometimes turn a branch so that it's
pointing toward the ground rather than skyward. In a few locales in
the tree's range, such as on Mount Washington in Nevada, you'll even
sometimes see trees so forced into position that they've been subdued
into a dense mat of growth close to the ground and unrecognizable
as a tree. The term for this type of vegetation is *krummholz*, from the

German "crooked wood."[2] The tree's capacity to twist into gnarled forms in response to environmental forces has meant that humans can't use it for lumber, or for much else. Nevertheless, it retains a right to live, and to succeed.

While humans don't scavenge the tree, other creatures do. Porcupines girdle the bristlecone by eating the bark, which can kill the tree. Bark beetles can cause extensive damage beneath the tree's outer layers. Lightning strikes on high mountain ridges can burn down a tree, or severely damage it; and the endless freeze-thaw cycles crack limbs and roots. The effects of age and brutal conditions on the bristlecone make it breathtakingly, sculpturally beautiful. At the same time, the oldest individuals look like hell, having taken an intense beating from the elements—the only conditions where they're adapted to live. But we have convincing evidence that the trees don't lapse into senescence. Their difficulties stem from the circumstances in which they grow, but not from any inherent biological decline. Old trees form and grow buds with the same vigor as much younger trees, and they make functional cells for thousands of years. Researchers believe that the tree has no upper age limit. Under the right conditions, a bristlecone could survive indefinitely.

But bristlecone pines have been manifesting strange behavior in recent decades. They have started to grow more quickly, especially at higher elevation. Scientists have discovered that the trees' growth has been greater in the past half century than at any other time in the paleobotanical record. Tree specialists studied, and then rejected, a number of possible reasons: that they had been fertilized by the greater quantity of carbon dioxide in the atmosphere; that we've somehow changed the ways we've counted tree rings as we've worked to refine and standardize our counting techniques; that their freakishly asymmetric, noncircular nature has messed with the count of rings; and so on. Curiously, these fast-growing trees occur within a relatively narrow range, almost all within about 150 meters of the upper tree line. Scientists finally determined that their rapid growth is related to high temperatures at higher elevations.[3]

It's now incontrovertible: global warming is a particular danger to the bristlecone pine. Higher temperatures mean that photosynthesis, the chemical process by which green plants convert sunlight into nutritious sugars, occurs more rapidly. The tree then undergoes respiration, using those sugars to produce energy for plant growth. But the bristlecone is a tree that has evolved to conserve resources, not use them up rapidly. If the tree had a motto, it would be "Not so fast." But growing quicker and bigger doesn't begin to cause problems until a frost occurs in late spring or early fall, destroying a tree's tender tissues at their most vulnerable stages. Warmer temperatures also mess with a tree's sexual reproduction, lowering its ability to form newer seeds. Higher temperatures also lower the presence of moisture in the ground. Water-stressed trees have fewer defenses, providing an opening for fungal invasions. And snowmelt is less present with higher heat, disrupting the tree's strategy of absorbing snowmelt over many weeks or months.

The list of recent climate-related woes continues in a cascade. Bark beetles have been a well-known threat to the bristlecone for a long time. Normally, it takes two harsh winters for a new generation to emerge, because the beetles are slowed by the cold. But warming has shortened this gestation period to a single year, so more beetles are produced, and more survive. One attack leads to another, and then another, for the trees cannot evolve fast enough to defend against a rapidly heating planet.

Modern tools and techniques aid our understanding of individual trees' responses to climate change. Researchers are attaching data loggers to individual trees to track temperatures. These tools can record micrometeorological details not available with older, less precise devices. We can now quantify how cold air can pool in particular divots in the earth; how hyperlocal wind patterns can affect temperature and humidity; and how water from snowmelt can flow in variable routes down the sides of mountains, providing some trees with ample hydration while leaving others high and dry. This fine tree-by-tree analysis wasn't possible until dendrochronologists started to make use of geospatial data and miniaturized technology. People studying ancient trees are very concerned about present conditions. Their work connects the dots from deep time up to the present, and extrapolates a future for trees.

The precision these tools provide is matched by the complexities of the tree and its workings. Scraping at the simple uncovers the intricate. Take the pine needle. It's a slender green pin. But it's not homogenous, for a pine needle is akin to a skyscraper, bustling with movement and life. It has a rigid outer skin, the metaphorical equivalent of the outside cladding of a building. This outer layer is marked by many microscopic holes, called stomata. These holes, analogous to windows in a building, provide access to air. Within the column of the skyscraper are hundreds of flat plates, akin to the floors of a building, which consist of chlorophyll-bearing cells. There is also plumbing in the pine needle: vascular bundles and resin canals that move fluids. The vascular bundles move water into the leaves, and also conduct the sugars formed by photosynthesis back down to the tree's larger parts.[4] So it is with all trees: Push the lens in closer, and various forms of biochemical joinery come into view. Lean back for a wider look, and other events swim into focus: the sway and density and variegation of color from cone to cone, from tree to tree, the whole forest standing against an uncertain future.

The most necessary of the tree's partners is the Clark's nutcracker (*Nucifraga columbiana*). The nutcracker is a light-gray, crow-shaped bird renowned for its campground-scrounging ways. It can recall thousands of caches it's placed in trees, including the bristlecone pine. Individual birds cache more than thirty thousand seeds and can relocate them up to nine months later. And the birds can locate nuts not only within the vertical confines of a tree, but also under the snow.

Biologists and animal behaviorists started studying this phenomenon in the late 1970s. After much speculation, and then experimen-
tation, to resolve just how the birds knew the myriad seed locations,
they eliminated various possibilities: it wasn't done by watching other
birds; it wasn't done by smell. It didn't involve them visually identifying unique features about the specific locations where seeds were
cached. Nor did the task involve random searching. It was all about
spatial memory, in the face of enormous, redundant seed production.

As with sea turtle eggs, or tadpoles, or octopi babies, or the offspring of African driver ants (three to four million eggs every month
or so), nature often runs on redundant systems. The mortality rate
for bristlecone pine seedlings is close to 99 percent because new trees
have a tough time in the extraordinarily harsh, windy, high-elevation
environments. But having many offspring means even a tiny percentage of survivors can keep a species alive, and the cached seeds, protected from the elements, keep the tree's reproductive futures intact.[5]

A single Clark's nutcracker can bury its hoard of seeds in up to
five thousand different locations that sprawl across a territory that
can range from dozens to hundreds of square miles. Small wonder
it forgets a few.[6] Known as scatter-hoarding to ornithologists, this
caching strategy involves the nutcracker gathering up thousands of
seeds, usually during the warmer summer months while the trees are
germinating, and carting them away in a pouch under its tongue. This
pouch can hold somewhere between 50 and 150 seeds, depending on
the size of the bird. Although the seeds are not the birds' offspring in
the usual sense, the strategy is the same: overreaching in their hiding
tactics to avoid predation by other opportunists such as squirrels or
other birds. The tree's wingless seeds, unable to be borne along by
the wind like those of many other pines, are evidence that the tree and
the bird probably coevolved: the tree benefiting from the nutcracker's
distribution strategy, and the bird benefiting from the enormous
nutritional bounty of the tree's seeds.

This caching process also helps to increase the tree's genetic variety: a key hedge against the difficult-to-predict effects of complex climate change. Every seedling is a unique genotype, and the more genotypes, the more potential variability exists. As the birds make their choices, they unknowingly shape the genetic diversity of the pines they scatter along the Rockies and across the ranges of the Great Basin.[7] Rapid diversification in nature can frustrate taxonomists, because it makes tidy categorizing of species difficult. Populations of trees evolve into new species, and in the case of the bristlecone, a chain of varying populations has confused taxonomists and foresters for a century. But move a tree's seeds around a lot, and they grow in varying conditions that exert a variety of differing influences on the tree's evolution, as it adapts to a variety of microclimates, subtly or dramatically varying soil, and much else. And while the bird shapes the tree's future, the bristlecone's environment might also somehow shape the nutcracker's caching ability, for recent studies have shown that there's a correlation between harsher environments and birds' better spatial ability to cache food.[8]

And just as birds hold deep memories, so do trees. The study of tree rings lets scientists dip deep into the past to make inferences, and reach conclusions, about deeper time, and much else. To understand the study of tree rings better, I spent a couple of days at the world's first, and still the leading, facility for the study of tree rings, the Laboratory of Tree-Ring Research (LTRR) in Tucson, Arizona. Andrew Douglass, the originator of the science of tree-ring research, founded the laboratory in 1937. An astronomer by training, Douglass had come to the desert for the clear skies and good seeing, and then developed a hypothesis that tree rings could trace past solar activity, based on the sun's potential influence on rainfall. He began collecting hundreds of tree-ring samples to build a time series to study these aspects of astronomy, and the study of tree rings in Arizona began. The LTRR has grown into a purpose-built thirty-five-thousand-square-foot multistory spectacle of a building, constructed in 2012, that engages in research programs in dendrochronology. With some fifteen faculty scientists and another fifty staffers, the LTRR is the largest of more than a hundred data-producing tree-ring laboratories around the world. The lab's work includes investigations into climate, fire history and ecology, paleoecology, multiproxy paleoclimatology, archaeology, biogeography, isotope geochemistry, biogeochemistry, geomorphology, numerical and statistical modeling, human societies and their interactions, carbon cycles, and even public health. David Frank, the director of the lab, took me through the enormous space and gave me full access to his scientific staff. I could see the draw of the work. The tangibility of wood is thrilling. You can touch it, smell it, hoist it up.[9]

David noted that in his dendrochronological interactions with thousands of people over the years, people tend to be receptive to the interdisciplinary aspects of the field. However, climate change deniers and people suspicious of science provide challenges. The LTRR communicates volumes of information related to climate change, and beyond the science, it can be a very volatile, emotional, and politicized topic. "We find that the tree rings' data is actually very good at avoiding that whole dimension of dialogue," David noted. Talking audiences through the copious forms of evidence provided by the innards of trees, and detailing the effort involved, has proved to be an important form of education. If there's common ground across human audiences, it's the truth of physical work. We all have bodies, we all understand labor, making a living, getting work done, seeing for ourselves.

In 1964 Don Currey, a grad student at the University of North Carolina, killed what turned out to be the oldest tree discovered until then: a Great Basin bristlecone pine, known today as Prometheus—the figure from Greek mythology who stole fire from the gods and gave it to man. Currey had been on a quest to date and analyze the bristlecone pines in eastern Nevada for his studies, and the first tree he came upon when he reached Wheeler Peak in the White Pine mountains was Prometheus. The story is often told in stark tones: Currey cut down the tree to better count its rings, understanding that it was an old specimen, but not knowing just how old. A 1968 article in *Audubon* magazine called him a "murderer." But he apparently tried to take a sample from the tree's core first, and he did get the Forest Service's permission, and, probably, their help in cutting the tree down. The mistake also helped lead to the establishment of the Great Basin National Park, which provides legal protections to more than seventy-seven thousand acres in Nevada. The remnants of Prometheus ended up at the LTRR, and sections of the tree have had a long, rich research life there over more than a half century, revealing far more details than if it had remained standing. It would be nearly another half century before researchers found a bristlecone pine tree older than Prometheus, a feat accomplished by the LTRR researcher Tom Harlan in 2012, who used a tool called an increment borer to take a sample and determined that tree to be 5,062 years old.

Although it's lost its place as the oldest tree known, the Currey tree still carries emotional and physical freight. I'm struck by the huge remnant laid out in front of us on a workbench. It has been polished, cleaned, a mirror of the past. The remaining pieces show why cutting down a tree is so much more useful than trying to core it. You can look at its entire life history, count its rings with unmatched precision, and examine its cellular structure in extravagant detail. It's like looking out over a landscape versus squinting through a periscope or peephole. Sitting under the workbench in a box are numerous other polished sections of the same tree, some with complex measurements marked on their surfaces. No part of the animal has gone unused.

I've always been a counter. As a kid, I had a pogo stick, and would spend a solid six or seven or more hours in my driveway trying to break the world record for nonstop pogo stick jumping. I would time myself emptying the dishwasher, trying to break my own personal best, day after day. There was something about the steady accumulation of numbers through counting that helped me make sense of a chaotic world, and I find comradeship with these tree-ring talliers.

A full slab of tree is a counter's delight. You can see it all: fire scars on different sides of the tree, insect damage, irregularities, changes in color and density radiating out from the tiny dot that marks its beginning. Polishing the slab clarifies the view of the rings, and provides better access to microscopic details, such as the cellular structure of the wood.

In contrast to cutting down a tree and creating a slab, coring a tree to count its rings and examine its wood allows the tree to survive, and reveals a lot about living trees. Coring a tree is both science and art. As long as the tree is big enough in diameter, coring doesn't kill it because the process doesn't remove enough living tissue to hinder the tree's ability to absorb water, photosynthesize light into fuel, and continue to grow. The whole coring process is old-school, done by hand, using an increment borer of the same kind initially used by Don Currey. This technology has changed little over the course of a century. The bit is assembled by taking the corer and attaching it to a large handle to provide leverage; then you simply press it into the tree at about chest height and rotate the handle, screwing it into the tree—a vintner putting a corkscrew into an enormous wine cork. Sometimes it takes two people to do the job, given the difficulty of penetrating the bark as well as the challenges of biting into what is sometimes very hard wood. After penetrating the tree to the desired depth, you crank the handle a couple of times in the opposite direction, breaking the sample free, and then gingerly pull it out. Voilà! The core, typically about pencil-thick and about half the diameter of the tree being sampled, is then placed in a paper straw, stacked with any others, and transported back to the lab.

Beyond cutting and coring, there is one more fundamental approach to collecting raw material for later analysis: the gathering of old pieces of wood lying on the ground at the base of the bristlecones. The information within those ancient samples of wood allows researchers to build up tree-ring chronologies. The living tree is the anchor, and the remnant wood lying on the ground allows researchers to push a chronology further backward in time. The ways that a bristlecone pine records many hundreds of years of weather leaves an indelible pattern, unique to a region and even to a specific tree. Rainy-dry-cold-very-dry-dry-cold-rainy-rainy-warm, creating a wooden fingerprint that can be compared from piece to piece. These overlapping reference chronologies let researchers stitch together, and thus extend, the tree-ring record, even from long-dead trees. The remnant wood chronology now goes back nearly nine thousand years. As Douglass noted in a 1929 article, "The closeness with which timbers of the same age corroborate each other's testimony about common experience would delight a trial lawyer's heart."[10]

Tree rings can tell us many stories beyond the simple facts of antiquity. A tree with rings offset to one side was probably exposed to high winds in one direction, because wood on the side away from the wind grows faster than on the side facing the wind. A tree with lots of closely packed rings from its early years might have faced difficulties and grew slowly; perhaps it was under larger trees and received scant light—and later, as shown in wider rings, grew in much healthier conditions, either because trees around it had been cleared to let in more sunshine, or because some natural disaster had thinned out a forest, or changes in the weather helped the tree to grow more freely.

Dendrochronology has many interdisciplinary applications, and some allied fields of scientific study. One of these is dendrohydrology, which uses evidence within ancient trees to tell us about drought, river and stream flow, the height of the water table, and the abundance or scarcity of water in particular areas over long periods of time. Another is dendroclimatology, which uses tree rings to tell us about climatic and atmospheric conditions and changes over centuries. Distant events, such as volcanic eruptions, or even gigantic solar flares, can be discerned in the rings of a tree. Detailed historic water and climate data are highly practical, because water managers today can add this information to forecast models to better predict future water and weather conditions.

One of the most interesting aspects of the LTRR's research is archaeological work, including the study of human settlement and cultural activities involving wood. Reference chronologies have been used to confirm or deny the dates of priceless musical instruments, and the age of the wooden frames and boards used by painters to settle questions of forgeries; and to pin down the precise dates of archaeological settlements, as with Douglass's work in dating the establishment of Chaco Canyon, Mesa Verde, and other native cliff dwellings in the American Southwest back to specific years in the thirteenth century. Some of these dates, Douglass noted, were "as reliable as if they had been dated at the time and sworn to before a notary."[11]

Tree rings have also resolved other perplexing historical problems. Data from bald cypresses in Virginia confirmed that the settlers of the Roanoke Colony, the first attempt at English settlement of North America in 1585, sponsored by Sir Walter Raleigh, had the awful luck to arrive in the midst of summer during one of the driest thirty-six months of the previous eight hundred years—an agricultural catastrophe for the settlers. The entire colony of 115 men, women, and children all disappeared; when a resupply mission arrived in 1590, delayed by war with Spain, the men found not a single settler. Various theories emerged well into the late twentieth century that they had somehow assimilated with, or were perhaps massacred by, local tribes, or were poisoned en masse, or met some other malicious end at the hands of humans. But in 1998, tree-ring evidence revealed the environmental catastrophe that must have unfolded, as food and water became increasingly scarce, upending, and then ending, what would have already been a tenuous existence in a new land.

Even wood that's already been burned so extensively that it's just charcoal is illuminating. Dendrochronologists work with what they can get. Lightning strikes frequently start fires, especially near the tops of mountains, where the route from sky to ground is most direct. A good deal of what dendrochronologists encounter are thus burnt chunks of wood: charcoal, which is physically delicate but chemically stable. It's possible to identify the species of a tree simply from a charred hunk of wood, and the rings' secrets can be coaxed out. It's patient, expert work to piece the puzzle back together. The burnt rings are easy enough to see, but rather than sanding the wood to clarify its ring boundaries, scientists can snap pieces off, and the boundaries from year to year are evident in the segments in their hands.

As we walk through the lab, the conversation returns, over and over again, to fire. Laying out a long cross section of a tree's trunk reveals, in an instant, a landscape of fire across millennia. Low-intensity fires and bigger conflagrations alike reveal themselves through wounds to the tree, and the subsequent healing of those wounds. We look at a sample of a ponderosa pine, where there was a flurry of fire in the last two decades of the nineteenth century. But suddenly, there's a big, dramatic, pale blob that appears early in the twentieth century. It looks like a breaking wave, and it's what tree-ring researchers who study fire call "the twentieth-century curl." As the rings progress, you can see the dynamic that's been at play in a world before humans: one of fire-created wounding, repair, wounding, repair. The twentieth-century curl looks radical compared to the tree's previous life, where fire is frequent. It's bland and scar-free, and looks out of place, like a tumor. One giant section we examine shows evidence of more than 125 fires before the dawn of the twentieth century, marked by blackened scar events over a fifteen-hundred-year life span—and then the cool, blank twentieth-century curl. It's obvious here that trees and fires have coexisted for a very long time. But the exclusion of fire from the land from the twentieth century onward, combined with the hotter climate, is causing radical changes to tree ecosystems, turning fire from a curative into a killer, hungry for long-unburned fuel.

A big graphic on the wall shows four hundred years of climate based upon tree-ring reconstruction in what is now the American West, from about Mississippi to the West Coast, stretching north to Canada and down past the tip of Baja California. The map represents a measuring tool called the Palmer Drought Severity Index, where browner colors indicate drier years, and greener hues indicate wetter years. Thousands of colored dots on the map show where LTRR scientists have identified trees with fire scars. These points are all assembled from a massive database of tree-ring data across the western half of the North American continent. "You can step back and get a sense of this very strong spatiotemporal variability," David notes.[12] In other words, circumstances can change a lot, especially over longer periods of time. David grew up in New Mexico, and he remembers watching developers build ski areas during wet stretches, only to see them fail when longer dry spells emerged. We extrapolate over shockingly short periods of time, creating tiny chronological snapshots— barely a flicker, even—which leaves us at a continual disadvantage. It's human nature to assume that what we have today is what we'll have tomorrow.

The graphic shows a huge stretch of green across numerous years in the first quarter of the twentieth century, corresponding with the years that water allocations were first worked out for the Colorado River. The Colorado River Compact was made in 1922, based on a fairly short period of data, and later found by climatologists to be reflective of an anomalously wet period. A useful generalization emerges from these discussions: be both chronologically and geographically broad in your surveying of nature's processes to reach accurate, meaningful conclusions. Seeing your neighborhood saturated with lawn signs for a presidential candidate doesn't mean that you've accurately taken the national temperature.

Short-term memory is never a substitute for long-term evidence, and this is one of the enormous strengths of tree-ring data: its ability to inform us about just what has constituted a longer-term trend, a process known as hindcasting. I ask David how dendrochronology might be usefully predictive. For him, and for other scientists at the lab of whom I asked this same question, their endeavors are centrally about deepening our understanding of how systems work: how has climate changed, what has caused climate to change, at what pace, and under what conditions? To examine these interactions over the course of a year, or ten, or a hundred, or a thousand, provides outcomes that let us test climate models. If we don't understand how systems have worked, we have no chance of predicting them. Do the climate models they describe have a reasonable sensitivity, or environmental variability? We can test current forest growth models: do they match the past dynamics of these ecosystems? If so, then we have more confidence in such models to be used to predict the future. If we can't get the past correct, how can we get the future correct?

I feel at home in the basement of the archives, where we land at the end of our journey. The spaces look very much like the archives for manuscripts and rare books where I spend my days: movable compact shelving, tidy rows of gray metal shelves, holding box after labeled box of pieces of wood—examples of more than a century's worth of collected material. As with research libraries, live plants are a no-no; an insect infestation could be disastrous. Pest traps line the floors. One large section consists of archaeological wood, pieces of timber and lumber used by humans. Following this area are others where the wood is used for ecological studies. There are ranges marked "Fire History." In other parts of the archives, big, heavy cross sections of wood sit on metal racks. Many slabs of wood rest on shelves, looking for all the world like misshapen books, complete with call numbers. They're just small enough to fit on the shelving, grouped by size, just as with rare books. The twentieth-century curl shows up again and again in the wood record; it's so obvious that I can now identify it at a glance as I walk down the aisles. We come upon yet another section of the archives, consisting of what look like bundles of firewood, collected in Colorado. These ordinary-looking pieces are shrink-wrapped in plastic and sitting on pallets, just as they're sold in supermarkets. The difference is that this wood is twenty thousand years old.

We open some boxes, and David shows me samples that were cut by a stone tool; it's obvious how the marks differ from those made by a metal axe. The evidence of the type of tool used to cut the wood immediately helps you narrow down the cutting era, even before you polish and examine any of its parts. He shows me a piece of wood not cut by a human tool but gnawed through by a beaver.

It's been a full day. The archives are giant slices of the past, occupying what feel like miles of shelves. There are still more sections from the Currey tree in the archives. David tells me about an artist in Los Angeles who has created a digital reproduction of Prometheus as it looked before the Currey cutting, and made a facsimile, created as a cast using 3D printing, and then placed in a snow globe, which I spot in at least one staff office. The Currey story has reach and resonance, with echoes of all of our failings, and I think that's one of the reasons for its appeal. Anyone can make a bad mistake; we all have, at some point or another. We hindcast: what could we have done better, and if we had a chance to reconstruct some previous aspect of our lives, what else might we have learned, or even lost anew?

Imperfection is life, and life is filled with beautiful imperfection. No tree's rings are ever perfectly, mathematically round, or perfectly even. The record of life limned on them, and within them, is splotchy. The planets might spin with precision, and Newton's immutable laws apply. On the living planet, however, it's messy business. Seasons shift, temperatures tremble between extremes, climate dips and rises. Humans charge in and out of the frame, using wood, our longest-lived and most versatile tool. The tree is a witness, recording evidence, and it accounts for these changes, presenting a record of the days and all their parts as they tumble into centuries. The oldest bristlecone pines have seen close to two million dawns and dusks. But nothing lasts forever, although the Great Basin bristlecone pine gives it a good try. Longevity seems to be an ideal for all organisms, even when it involves contorting yourself into something defiant. Trees are like books, and they leave a record that runs backward, as time runs forward, from the first page to the last. These ancient trees offer a story of losses and gains—theirs and ours—a simulacrum of the gorgeous jumble of the world.

CHAPTER 2

Awesome Matters:
The Coast Redwood

*"I am pleading for the future. I am pleading for a time . . .
when we can learn by reason and judgment and understanding and faith that all life is worth saving, and that mercy is
the highest attribute of man."*

—Clarence Darrow, "A Plea for Mercy,"
Chicago Daily News, August 25, 1924

The big coast redwoods (*Sequoia sempervirens*) are magnificent,
like news from another world. A few individuals grow to just
shy of four hundred feet, making them the tallest carbon-
bearing organisms on Earth. We still don't know why they get so
high, nor why they're not even taller. But their sheer bigness—their
height, their circumference, their massive bulk, their huge payloads
of tissue and carbon and ancient wood—relocates us. If we pay attention, they can lead us to our better selves. They can confront us with
our frailties, our smallness, and our puny life spans, while reassuring
us that life can go on, and that if we are part of the living world, we
too can go on. I find it reassuring that an entity this extraordinary can
live while we live, in a sliver of shared time.

We gather around the tree, we take photos, we mug for the camera, we grin as we pretend to try to encircle the tree with our arms.
It's like taking a photo with a president. Each visitor is just one of an

uncountable number of supplicants for the tree's brief attention, and it will have a life far beyond ours. There's something congregational about the redwoods in their groves: a group of worshippers, petitioners standing solemnly, upright before an even higher power than themselves—the calculus of wind, rain, sun, oxygen, carbon dioxide, and time. The coast redwood is about wonderment, delight, and, ultimately, the right of a tree to exist, to not have to serve as a means to human ends. Awe isn't the exclusive property of tourists, monks, and rubberneckers. Scientists are driven not only by intellectual pursuits but also by astonishment, and by its cousin desire. To claim that science is impartial and bloodless is incorrect.

There are only three redwood species in the world, despite a fossil record littered with others from the dim past. One survivor is the dawn redwood, which is native to just one valley in south-central China, although it plants well around the world. The second is the coast redwood's cousin, the giant sequoia (*Sequoiadendron giganteum*) another huge tree often mistaken for the coast redwood despite no overlap in their ranges, and different biology. The coast redwood lives almost exclusively along the upper California coast in a maritime climate, running northward from midstate for about nine hundred miles and occupying a narrow rind of land approximately seven to twenty miles wide for most of its length. Most of the trees live within the Humboldt Redwoods State Park. A small population, wantonly ignoring state lines, has pushed up into Oregon, and down to Southern California, and to other scattered locations worldwide, where the coast redwood was introduced as an ornamental species decades ago.[1]

A mature redwood adds, on average, a ton of wood to its mass every year. It can be up to twenty-five feet in diameter near the ground. Explorers in the 1840s immediately spotted the big tree and went to work monetizing it, eager to make their fortunes in the new lands of California. These visitors logged the trees extensively; by most reliable accounts, there were about two million acres in existence when first "discovered." More than 96 percent of the tree's earlier acreage was lumbered down to about ninety thousand old-growth individuals. These giant conifers are now all within areas protected by the state or the federal government, sheltering in place against the multifarious threats of the outside world.[2]

The constrained boundaries of the redwood population, and the trees' proximity to roads, means that it's easy to encounter whole groves in person. Up close, the biggest trees transform. Our eyes are accustomed to being able to take in the extent of a tree, to make sense of its tree-ness. But upon my seeing a redwood for the first time, it struck me that the trees were more like massive, notched slabs of rock. They're unmoving under your hands; they are striated and rough, and stretch off to both sides, more akin to a wall than a tree. People climb them, and speak of their heights with wide-eyed reverence. You crane your head up and can't see the top. Mossy ledges higher up on the trees look for all the world like ledges on a rock face, with other species of trees growing on flattened protuberances.

The coast redwood holds up the sky. And what holds up the tree? Soil, and lots of it. The alluvium from which the trees grow—clay, sand, and silt, the remainder of long-gone riverbeds—is some twenty feet deep in places. The root system of the tree spreads roots laterally for ridiculous distances of nearly one hundred feet, although in relatively shallow fashion. The redwood's bigness means it takes up a lot of ecological real estate. There are soil, air, water, and chemical dramas. There are pollinators, incubators, microbes, contributors, givers, takers. All are actors in the production that stretches from the tips of the coast redwood's roots to the tops of its canopies, and then radiates out from there to the bigger world: the forests the tree makes.

Every species of tree is unique, but with the coast redwood, oddities and contradictions proliferate. It's what botanists call a late-successional species, or a climax species: having survived for a long time, it's reached a state of equilibrium, and is as ecologically stable as can be. But at the same time, it's also adaptable to disturbance. Those two aspects of trees are usually mutually exclusive. And then there are the oxymoronic white redwoods. There are about four hundred known albino trees, white drops in a big lake of green. They're usually small, often no more than shrubs, although they can rise up to about thirty feet. Due to a mutation, their needles can't produce the chlorophyll that gives trees their green raiment. But nature provides, and the tree can draw its energy from a photosynthesizing mother plant, or through higher stomatal conductance: the process of cycling CO_2 and water vapor through the stomata, or tiny pores that plants require to undertake the tree equivalent of breathing. These albinos are found across the tree's range, and their albinism is a useful trait that allows geneticists to study mutation rate and the trees' relationships with water and light.

There are also ten known individual trees in the wild that contain more than one genotype, and are thus both albino and not-albino, with green and white foliage interspersed. These chimeras aren't quite jackalopes or turduckens. But they are oddities, and the chlorophyll deficiency leaves them with leaves that range in color from white to yellow to silver. These genetic oddities are the subject of considerable research.

You would expect a tree this big to be old, and though size and age aren't necessarily correlated with trees, they are with this one. Long lives are inscribed all over the coast redwood. Big is beautiful, as is living long, but it's also hard work. Root systems are under constant stress from the trees' weight, and from the leveraging effects of wind and other adjacent trees. Huge boluses of bark and wood bulge out from some of the trunks. Burn marks from lightning strikes and gaping cavities are abundant. Notches from the dawn of the twentieth century, evidence of wood extracted for railroad ties without cutting down the whole tree, are frequent. Even with these stresses, the oldest-known coast redwoods clock in at twenty-two hundred years, making them some of the planet's most ancient trees.

Every species of tree offers lessons to the world, both humanistic and scientific, and they all fill the spaces between those two often arbitrary poles. The tallest redwoods continue to grow at a rate of about a quarter inch a year. But even with abundant rainfall, the upper leaves on the tallest trees are stressed from a relative lack of water. The answers to the why-so-tall and why-not-taller questions seem to involve water, as is the case for so much about trees. Ultimately, it's most likely a matter of hydraulics: a tree's height appears to be limited by the enormous effort needed to lift water up through the tiny tubes, or xylem, the transport tissue that constitutes most of its mass. However, we have no certainty about these higher powers, because there are no hydraulic systems built by humans that have sufficient capacity to let us test some of the finer theories about this water-raising process.

As a rule, less water at the top of a tree means it's harder for leaves to photosynthesize and expand. Individual trees in the drier, southern parts of the redwood's range are shorter. But climate change will also modify the height equation in the coming decades, as higher CO_2 levels, the carbon balance, and changes in temperature and moisture will probably mean shorter trees. It takes redwoods weeks to pull water up from their roots to the tops of the trees. Sucking water up a straw from a drinking glass is a trivial task. But as the straw gets longer and longer, the pressure needed to raise the water gets greater. The tree pulls mightily against the negative pressure generated by passing liquid through wood. The tallest redwoods probably generate some two million pounds of negative pressure.

The tallest of these trees is so tall that if you were tethered at the top and swaying in the breeze while praying for your life, you'd be able to look down and see the Statue of Liberty's bald spot, if she had one. That is, of course, if the Statue of Liberty had been relocated to a spot adjacent to Hyperion, the tallest known redwood. And moving Lady Liberty would be easier than relocating the tree, simply from a weight perspective, not to mention all those roots.

Loggers weighed, segment by segment, one huge fallen redwood, the Lindsey Creek tree in Fieldbrook, California. The tree was 3,630 tons, more than twenty times heavier than the Statue of Liberty.[3]

I had planned to climb one of these trees, but I felt decidedly unenthusiastic at the prospect. Besides being anxious about heights, I haven't had great luck in the past at upper elevations. I've climbed a fair number of mountains, some of it using technical ice-climbing and mountaineering gear. But 18,700 feet appears to be my limit. Aconcagua, the tallest peak in the Western Hemisphere? I got cerebral edema at 18,700 feet. Mount Kilimanjaro, on the other side of the planet? I made it to 18,700 feet, to the so-called false summit of the mountain, before running out of steam. But a tree less than four hundred feet tall? Pffft. And then I saw a *picture* of people climbing the tree and was deterred. Talking to others about the view from on high was enough for me. We all have our limits.

But others have climbed far up into its high embrace, including Jerry Beranek, a pioneer of coast redwood climbing who first ascended one in 1971.[4] As Jerry described his own time near the top of the canopy, "The views from the vertical column have a stunning three-dimensional effect: distance, depth and space filled in with the trunks of giant amber columns stirring and swaying."[5] Few people have had an opportunity to get that high up into a tree. More humans have summited Mount Everest than have gotten higher than three hundred feet up a coast redwood. In the canopy, amazing worlds emerge. Different species of trees are thriving in soil up to three feet deep within the inner folds of some of the redwoods. One tree climber found an eight-foot-tall Sitka spruce growing in the upper heights of a giant redwood.

Beranek described the tree and its environment as a world unto itself. He told me, "Other than a few lichen and mosses that are adapted specifically to life in the canopy, everything else—and I do mean everything—that you see growing in the redwood forest can be found growing in the canopy of our old-growth redwoods." He's even seen grass growing on high.[6] Epiphytes (plants that grow on other plants, a common strategy for botanic life around the world) build up bulk and size, drawing their moisture and nutrients from the air, rain, and nearby debris. As those rafts of plant matter accumulate, they create a carpet-like layer that collects falling organic material: leaves, twigs, bird poop, and other debris shaken loose by the wind or birds. This organic material starts to decay, with help from omnipresent microbes, and soil is born. Not only does the soil host other forms of life, including small creatures ranging from crickets and beetles to mollusks, amphibians, and earthworms, it also regulates the climate within the canopy, providing insulation against temperature fluctuations, sound, and wind.

These canopy soils aren't unique to the coast redwood. They exist in big trees all over the world, and they provide homes for any number of organisms: interactions we need to understand better. But the sheer size and volume of the redwood's inner structures means that the quantity and variety of its inhabitants are unique. And it's not just plant material up in the canopy. The zoologist Michael Camann has found aquatic crustaceans called copepods living in the fern mats—lush, large epiphytes that grow atop branches, or inside of tree cavities. Other surprise animals have been found, including a new species of earthworm, and wandering salamanders (*Aneides vagrans*), which spend almost all of their lives up in the canopy.

As amphibian populations around the world decline, learning their survival strategies becomes more urgent. A 2022 study described the wandering salamander's ability to glide and parachute out of the crowns of the redwoods when disturbed. This behavior had been observed before, but the new study focused on their specific aerial maneuvers and evolutionary adaptations. Jumping out of a tree is a risky way to escape a threat, because the salamanders have no obvious aerodynamic control mechanisms to slow their fall: no flaps, membranes, wings, or other obvious speed-slowing tools. Dropping the salamanders into a wind tunnel and using high-speed cameras, researchers showed that the amphibians assume a stable skydiving posture, allowing them to maintain a steady speed, and to control their direction. Falling at about a meter per second, the salamanders can take up to two minutes to fall from the tops of the tallest trees to the ground. It turns out that the salamanders' shape helps them survive this aerial enterprise: a body that's just flattened enough, and large feet with long toes, helping to create drag and balance.[7]

Discoveries in and among the redwoods demonstrate other survival tools of the redwood's residents, helping to counteract the narratives of decline. A 2018 survey of nine large redwood trees yielded a total of 137 species of lichens, several new to science.[8] One of them was *Xylopsora canopeorum*, its specific name celebrating the canopy in which it was discovered. The lichen seems to be unique to the warmer and drier forests in Sonoma and Santa Cruz Counties—an exciting finding. As climate change affects trees everywhere, that warmer climates have fostered a lichen new to science is encouraging.

Much larger organisms also find purchase within the redwood ecosystem. One of these is the California condor (*Gymnogyps californianus*), a cavity-nesting bird with a wingspan of nearly ten feet. There are slightly more than five hundred condors alive today, both in the wild and in captivity. Formerly spread across the American Southwest, the population of these giant birds was down to twenty-two individuals in 1987, leading to a decision to capture every surviving bird and bring it into captivity. My friend Mike Scott, the former director of the California condor program during these critical years, told me that at one point he had more people working on the project than there were living condors. It makes sense that a bird this big would want a big tree in which to nest, and the redwood's giant fissures provided this kind of room. The condor recovery program, now run by the Ventana Wildlife Society in Monterey, California, tracks every one of the birds in the wild, and gives each a name. One of these condors, known as Redwood Queen, was first discovered in a nest in 2006 in a coast redwood. Joe Burnett, the manager of the recovery program, explained to me that the redwoods had been used by multiple pairs over the years in the cavities, which were created by burns from lightning strikes.

The tree also has its ghosts. One of the redwood's most mysterious residents has been the marbled murrelet (*Brachyramphus marmoratus*), a small endangered seabird whose secretive ways meant that its nests went undiscovered for a very long time. The bird has long seemed to have otherworldly powers. Flying close to the ground, a murrelet is one of the fastest birds in the world; it can reach up to a hundred miles an hour, a passing blur to people on the ground. Indigenous peoples called the birds "fogbirds" and "foglarks" because of their preference for cloudy, misty habitats. They nest in solitary fashion, and in low light. Captain James Cook first collected the bird in Prince William Sound, in the Pacific Northwest, in 1778. It was described in print a decade later by the German naturalist Johann Friedrich Gmelin— no zoological slouch, for he updated the key edition of Linnaeus's *Systema naturae*. But Gmelin's description lacked one important fact: details on the bird's nesting habits. One hundred and eighty-five years would pass between Gmelin's assiduous, learned, imperfect description of the bird and the location of its home. Energetic professional and amateur bird people began the long search for the bird's nests. Theories abounded, each crazier than the last. Some were convinced the bird was a ground dweller. Others, knowing the murrelet had been seen on lakes, proposed that somehow it lived *under* the water, in some kind of wet subterranean home. It began to be an embarrassment to ornithologists. In 1970 the editors of *Audubon Field Notes* offered up a hundred-dollar reward for the first verified and documented discovery of a nest.

For four years, concerted efforts turned up nothing. It wasn't until 1974 that a wiry, strong tree trimmer named Hoyt Foster, cleaning up debris from a big winter storm in a mixed grove of redwoods and Douglas firs, nearly stepped on a baby bird in a tree he was trimming. Foster was very experienced but had also suffered from a bad fall from a big tree twenty years earlier, puncturing an organ, breaking ribs, compressing vertebrae, and fracturing his skull. He returned to the craft of trimming but became more meticulous, a close observer. The little bird was nesting on what looked like a patch of moss, and "it looked like a squashed-up porcupine with a beak sticking out," he recalled. "I'd never seen anything like it." He wasn't sure what to do. It was a strange and pugnacious creature, pecking repeatedly at his saw. After trying to cut around the bird, he accidentally dislodged it, and it fell, landing—unlike Foster in his previous aerial exploits—completely unharmed, after a drop of nearly 150 feet. His colleagues took it to the ranger station, it was quickly identified and passed along to professional ornithologists and systematics experts, and the jig was up. Foster had inadvertently solved what one ornithologist called "one of the last great ornithological mysteries in North America." Past bird experts had come close but hadn't hit the mark. The legendary California ornithologist Joseph Grinnell's last field notes on the murrelet, written in 1936, noted that "there is no evidence . . . that the birds ever occur in redwood trees, as once guessed by someone." After Foster's discovery, the murrelet's nesting site was no longer a puzzle and a vexation. Neither he nor anyone else ever claimed the hundred-dollar reward.

The murrelet's foggy habitat is also one of the key reasons for the tree's long-term success; California's coastal fogs have provided stable moisture for millions of years. But while fog fosters the tree's survival, fire has helped make the tree fit more effectively into its environment. The tree's persistence story gains a new layer at the intersection of fire and indigenous populations, some of which have had a twenty-thousand-year tenancy on the land. Unlike the later Euro-Americans, who considered fire to be destructive to the tree, the indigenous residents embraced the benefits of burning and used fire to their advantage. Fire regimes have existed among the coast redwoods for centuries. The tree has thick bark, which makes it resistant to most fires, and other traits that allow it to rebound, and even thrive, after a blaze. Native Americans burned among the redwoods for a variety of purposes, including increasing the efficiency of food gathering (less undergrowth to travel through), and reducing acorn-eating insects that flitted among the understory.[9] The Yurok, Tolowa, and Wiyot tribes revered the redwood, and used its wood for buildings and for constructing canoes. The tree had a deep spiritual significance for the earliest humans: living and seemingly timeless, with its own creation stories and myths.[10] There is even an indigenous turn to the name "Sequoia"; it is thought to have come from a Cherokee named Sequoyah, a man of high linguistic talent who created an official and effective writing system, a rare event for a preliterate people. He created his syllabary, as a set of written symbols is called, after seeing soldiers reading paper—what he called "talking leaves." He determined to make his own syllable-based language, which has proved successful and durable into the present. This tie is resonant and relevant to the giant whose genus bears his name. The species name also resonates: *sempervirens*, meaning "ever living."

We think of these trees as immortal because they can outlive us by so much. But despite their presence in deep time and their ageless relations with other organisms, the redwood is not impervious to destruction. Modern humans with their steel instruments have harvested millions of board feet of redwood lumber, using the wood to build entire housing developments and business districts. Trees built our nation, and the biggest coast redwoods made a lot of lumber—more than a half million board feet each. All told, a tree could yield thirty-three homes, a street's worth of residences from a single redwood. The tree's harvest is also a story of variety as well as volume. People have constructed sheds, docks, bookshelves, tables, caskets, roadways, flumes, egg incubators, cesspools, and the pipes used in municipal water systems from Hawai'i to Florida, out of wood from *Sequoia sempervirens*.

Lumber-loving humans aren't the only complications for the trees' lives. The earth on which the trees rest, its silent foundation, can also subvert the redwoods. A massive earthquake, a near certainty for the trees given how long they live, can end their lives like so many match-sticks falling out of a box. The Cascadia subduction zone, running from Vancouver Island in Canada down to northernmost coastal California, lies beneath the world's highest concentration of old-growth redwoods. One writer has described a subduction zone as the biggest crash scene on Earth. It's the collision of two tectonic plates, immense pieces of the Earth's crust that are slowly but inexorably in motion. When they run into each other, something has to give. One slides down, or subducts, beneath the other. The violent movement of millions of tons of rock twists a coast redwood's root ball against the axis of the tree itself. This subduction can unleash a circular motion, a catastrophe trees probably never evolved to guard against. The tree rotates, and whipsaws, and then, like a cook snapping a length of celery, the ground movement shears off a huge part of the tree. In nineteenth-century accounts, the Bay Indians in Humboldt County described trees buried up to two hundred feet by earthquakes, fallen straight into fissures in the ground.[11]

At some point prior to being photographed for a postcard in the 1970s, one tree's huge lignotuber (the woody base of the tree that provides extra nutrients and a reserve of energy) washed up in a fresh-water lagoon in Northern California. The burl, as it's also known, was forty-one feet across and half that tall, and thought to weigh about 525 tons. These burls give the redwood regenerative powers, because new clones from the burls of fallen trees can rise out of them. The six people lined up in front of the washed-up burl seem a bit stunned, perhaps hastily assembled to pose with a house-sized piece of tree sitting on the beach.

Other elements can also affect the tree's survival. There is strong evidence of a major tsunami that reached much of western North America. The wave was triggered by an earthquake in 1700 that originated in the Cascadia subduction zone. There's no doubt that other mega-tsunamis from powerful earthquakes have come ashore, likely leaving coast redwoods under a hundred feet of water or more, and leveling great stretches of forest.[12]

Coast redwoods can also lose the fight against gravity in many other, more irregularly regular ways. Sometimes, a root plate—the heavy mass of roots that forms a flat carpet at the surface of the ground—will sink slowly into the ground, on one side or the other, tilting the tree. This tipping usually happens because subsurface water has saturated the alluvium in which the roots rest. Sometimes, the tree's taproot—the long central leader running straight down under the trunk—dies back, leaving a shallow series of roots unable to sustain the tree under the regular stresses of the local climate. And sometimes redwoods fall like dominoes, when one topples and hits another, bringing down others in a ragged cascade. The trees, as Beranek noted, are "chock-full of defects: old wounds, new wounds, fire scars, splits and large open breaks." All of these injuries give an opening to organisms that contribute to the trees' decline, hastening rotting and large cavities. Just as humans stretch and wrinkle and sag, so too with these trees.

So the redwoods can be fragile, a quality we don't really associate with such solid, monolithic structures. The effects of gravity, and then death, are everywhere, even as the trees push upward. Bark can slip from the trunk like loose, heavy sheets of fabric, coming off in unpredictable sizes and shapes. To walk through a big redwood grove is to see the fascinating effects of hundreds of years of activity. But a fallen tree can live on, often becoming part of the forest ecosystem by sprouting up new growth or serving as host to other plants, a garden of its own. The redwood forest's complications are well described by a Zen word, *Ensō*. In the West, we might reach for the cliché "circle of life" to describe it, but that's an old saw, dull from overuse, and it's more than that. When drawn with an uninhibited brushstroke by a Zen calligraphy master, it's sometimes a closed circle, but sometimes not quite closed, the very imperfections and inconsistencies of the shape symbolizing enlightenment, strength, and elegance. Ensō also relates to another Japanese concept, *wabi-sabi*—the beauty of impermanence. To be born is to die is to be born, as the trees engage in a quiet but pitched battle. As the stem and roots break down into mulch and duff, enough organic material assembles to support other life. Vines, ferns, and other trees rise straight up. Sometimes, though, fire or rot consumes the trees entirely and leaves just a telltale pit, the only evidence they once existed. No one seems to have done it yet, but plotting the thousands of pits left along the Lost Coast would enable us to see the footprint of ancient groves, providing detailed evidence of their previous density. Even a shadow leaves a mark.

While the more recent treacherous and relentless changes to our environment pose even greater threats than the movement of earth and water, we can find surprising oases of hope in a landscape of climate dread. The survival and growth of more heat-adapted organisms within the redwood's ecosystems, such as the aforementioned lichen, offers one example. Another is evidence that after recent fires of unprecedented severity, 95 percent of the coast redwoods survived and regenerated. This percentage is much higher than it is for other species of large trees in the fire areas studied. Conflagrations of this magnitude have given scientists an opportunity to study the redwoods' response to these events.[13] It's at times like these that the coast redwood seems invincible: able to weather some of the worst natural disasters possible.

Not all changes to the climate have been driven by humans, for we are newcomers, and our ball of rock and water is ancient. Scientists can look deep into the trees' past lives to see how they fared in very different conditions millions of years ago, and they can make these examinations in a laboratory setting that allows them to re-create ancient environments. For instance, how would the coast redwood do if it was starved of carbon dioxide? Despite its reputation as a bad actor, CO_2 is mandatory for trees—else they wouldn't sequester it by the gigaton. They're not doing it for us but for themselves. A 2013 study demonstrated that as CO_2 declined during earlier epochs of climate change, the tree's range also declined. Carbon starvation is bad for the redwood, as it turns out, which is what you might expect. Climate change that creates high rates of carbon dioxide helps trees, but the associated knock-on effects—fires, increased heat and its accompanying trials of insect infestation—are bad for trees. Too little carbon dioxide and the tree suffers. Too much and the planet suffers.[14]

Humans have also helped the tree to survive in a hotter world. In one 2016 test, researchers studying the redwood's genetic variation collected seeds from specimens on hot, dry ridges, presumably ones that had undergone some genetic adaptation to the warmer, drier climate by dint of their survival there. They then moved the thirty-four seedlings grown from those seeds to a pair of test sites at the eastern, inland limit of the tree's range, an even warmer region where no other redwoods occurred, to see whether they could take root and thrive. Many of the clones performed well at each of the test sites.[15]

All of these hydrological, geological, and biological considerations are key to understanding the redwood. But to know the tree best, it's important to move beyond its biology and to the emotions and sensations it stirs. Beauty as a branch of biology is underrated. Some of the loveliest elements in the redwoods' ecosystems are the tiniest. The range of small, close-to-the-wood species, and their visual presentations, are exquisite. There are the *Lepraria*, crusty silver-green-gray lichens named because they resemble the skin of leper patients. Beauty from pain, or beauty because of pain. Bryophytes abound: moisture-loving plants, including sporophytes of *Buxbaumia piperi*, shaped like a green T. rex tooth. And the lichens! The writer Richard Preston has described the *Cladonia* lichens growing high up on coast redwoods as "among the most beautiful of lichens. They come in wild shapes: trumpets, javelins, stalks of pinto beans, blobs of foam, cups, bones, clouds, and red-capped British soldiers."[16] Lichens are also biologically confounding and deeply complex—shape-shifters, microbiomes that are networks as much as they are individual organisms. They start to mess with our notions of where the physical boundaries of an organism begin and end.[17]

We marvel at the trees' tiny fungal beauties, and then step back to take in their immensity. I find their size and presence deeply comforting. Redwood groves are quiet places; there is a distinct sense of the sacred. As the writer Anne Lamott notes about the redwoods, "The trees are so huge that they shut you up."[18] Their mass dampens sound, and people in and around them tend to speak in quiet, reverent tones, as often happens when walking among giants. But they provide a world of sensations: you don't just drink them in visually; you see their colors and take in their smells.

And the smells! They provide a riot of sense data, which changes depending on your proximity to the tree and its different parts. They are aggregations of fragrant, bitter, sweet. Although not trained as a scientist, Beranek has worked among the redwoods for decades and has developed a deep affection for them. He's felled trees, climbed them, and cleared them for rights-of-way for forty-two years. In some ways, he's the walking contradiction inherent in many tree people, and the walking contradiction we all are when it comes to conserving the planet: we use it up at the same time we work to save it.

Jerry noted that trying to describe a smell to someone is akin to trying to describe a color. The redwood forest has a wide range of odors, which vary depending on the season and on what is most biologically active at the time. But the scents are always there, literally in your face, because of the immense biomass and the resulting volatile organic compounds (VOCs) that the trees emit. Take cold, dark, damp winter days in the redwood groves: there are a lot of fungi and molds at work in the forest, and the air can become acrid, funky, moldy. The smells aren't just odor dead ends. VOCs are signaling chemicals, communicating with other plants, and attracting insects to pollinate and disperse seeds.[19] It's not very pleasant for humans, and you wrinkle your nose, but nevertheless, there is still a quiet, healthy quality to it. "You go on about your business like it wasn't there," Beranek told me, but still, it's an inescapable part of the tree's ecosystem.

In the nineteenth century people had monikers for many redwood clusters or individuals: Three Sisters, Siamese Twins, Bachelor, Hermit. During the Civil War, discoverers attached a raft of heroes' names to the trees. Even trees that had toppled over got named: Fallen Monarch, Noah's Ark, and so on. This naming business is not new and continues apace today. The biggest trees are now usually named by the small coterie of biologists who regularly climb them. No one has to agree to them, because there's no scientific route to claiming a name for an individual within a species. More recently named trees include Adventure, Brutus, Nugget, Paradox, and Atlas—each so tall that the temperature is noticeably cooler at the top than at the base. And there are many more. It's probably the exception to have a tall redwood that *doesn't* have a nickname.

Maybe names give them extra gravitas, but talk about gilding the lily. More likely, today at least, they're simply a form of affection on behalf of the scientists who study them, as well as a practical handle to distinguish one huge tree from another. But zoological history is full of nonhuman names: there's Lassie, and also Koko the sign language–fluent gorilla, and Pepper the famous talking parrot, and, of course, Mickey Mouse, and even my son's long-lived pet goldfish, President Obama. Only a handful of people know the precise locations of these tallest trees, which protects them from the curious who'd like to try to climb one, or remove a part, or otherwise vandalize them. I considered sidling up to the biologists who know the locations to try to visit some of the tallest, but their coordinates are guarded like crown jewels, and I refrained.

The trees' Linnaean lessons about photosynthesis, growth, organic compounds, and water transport are softened by their nonscientific roles. Although the coast redwood grows in the United States, other cultures have made sense of the tree and appropriated it. Bonsai, the

Japanese art of making miniature trees, creates tiny simulacra that have lessons to teach about patience and the long view. Dating back to the thirteenth century in Japan, bonsai is an ancient and complex art form, but at its heart, it promotes emotional well-being and a sense of peace and tranquility. One study of 255 bonsai artists showed that practicing the art of bonsai improved the mood of most of the practitioners.[20] But can we consider the bonsai redwood to be as "natural" as the full-sized version? Perhaps not. After all, it's a carefully managed activity designed to create a miniature version of the full-scale tree. They're wired, pruned, and very consciously shaped to fit a human's vision.

But there are still numerous commonalities between big and little. As with the full-sized trees, bonsai can have human characteristics. "You start referring to them as hes and shes, and they have personalities," the Huntington Gardens bonsai curator, Ted Matson, told me as we walked through the botanical garden's back-of-house bonsai collection. They also have curative powers that echo the peacefulness of the full-sized groves. Ted noted that he found that if he was dealing with writer's block, or couldn't figure out how to phrase a paragraph, working with his bonsai could turn him in a new direction. "I learned quickly to get out, go walk among my trees, go do a little pruning, do a little pinching, and inevitably, within minutes of doing that, whatever solution I was seeking would pop into my head, and the copy would just flow out of me."[21]

To grow a bonsai, Ted observed, you need to resist the urge to do something. You have to respect the pace of the tree.[22] We can't resist bottling nature, making it manageable and graspable, sitting in front of us, able to be seen in one glance. "One of the first bonsai shows I went to, a tree that was absolutely the most stunning and inspiring was a coast redwood," Ted noted. "And at that time, it was probably about three feet tall. The proportions were absolutely perfect for a redwood. So that was one of my first inspirations."[23] It's as if the giant redwood has given birth to its smaller congener. That's literally true, because the process of bonsai begins by going out among the redwoods, finding and digging up the stump of a small tree, and taking it home. Ted reminded me that bonsai is an abstraction—a representation, what he termed "the ultimate example of bringing nature into your personal space." It's also an interpretation. The Japanese did a great service in studying the characteristics of very old trees, and codified those into design principles. And the big trees don't have much of an advantage over the bonsai when it comes to antiquity; the Huntington contains bonsai that are more than a thousand years old, and one that's crowding two thousand years. They're artifices, but they're also a part of rambunctious life.

Bonsai trees and humans have formed ancient bonds. But a new concept has built momentum for just over a half century: the natural world has legal rights all its own. Some species have sued in court to protect their rights, in litigation brought, of course, by humans. The stage for this had been set in 1971 when the USC law professor Christopher Stone, trying to roust some bored students in one of his classes, put forth the radical notion that the natural world might have legal rights. He then published a seminal article in a law journal, titled "Should Trees Have Standing? Toward Legal Rights for Natural Objects." (And I use the word "seminal" in its etymological sense here, as in, "from seed.") The article might've slid into legal obscurity but for the fact that it was soon cited in a famous Supreme Court case. Stone's article would launch a rationale putting forth the rights of the natural world. In building a careful, stepwise argument through example and precedent, Stone noted: "Increasingly, the death that occupies each human's imagination is not his own, but that of the entire life cycle of the planet earth, to which each of us is as but a cell to a body." Others have taken his arguments and reasoning and extended, supported, and clarified them in the ensuing decades.[24]

Stone's single radical, rhetorical match lit a fire that continues to burn brightly, as a way to consider not just ethical imperatives for the survival of trees but also legal ones. Put in technical terms, it's a huge deal. As the legal maxim goes, *de minimis non curat lex*: the law is not concerned with trifles. It's a strange proposition, though, to the uninitiated, and just as Charles Darwin chose to speak disarmingly of his radical new idea of evolution by talking about just how improbable it must seem to many, so too did Stone take a similar tack. "There will be resistance to giving the thing 'rights' until it can be seen and valued for itself," he noted, "yet, it is hard to see it and value it for itself until we can bring ourselves to give it 'rights'—which is almost inevitably going to sound inconceivable to a large group of people." However, the concept continues to gain traction.

Other writers have offered different valences for the ways we speak, and thus think, about nonhuman entities. Robin Wall Kimmerer, in her book *Braiding Sweetgrass*, talks movingly and convincingly about the grammar of animacy. "To name and describe you must first see, and science polishes the gift of seeing," she notes. But when we tell someone a tree is an *it* and not a *who*, "we absolve ourselves of moral responsibility and opening the door to exploitation." It's much harder, she points out, to turn a chain saw onto a "she" than onto an "it."[25]

The writer Elizabeth Kolbert has pointed out that for most of history, people keenly understood how much they were at the mercy of their environment, dependent on the natural world for their very survival, and rivers and mountains had the last word. But the power of law, more than issues of moral suasion, may now be the tool that finally urges us, even coerces us, as a civilized world, to take action on the idea that nature deserves to live on its own terms, not ours. Ultimately, it's a survival strategy for humans as much as for the trees.

Humans live and die by their justifications. We need reasons for things, damn it. The issue of intelligence among nonhuman species gets our attention, because we instinctively think, perhaps, that we are the only entities that have what we construe as intelligence. But nature provides many counterexamples, such as the New Caledonian crow, with its ability to make and use tools to get at food, and its skill in working out sequences of tasks to feed itself. Talking about intelligence and trees is riskier, for we've come to consider comprehension as relevant only to other animals with brains. Human intellect has been used for centuries as the benchmark by which all other understandings are measured. These "vexed hierarchies" of intelligences, as the biochemist Merlin Sheldrake calls them, are now being tempered by new understandings of what trees, and other organisms, can do in terms of cognition, making decisions, and other classic markers of intelligence. Cognition, the ability to detect environmental variables, is sometimes confused with consciousness, which leads to its rejection as being present in plants. But philosophers of biology have argued convincingly that plants have consciousness as well: in the simplest sense, consciousness is an awareness of the outside world.[26]

The collective crucible of law, biology, beauty, awe, common sense, and something we can recognize as intelligence can forge humans into creatures able and willing to give trees like the redwoods their own due. We move toward a kind of newfound affinity, or at least it snags our attention, when we find clues that we're not alone in our ability to express intelligence. For the natural world to survive, it needs long-term empathy. The future of the planet's health is an abstraction to almost everyone, and the longer the arc of time, beyond our lifetime, the greater the abstraction. I'm betting that you don't care all that much that the planet will finally be absorbed into the sun in 7.5 billion years. But if that was the plan for next week, you'd suddenly have it front of mind. And someday, it will be next week, even though the concept of a week will be long gone. We need to find ways to extend our compassion just a bit further into the future, and make it less abstract. Just as the past existed, whether you want it to have existed or not, so too is the future coming, whether you like it or not, and if you care about life on Earth, you will find a way to care about the future. Work your empathy muscle through contemplation and discussion. For trees to survive, we need to have sentiment along with sediment. Philosophers now propose ethical models of intergenerational heritage, building emotional connections across generational divides: a tall order. These models offer ways to stitch together current communities with the generations that will immediately follow, and then tying those to the generations that follow them, and so on— a reference chronology that ties past to future.[27]

And back to the Earth: we all come from it, and we will all return to it. It roots everything. In the time in between, we're awfully busy. We name, we search, we scurry, we work. And as we live, we sometimes too easily slip away from nature, bound up in our offices and cities. But fortunately, we have a very hard time removing ourselves from the fibrous equations of the natural world, because we are always a part of it. It's just that it's often difficult to see the biosphere from a new vantage point, high up in a tree, say, after being on the ground for so long. Despite how human we are, it is still possible to understand the world from a tree's perspective. I don't find much traction with anthropomorphic approaches to trees; I don't think of them as "affectionate," or "tender," or having other attributes more applicable to humans. That's not to say that I don't have abundant shovelfuls of my own tenderness and affection for trees, and I think that's the right direction: we can feel kinship with trees, without requiring it from them. They owe us nothing; we owe them everything.

Thomas Berry was a US cultural historian who introduced the broader legal concept of Earth jurisprudence early in the twenty-first century. Earth jurisprudence is the philosophy of law and human governance that says humans are just one element in a wider community of beings, and that the welfare of one speaks to the welfare of all. "The universe is a communion of subjects, not a collection of objects," Berry argued, and it's through the work of people such as Stone, Berry, Kimmerer, Kolbert, and others that we are moving our collective understanding, and our will, toward a more environmentally just world. In the face of the ecological catastrophes bearing down on us, we must remember the collective good of countless people as well as the rights of trees, and of the land that supports and nurtures us all.

CHAPTER 3

Earth Work: The Nearly Lost Tree of Rapa Nui

"In regeneration nature is not ruined, but rectified."
—George Swinnock, *The Vanity of the World*

Survival takes many shapes. Occasionally, it involves standing your ground. Sometimes it means returning home. At other times, it requires leaving altogether. While the coast redwood is irrevocably rooted in its home in the Pacific Northwest on the North American continent, one tree has been a fragile expat for more than a half century: the little *Sophora toromiro*, which lacks a common name and goes by toromiro. It is far from home, no longer present on Rapa Nui, the Pacific island where it evolved. Also known as Easter Island, or Isla de Pascua in Spanish, Rapa Nui is a speck of land in the Pacific, about thirty-five hundred miles from the west coast of Chile. It's tiny, encompassing just sixty-three square miles, and quite flat, with a maximum elevation of five hundred meters. The tree's story, and its struggles, are grounded in the literal earth on the island: difficulties the soil has posed for reintroducing the tree. But in this story, oceans also loom large.

The last date of the toromiro's tenure on Rapa Nui is uncertain. Some accounts say it went extinct in the wild in 1960. Others note that it was gone by 1962, when Karl Schanz, a German meteorologist,

clambered down to see the tree in the crater where it had last been
spotted, and it was gone. Was it removed? Did it die, tip over, and
return to the earth? We will never know. Although the toromiro is
gone from Rapa Nui, it survives elsewhere through luck, and pluck.
Over the past century the intermittent collecting of the toromiro's
seeds and their replanting in mainland locations have given the species purchase elsewhere. Each tree is a member of a small diaspora,
with only a handful surviving in about a dozen different public and
private botanical gardens around the world.

The first few years of the 1960s were sobering times. Rachel Carson's
luminous, chilling book *Silent Spring* came out. The Mexican grizzly
bear disappeared forever. Ornithologists last reliably saw Bachman's
warbler, a bird once common across the southeastern and midwestern
United States. Plants and animals blinked out by the dozens around
the world, or dipped to precariously low numbers.

Out on another island in the Pacific, I was a year old, and I nearly
went extinct myself around the same time, when a tsunami struck the
eastern side of the Big Island of Hawai'i. In the early hours of May
23, 1960, three great waves originated from a gigantic 9.5 magnitude
earthquake off the coast of Chile. It was the largest earthquake ever
recorded, and one that had killed thousands of Chileans the previous
day. Tsunamis are a slow-motion disaster; waves take a long time to
travel long distances. But they're inexorable liquid extinction events.
The temblor, caused by a massive shifting of plates underground, tore
rifts hundreds of miles long through the sea floor, generating a series
of waves that struck Hawai'i around midnight, and on into early the
next morning.

Warning sirens began around 8:30 p.m., part of the civil defense
system in place to this day. The first wave arrived just after midnight, barely three feet high. The hubbub emboldened people, awo-
ken by the eerie howling of the civil defense sirens, to walk back out
to explore the now-exposed shore, as the water receded in advance

of the next wave. This second wave, nine feet tall, arrived around 12:45 a.m. The third wave was the biggest and most devastating. Part of what seismologists call a wave train, it roared over a ten-foot-high seawall, moving twenty-ton boulders more than five hundred feet as it entered Hilo Bay, and reaching a height of thirty-five feet. It hit the power plant sitting on the bay, which exploded in a shower of sparks. The little town went dark. We lived on the water on Hilo Bay, on a cliff above the pounding Pacific Ocean. Although the wave spared us and our house, the three waves that churned up Pukihae Stream, the southern boundary of our property, reconfigured the river for hundreds of feet inland. For years afterward, my brother and I found broken pieces of pottery, parts of boats, cryptic bits of vulcanized rubber, and other debris that probably originated with the immense churn of water. Photos of downtown Hilo show row after row of thick, sturdy parking meters bent flat to the ground on Kamehameha Avenue.

Sixty-one people in Hilo, population twenty-six thousand, died—fishermen, blue-collar laborers, residents of apartments and houses close to the water. My father, a general surgeon at Hilo Hospital, worked for days without sleep, saving some lives and losing others in the chaotic aftermath. Nearly three hundred people were injured severely but survived. Dad repaired broken bones, removed damaged organs, amputated, stitched, and comforted patients with missing relatives. His fellow doctors in the small rural hospital in Hilo did the same. He received bottles of expensive liquor every holiday season from survivors, and their descendants, for decades afterward.

There is rarely a single factor that yanks a species out of existence, but instead a succession of slower and more diffused pressures. In the case of Rapa Nui, the entire island suffered decline both before and during human occupation and afterward. Scientists still debate some of the causes of the island's biological deterioration. Rapa Nui's and Hawai'i's circumstances offer useful points of comparison. Both have biota that evolved in isolation and have had to confront the sharpened

risk of extinction. Large parts of both islands were remade in the mil-
lennium after the arrival of Polynesians, who brought payloads of
pigs, rats, and other stowaways that quickly occupied ecosystems that
had never evolved defenses against the animals' invasive ways.[1]

Life in the middle of the ocean is both ferocious and fragile.
Almost all islands begin as upwellings of magma, turned to stone and
then fertilized by nitrogen from seabirds over eons before the arrival
of humans. On islands, life's tenancy, and its specific characteristics,
can change slowly, or rapidly. But change is the currency of islands.
Isolated life leads to countless in-betweens and variations, driven
over thousands of years by slow settlement of plants and animals, and
then by natural selection, climate, mutation, genetic drift, and, once
humans arrive, vast anthropogenic influences.

One especially powerful contributor to extinction on islands is
isolation. This at first appears contradictory, because evolutionarily,
isolation leads to radiation—the rapid formation of a multitude of new
species. Organisms can diversify wildly when lacking the restrictive
pressures and competitions found on mainlands. The trajectory of life
on islands, before humans, is thus a story of magnificent speciation.
These are places, more than any other, where "endless forms most
beautiful and most wonderful have been, and are being, evolved," as
Darwin noted in the last sentence of his 1859 book *On the Origin of
Species*. Millennia ago, organisms arrived on remote islands only accidentally, and only every several thousand years, on average. A plant
arriving as a seed in the dark belly of some wayward bird, or on a raft
of material caught in a current that brought it to an island, or a bat or
bird or insect borne a remarkable distance by the wind, meant that life
arrived in a foreign environment.

Biologists call this kind of forced relocation "sweepstakes dispersal." The odds of a new species arriving were roughly akin to those
of winning the lottery. But upon their rare arrivals, plants and animals
brought new tools. Newcomers could take advantage of fresh ecological niches, including food sources such as nuts that other birds
with weaker beaks were not able to crack open; and bats faced scant

competition for an abundance of insects to eat. Once established, these organisms continued the ancient evolutionary journeys they'd started in other places, but in new circumstances. Generally, on pre-contact islands, new organisms didn't have the predators they'd confronted in their lands of evolutionary origin. Mammals were usually nonexistent, as they were much less likely to survive a voyage of many weeks or months over water on some piece of flotsam. They would've had to come as at least a pair, too, of female and male, to propagate. But once they were there, life was good for these newcomers. Insect-borne pathogens, poxes, or viruses almost never appeared. Somehow the mosquito didn't arrive in Hawai'i until the 1820s, probably brought in a casket of egg-laden water on a whaling ship. On islands, flowering plants that came with thorns usually evolved into thornlessness. After all, thorns are a waste of energy if nothing is trying to eat you. Without other creatures chasing them, some birds evolved flightlessness, another huge energy-saving strategy. But most of all, there were no humans, the most pernicious invaders of all. So islands before humans arrived were exemplars of biological freedom. But after people arrived, they became prisons: organisms couldn't flee from people and their wanting ways, nor could they spread their genetic progeny elsewhere to keep their species alive.

Mention Easter Island to almost anyone, and if they've heard of it, they've likely heard of its statues. Imprinted in the popular imagination are its enigmatic, massive stone sculptures, or *moai*. Curious investigators have speculated for more than two centuries about how more than nine hundred of these mysterious statues—the largest being more than thirty feet tall and weighing over eighty tons—might have been moved to locations around the island, traveling miles from the site where they were quarried. The toromiro, though, is an invisible tree on the island, its story known to very few, and its existence marked more by its absence than its presence.

The tree does have many close relatives. The *Sophora* genus is speciose, as biologists say—a crowded taxon consisting of some sixty different species, including a dozen closely related oceanic ones scattered across the Pacific. None of these trees is large, but the toromiro is more of a shrub than a tree, at least from descriptions over the past century. The northernmost outpost for the *Sophora* genus is in Hawai'i, where its cousin *Sophora chrysophylla* is the primary food source for the palila, a critically endangered honeycreeper. The bird's beauty and rarity led my wife and me to give our second child the middle name Palila. Without *S. chrysophylla*, known as *māmane* in Hawaiian, the palila would not have survived the last century as its range dwindled.

The subterranean pollen record reveals that the toromiro was abundant across much of Rapa Nui, where many other now-extinct plants also thrived. Paleobotanical evidence shows that the tree's presence on the island dates back at least thirty-five thousand years. Its seeds are both buoyant and salt-resistant, and they probably first arrived by water, floating onto the island, probably from another Pacific island, and then it did what species do: continued its evolutionary journey in a new place to become the tree we know today. But even before the toromiro disappeared from the island, it had been without a lot of endemic companions. Fewer than thirty indigenous seed-bearing plant species have survived on Rapa Nui to the present day, and weeds, along with naturalized, cultivated shrubs, are now the main plants growing there.

The toromiro did not disappear precipitously but experienced a protracted decline. Humans arrived in Rapa Nui around the twelfth century CE, probably not long after Polynesians reached the Hawaiian archipelago. Some hundreds of years after humans' arrival, the island experienced a painful drop in biodiversity, and its carrying capacity plummeted as the native palm forests disappeared, replaced by grasslands. Food grew scarce, and occupants fled, thinning down to just several hundred humans at one point in the nineteenth century.[2] In his deterministic 2005 book *Collapse: How Societies Choose to Fail or Succeed*, Jared Diamond claimed the occupants were lousy land managers. His analysis of why Rapa Nui became denuded of its plant life is now out of date, as later studies have revealed the island's complexities. It's tempting to sketch the story of the weakening grip of native plant life on Rapa Nui as a predictable story of human arrogance intersecting with a small, remote, and evolutionarily vulnerable spit of land, but it's more nuanced than that.[3] Natives there recorded centuries-old histories of careful but intermittent conservation strategies. Some scholars have asserted that the Little Ice Age stressed resources on the island between the sixteenth and nineteenth centuries, leading to the disappearance of palms and other important contributors to the islanders' activities and well-being. Others have pointed to prolonged droughts, while still others have continued to argue that humans were highly complicit in the island's declining biodiversity. Were groves of palm trees decimated to create systems for rolling the giant stone carvings from quarry to coastline, where most of them have sat for many hundreds of years? Perhaps.

However they disappeared, the loss of palms seems to have been a factor in the tumbling downturn of the island's other trees, including the toromiro. The palms had made up the great majority of Rapa Nui's tree cover, some sixteen million trees that blanketed about 70 percent of the island. There is some controversy about the particular species, but many believe it was *Paschalococos disperta*, the Rapa Nui palm.[4] Jaime Espejo, a Chilean botanist who's written extensively about the toromiro, noted that it probably lived in the undergrowth of the palm, lodged in an ancient ecosystem that no longer exists. Paleobotanists and archaeologists studying the island evidence spotted the widespread loss of the palms in their investigations. At the same time, they found that the number of fish bones, found in waste middens around the island, dropped as fishing boats could no longer be constructed in large numbers from trees. The loss of access to fish must have been a devastating turn, because the human residents' main proteins came from the sea.

Soil erosion, likely exacerbated by deforestation and agriculture, led to further losses. Hooved animals, arriving with European explorers, were also certain culprits in the toromiro's decline and disappearance. On the island of Hawai'i, sheep consume that archipelago's species of *Sophora*. Another creature implicated in the destruction of much of both Rapa Nui's and Hawai'i's plant life was the Polynesian rat (*Rattus exulans*), as well as the bigger ship rat (*Rattus rattus*) and Norwegian rat (*Rattus norvegicus*).

Early European accounts and pollen records tell us that by about 1600 CE, forests in the island's craters had disappeared, and, with that, the toromiro's decline into long-term scarcity and then extirpation. The New Zealand anthropologist Stephen Fischer has noted that the last forest was probably cut for firewood around 1640, making wood the most valuable commodity on the island. Driftwood became precious. So scarce was wood, Fischer observes, that the pan-Polynesian word *rākau*, meaning "tree," "timber," or "wood," came to mean "riches" or "wealth" in the old Rapa Nuian language—a meaning not present in any other use of the word elsewhere in Polynesia, including in Tahiti, Tonga, Hawai'i, and New Zealand. It's ironic that after the deforestation of the island's trees, new linguistic meanings sprouted out of the island's impending botanical doom.[5]

Amid these centuries-long difficulties, but long before the toromiro disappeared, a wood-based culture thrived. The Rapa Nuians had a particular passion for carving; beyond their giant stone statues, they favored the toromiro for its durable and fine-grained wood and reddish hue. Although primarily used for ritual objects, the toromiro was also serviceable for building material in houses, household utensils, statuettes, and paddles. These artifacts survive in museums around the world. Some of them are hundreds of years old, and might provide unexpected addenda to our understandings of the tree's deeper history, offered up through dendrochronological analysis. Studying the annual growth rings in the wood could provide details we lack: the pace of growth of the wood, environmental pressures acting on the tree, its ultimate size, and many of the other clues revealed through laboratory work with wood specimens.

Part of our lack of knowledge about the tree's wood is because it has always been uncommon on the island, at least since Western contact. Rapa Nui came with inherent geographic disadvantages for plant survival, including few sheltered habitats with steep hillsides or deep ravines in which toromiro could remain hidden away from humans. The three volcanic craters on the island are the only such places. In 1911, the Chilean botanist Francisco Fuentes noted that the toromiro was rare, only to be found in Rano Kau, the largest of the craters. The Swedish botanist Carl Skottsberg, who also worked on Hawaiian flora, visited Rano Kau in 1917 and found only a single specimen. Other people rescued seeds from trees they identified incorrectly as *Sophora toromiro*, planting and growing these individuals elsewhere over the decades, further muddying the taxonomic waters.

The final contact with the tree on its native soil occurred when the Norwegian explorer Thor Heyerdahl collected seeds from the last surviving example. This was likely the same tree that Skottsberg had found in the shelter of Rano Kau. The egg-shaped crater is about a mile across and has its own microclimate, largely out of the winds and weather, and protected from grazing ungulates by a rock formation. There's not been a lot else in the crater to harvest or cut down in the last century, which has kept foot traffic down. It's also difficult to traverse, with innumerable swampy pockets of water. A beautiful, multicolored, shallow lake of open water and floating mats of peat cover much of the bottom of the crater. There, the tiny toromiro held on.

Heyerdahl, who had already been traveling around the Pacific Ocean in the 1940s, became famous, or infamous, for floating a radical new theory: that the islands in the Pacific had been populated initially by American Indians from the mainland of South America, rather than by people from Asia or from other Polynesian islands. In 1947, he launched an expedition with a primitive raft named *Kon-Tiki*, and made a five-thousand-mile journey, heading west from Peru. My parents had one of the several popular illustrated books about the voyage of the *Kon-Tiki*, and I reread it obsessively over the years. He looked to me like some kind of Norse god, eyes blazing as he rode atop his craft. I was drawn to the daring of the sea adventure, which took place in a raft that echoed those of prehistoric peoples, and to the length of the voyage, but mostly to the improbability of it all.

What's often lost in the voluminous writings about Heyerdahl and his oceanfaring obsessions was his interest in Rapa Nui. Björn Aldén, a Swedish botanist with the Gothenburg Botanical Garden, became friends with Heyerdahl and has worked to return the toromiro to its native land. In a letter to Björn, Heyerdahl decried the "tankelöse treskjaerere," or "thoughtless woodcutters." He noted how good it felt to have helped to save the species by collecting a handful of seeds that hung from the tree's sole remaining branch. Heyerdahl couldn't recount the exact date, or even the year, but thought it was sometime in late 1955 or early 1956. Heyerdahl handed the seeds off to a Professor Olaf Selling in Stockholm. They went to Gothenburg from there.[6]

There is a strain of national pride in Gothenburg for its role in the tree's cultivation and survival. But recently, researchers in Chile discovered that another botanist preceded Heyerdahl in getting seeds off the island. Efraín Volosky Yadlin, a Moldavian-born immigrant, participated in the first agronomic studies on Rapa Nui. Sent there by the Chilean Ministry of Agriculture in the early 1950s, Yadlin collected seeds, apparently from the same tree that Heyerdahl would come upon a few years later, and proceeded to carry out his own propagation tests on the toromiro.

The most active restoration efforts are now taking place in Chile, which is Rapa Nui's political and administrative entrepôt. CONAF, the country's national forestry organization, has planted hundreds of small propagated seedlings in Chile's Jardín Botánico Nacional de Viña del Mar. Still others survive in about a dozen disparate locations on various continents. Besides the Gothenburg population, you can visit the trees at Kew Gardens in England; at the Jardin botanique du Val Rahmeh-Menton, a tiny subtropical garden with a unique microclimate, nestled on the coast in southern France, less than a mile from the Italian border; and in several private botanical collections. Other examples may be in individual collectors' holdings, or in the far corners of public institutions, misidentified or unidentified. The institutions all share a goal: to keep the tree alive, along with the hope of reintroduction to Rapa Nui.

It seems as though returning the tree to its native land would be straightforward: simply plant it on Rapa Nui, tend to it judiciously, and see what happens. That's been tried, through more than twenty specialized botanical expeditions going back to 1965, with no luck. There are two obstacles to reintroducing the toromiro to Rapa Nui. The first is a diversity problem. The genetic makeup of the eighteen surviving Gothenburg specimens is the same from tree to tree, since they all came from the single survivor in the crater.

The second difficulty lies with the soil, and the toromiro's difficulties are best understood as a two-part problem: first, this issue of genetic weakness—the equivalent of the sickly, skinny kid on the playground, easy to knock to the ground—and second, a lack of a proper relationship between the tree and its native earth. The first issue may be resolved by cross-pollinating different individuals to create a more robust plant. The second problem is harder to resolve: getting the right bacteria into the soil so that it can help the tree take root. Mike Maunder, the executive director of the Cambridge Conservation Initiative in England, observed that the radically modified ecology of Rapa Nui is a fundamental obstacle because the soil has changed. "That's the challenge for these oceanic islands," he noted. "The soil would've been highly fertile, seabird-enriched. What we're trying to put it back into is an eroded, starved soil."

Many people think that soil is sterile dirt. But healthy soil is a dynamic mix of fungi, bacteria, viruses, decaying vegetation in various stages of decomposition, and minerals. A single gram of soil can contain billions of bacteria—more individuals than there are people on the planet—from thousands of different species. Soil is complex, and the mycorrhizae that have kept the toromiro from taking root constitute a key difficulty. A mycorrhiza isn't a tree part, strictly speaking, but a mutually beneficial relationship, an association between a fungus and the roots of a plant. It's a pact, a botanical agreement. Fungi give the plant minerals and water through the trees' roots, and the plant supplies the fungi with steady access to carbohydrates, which fungi need to grow.

The bristlecone pine gives the botanical equivalent of a shrug when planted in poor-quality soil, whereas the toromiro seems to need a particular recipe. And it gets weirder elsewhere in the plant kingdom. The white "ghost pipe" plant, *Monotropa uniflora*, has given up photosynthesis, relying entirely on mycorrhiza for nutrition. The kinship involved in these fungus-root interactions is staggeringly intricate. It's what the ecologist Merlin Sheldrake describes as flexible behavior. No wonder the toromiro's rerooting on Rapa Nui has proven challenging, given how much complexity has been stripped from the ground over the centuries. The toromiro's chances of survival will probably continue to increase as our understanding of the complex relationship between fungi and roots grows.[7]

Mike offered up several complementary and practical approaches beyond the mycorrhizal. "You'd also want to take a good gardener's approach," he observed. "You probably want some shelter from the wind; you probably want some initial shelter from the sun; you'd want a good, deep organic soil; and you need someone to look after them to water them and keep them fenced. And you'd need to put a couple of hundred down, because putting them down in batches of four or five means they won't survive."

Getting the toromiro to root on Rapa Nui might only be a matter of time: as the wheels of natural selection and evolution turn inexorably, the trees in captivity will eventually (and what "eventually" means is an open question) diversify from their siblings around the world, and can be crossbred. They'll evolve in isolation. But herein lies yet another complication: if too much time passes, the trees will be so different that they can't interbreed. Moving an organism means subjecting it to different selective pressures based on different conditions. Even over the course of mere decades, identifiable physical and genetic changes occur, not just among trees. The common myna, a raucous, cocky transplant from Asia introduced to Hawai'i in 1865, has evolved over a hundred generations into a bird that's genetically unique to Hawai'i, and on its way to becoming a new species, which may already make it incompatible with its brethren off the island. Complicating the work is the possibility of continued effects from climatic changes in the Rapa Nuian environment that will confound the reintroduction process. We cannot anticipate the effects of these changes. But evidence in other regions of the world indicates that climate change's effects on soil erosion, root growth and function, and root-microbe associations make planting prospects worse, not better.

In Chile, there is intensive research underway to identify the rhizobia: the bacteria associated with the species. (Bacteria are less complicated than fungi, but also play a key role in soil health.) One strategy has been to inoculate trials of the toromiro with rhizobia collected from other species in the *Sophora* genus. Does this scientific alchemy make it the same tree? Probably; the DNA sequences in an inoculated tree would be identical to those in an uninoculated tree. But modifying the rhizobia also sets the wheels of evolutionary change into motion, with unpredictable effects.[8]

Unpredictability is the watchword for a great deal of the difficulties the toromiro faces, along with its cousin uncertainty. We have no clear answer, only potential solutions. Conservation is slow, patient work, and every island has its own challenges and opportunities. With more surviving endemic species, Hawai'i has more to work with than Rapa Nui, and is an exemplar of the complexities of island conservation. Bob Cabin, an island ecologist, noted that the more time he spent in the trenches of Hawaiian conservation, the more he began to realize that conservation is not rocket science—it's much harder! In contrast to the relative simplicity of understanding and manipulating the inanimate physical forces involved with building rockets, conservationists must deal with the much greater complexity of interacting living species and the intractable world of human desires.[9]

People point to the strong hand of humans in effecting changes on islands. But tsunamis, which are globally disruptive, have unpredictably and dramatically reshaped island life. Historical records show that my homeland of Hawai'i has endured at least eighty-five tsunamis.[10] These big waves have also modified Rapa Nui, affecting the island's vegetation, including the toromiro. The same tsunami that struck Hawai'i in 1960 also roared onto Rapa Nui. One recent research article suggested that at least fifty tsunamis may have reached Rapa Nui in the last thousand years.[11] The 1960 tsunami was epic, but one in 1575 in southern Chile was also devastating, along with all those others for which we have no written record.

Tsunamis matter in the toromiro story because it's possible that they have been an escape valve for the tree.[12] The toromiro's buoyant, salt water–resistant seeds could have spread via tsunamis to other islands in the Pacific, leading to what biologists call vicariance: the geographical separation of a population, usually by a physical barrier such as a mountain or an ocean, eventually leading to a pair of closely related species. The toromiro could've thus jumped the prison walls and spread to other locations. The southern coast of Rapa Nui, all of it at lower elevations, would have been inundated by a tsunami originating along the South American coast, or from anywhere around the Pacific Rim. Tsunamis may have been the mechanism over eons that led to the transmission and subsequent evolution of some of the dozen Pacific species of the *Sophora* genus. Trees in this genus are never a dominant part of any region's vegetation, and given the recent quantity and size of tsunamis in recent centuries, I think it's possible that other examples of the little toromiro have survived elsewhere but not yet been identified.

Marine biologists and ecologists have begun to study and contemplate tsunami-driven plant and animal dispersal with newer statistical tools in recent years. Species typically have a vanishingly unlikely chance of surviving a pan-Pacific voyage from one of the regions along the Pacific Ring of Fire, as the region around much of the rim of the Pacific Ocean is known. But tsunamis appear to have changed the dispersal story. What was once a lottery ticket becomes more like a passage on an ocean liner. It's likely that Rapa Nui and Hawai'i may both have experienced a kind of settlement acceleration through tsunamis. After the 2011 tsunami originating in eastern Japan, at least 289 species of living organisms floated for thousands of kilometers over six years, ultimately reaching Hawai'i and North America. If one tsunami can disperse hundreds of species across the Pacific, imagine the colonizing effects over eons. And as a warming climate leads to more frequent tsunamis, they may increasingly reshuffle organisms across the oceans to new homes.

My own story was also one of escape from an island. There is a common term for someone born in Hawai'i: *kama'āina*, meaning "child of the land." But although I was from the islands, I was not fully of the islands. I had not descended from ancient Polynesians, nor could my lineage there even be traced back to before my parents' arrival from the US mainland in the middle of the twentieth century. I had a fitful foothold in Hawai'i and frequently felt like an outsider. Still, some part of me *was* of the islands. Hawai'i had nourished me, raised me up, colored me through its culture and its beauty. But upon finishing high school, I was washed back to the mainland, not under the power of a seismic wave but by the desire to seek a wider world, as a diaspora of one, glad to leave everything and everyone behind. My brother, Gene, who left the islands around the same time I did, did not survive the transition, taking his own life some years later on the mainland, a child without an emotional land to call home.

Belonging is burdened with complexities, but it's not a static condition; it's a problem to be worked. Explorations to diversify the toromiro's genetic footprint continue to the present day. Jaime, the Chilean botanist, recently discovered that the Smithsonian had an herbarium sample consisting of the tree's pods and seeds, and dating to a collecting voyage to Rapa Nui in early 1934. CONAF has asked for a single pod containing four seeds. If the request is successful,

Chilean foresters will germinate the seeds and produce seedlings. The resulting plants will allow for comparison of the DNA with recent progenies to better understand changes in the plant's DNA sequence or hybridization.[13]

So we have a story of a tiny tree from the middle of an ocean, extinct in the wild and now in the middle of a challenging international effort to translocate it back to that island. But the extensive scientific discussions of the tree never mention the reasons for returning it to Rapa Nui. I offer three thoughts as to why it's important work. The first is an ecosystem rationale: that every species that arrives, or rearrives, at a place that might become its permanent home brings some bit of biodiversification with it. It's not just the tree that brings new elements but the interactions and alliances: the microbiota in the vicinity; the birds, insects, and mammals that can make use of the plant for shelter, sustenance, survival. Another species on the edge of its own ability to survive can find a toehold in the form of an allied plant with which it can create some kind of symbiosis. What other animals and plants would make common cause with it, and on what scale? Every island has an ecological pulse, a series of rhythms and sequences. The toromiro had a place on Rapa Nui, and it should have a place again. But it wouldn't grow in the same density, or inhabit the same ecosystem from which it sprang. It probably wouldn't even be the same tree, given the long influences of the other places it's been. Sixty years is a long time to be a traveler far from home. But given how depauperate the island's flora is now, it will be an experiment, and it might bring new life to an old island.

The second reason is emblematic. The economic costs of all this work far outstrip any financial gain that might result from returning the tree. But the toromiro has value as part of the island's culture, and it belongs to the people of Rapa Nui. It's difficult to anticipate how humans would make use of the reintroduced tree as a cultural or practical element. But Rapa Nuians would celebrate its return, and it would serve as a strengthening element and a point of pride for an island people who have suffered privations for a very long time. Åsa

Krüger, the curator at the Gothenburg Botanical Garden who now stewards their toromiro, thinks that successful reestablishment of the tree could have great symbolic value. If the toromiro can serve as the poster tree for native species on Rapa Nui, the rest of the native flora—the fifty other native species that still survive—will benefit from a larger conservation undertaking and from broader ecological awareness of what it takes to maintain native plants there.

A number of vexations remain. It's an open question as to whether or not Chilean botanists should instead establish a closely related species on the island. One unintended effect might be that inserting a slightly different species would just be another invasive introduction, since we can't anticipate the subtle ecological interactions that would follow. What could go wrong? Maybe nothing, maybe a lot. And planting an approximation of the toromiro might give the appearance of a successful introduction, but it seems like offering up a facsimile of a museum object: nobody would flock to see the *Mona Lisa* if it was a copy, no matter how carefully done.

The third reason for repatriating the tree is an ethical one: it provides a chance to fulfill an obligation to shatter what have seemed like the inevitable shackles of extinction. For Jaime, the tree is an exemplar for other endangered trees. He praised the attempts at reintroduction as a way to lead by example, demonstrating the virtues of persistence, soil science, and problem-solving.

Along with the mycorrhizal obstacles, grazing livestock and some agricultural practices on the island continue to threaten any future establishment of the toromiro, and until those matters are resolved, the little tree will probably always have a limited presence on the island. But even a slight and steady footing on Rapa Nui would be much better than no presence at all, because it provides evidence of survival, and a return home, in the face of a changing planet: presence, not absence, a bush in the hand, and a harbinger of the future. There is an island of opportunity in the middle of every difficulty.

CHAPTER 4

Finding Time: Amber, Insects, and a Fossil Tree

"Great things are done . . . by a series of small things brought together."

—Vincent van Gogh, writing to his
brother Theo, October 1882

Animals don't get much stranger than the tardigrade. It's a boneless little creature, a chubby, eight-legged, microscopic organism that lives mostly in water, although it can live anywhere, and I mean *anywhere*. It's not what you'd think an unstoppable organism would look like. If it were bigger you might consider it cuddly. Despite its sharp claws and a megaphone-shaped snout where you'd expect its face to be, it's a cute, clumsy crawler, staggering along like a newborn puppy. The tardigrade has been reported to live in hot springs, deep under the sea, and beneath solid ice at both poles. In tests, it's survived being boiled, frozen, dried out, and even subjected repeatedly to the intense radiation of outer space. Its evolutionary past, and the futures it contains, are embedded in the amber from a tree that's so old it has no common name, known only as *Hymenaea protera*.[1] It's not an exaggeration to say that the tardigrade holds secrets that could offer salvation from the effects of climate change.

In 1773, J. A. E. Goeze, a German pastor with a zest for microscopy, first identified the tardigrade, which he named using the French adjective for "slow-moving." News of the animal's freakish survival abilities spread quickly; in 1800, *Edinburgh Magazine* called tardigrades "the colossuses of the microscopic world." Because tardigrades are micro-sacs of goo (albeit with mouths, rectums, and esophagi), they don't fossilize. But three of their intact remains from deep time have been found—all in amber, spread out over nearly sixty years of painstaking searching between 1964 and 2022. Tardigrades' evolutionary heritage had been previously inaccessible to paleontologists: a "ghost lineage" because of the lack of examples marching through the long ledger of time. But now that's changing. Scientists would like to understand how tardigrades came to be such extremophiles, able not just to survive radiation in outer space, but to suspend their metabolism when going dormant. Studying the biology of tardigrades over long time frames could provide new understandings of what selective pressures, what mutations, and what circumstances gave them such profoundly effective survival skills. The search for more tardigrades in amber continues.

Tardigrades, which can live for at least sixty years, are called water bears, although they can readily live on land, because there's a lot of water to be had there: in the watery layers between dead tree leaves; in lichens that trap moisture; and under solid layers of ice. Scientists have identified about a thousand different species, living just about everywhere on Earth. They've also been hardy extraplanetary travelers for some time. Russian scientists sent them into space in 2007, and NASA astrobiologists packed them off to the International Space Station in 2021. They've also been flown on other spacecraft to expose them to various conditions, including radiation, extreme temperatures, and zero gravity. They even reproduced while in these circumstances. Coming to understand how they can survive UV radiation a thousand times higher than on the surface of the Earth, without oxygen and in freezing conditions, might also prove useful for acting on our own desires for space travel. (An Israeli lunar lander that crash-landed on the moon in 2019 when its gyroscopes failed might've even accidentally spilled a bunch of them. Among its payload were thousands of tardigrades, accompanied by a digital library designed to serve as a primer for humanity in case it was discovered by future civilizations. The library appeared to have survived the crash, so the tardigrades probably did, too.)

Ideas about how the tardigrade could help humans are more than speculative. Japanese scientists have already studied tardigrade proteins to see whether they can come up with a more effective sunscreen, binding tardigrade proteins to human cells in the laboratory to develop a more radiation-resistant product. This work produced cells that showed a 40–50 percent reduction in X-ray damage to skin: useful if you're prone to sunburns, but essential if you're at risk of, say, radiation poisoning. There is no organism hardier than the tardigrade, and none potentially of greater use.[2]

H. protera grew across large portions of what was once the combined continent of Africa and South America. The tree lived about twenty-five million years ago, probably growing tall and leafy, branching out with a large crown, reaching above 120 feet and occasionally emerging above the surrounding canopy. It had tan-colored petals, and provided leaves and fruits to a menagerie ranging from tiny insects to large mammals. Bats, bees, butterflies, moths, and other insects pollinated its flowers.[3] *H. protera* has a messenger in its biology: amber, an ancient substance that began as a sticky resin, exuded by trees from wounds, and then hardened into rocklike form. Amber has conserved abundant and diverse biological evidence of ancient species from millions of years ago: a map of the planet's ancestors that offers a route to better understanding evolution and current life on Earth. We now know well that the natural world is reliant on parts working in approximate harmonies with one another. But our understandings of the linkages between past and present life are nowhere near as clear, in part because the record from deep time is so incomplete.

The passage of time is a lubricant: given enough of it, change is irresistible. Even though fossil trees have existed for tens to hundreds of millions of years, we can learn a disconcertingly detailed amount about changes in past climates on Earth from the trees, but especially from their remnants. Tree parts typically end up on the ground, and then, covered over with water and sediment, live on as exquisite casts, typically taking hundreds of thousands of years to become stone, through permineralization and the actions of water and time. The details paleontologists glean from this evidence from the past are called proxies. Since it's not possible to directly observe ancient climates, paleontologists study the imprints climate has created. Fossilized proxies can include not just trees themselves but their residual efflorescences: leaves, bark, roots, flowers, and pollens, which are often highly localized, and thus can help connect organisms to particular elevations, latitudes, and effects from past weather conditions. Unlike fossils, however, the specimens trapped in amber offer a more direct voice from deep time. These nuggets of amber are not fossils but, rather, contain the original organisms: flesh, bones, tissue, and even blood, trapped in an oxygen-free structure for millions of years. The contents of amber are a message in a bottle, cast over the immense oceans of time.

Amber first came to people's attention not because of its contents but because it had a powerful cultural pull. It's beautiful stuff, amber, and fortunately for artisans as well as scientists, it survives in enormous quantities. Ranging from pale yellow to brownish red, blue, and green, amber has been in demand since humans first used artifacts. A palace built in Germany in the seventeenth century used more than six tons of amber to line the walls and ceiling of one of its rooms. It has been talisman, jealously guarded prize, and object of obsession. As my colleague Faya Causey, an authority on cultural uses of amber, told me, "Jewelry is never just jewelry. It can signal allegiances, ward off danger or illness, provide self-identity, and so much more." In a recent book she wrote about amber and the ancient world, she observes that it has also served as amulet, incense, decoration, and funerary object.

A great deal of *H. protera*'s amber has come into human hands from one location: the La Toca mine in Santiago Province in the Dominican Republic. It's thus come to be called Dominican amber, and out of this mine, amazements have emerged. One variety of Dominican amber is a deep, hypnotic blue. In the art world, blue resonates like nothing else. My jaw sagged the first time I saw a piece of Dominican blue amber, and lust rose in my heart. Although it's not been determined conclusively, paleobotanists think that the color comes from forest fires among *H. protera* trees. Because blue amber contains virtually no inclusions—no plants or animals—it makes sense that fire raged, because the contents would've been cooked and burnt up before the amber had a chance to solidify.

There are other sensory delights with Dominican amber, and with any kind of genuine amber. Cut a piece of it and you'll smell the odor of pine tree sap, or sometimes a whiff of turpentine, or, as one amber salesperson described it, "church incense." Others say it smells like cloves. It's amazing that anything millions of years old could retain some of its original odor. Heft a bigger piece in your hand and it's chunky, solid, and safe to handle—although be prepared for a crackle of static electricity. Amber's ability to generate static through rubbing was probably its primary practical interest to people thousands of years ago, as a potential cure for numerous ailments. The Greek word for amber is *elektron*. The substance's origins were unknown for a long time. Pliny thought it was a liquid produced by the rays of the sun, striking soil and "leaving upon it an unctuous sweat." It is a kind of sweat, perhaps, one caused by trees as a protective response to injury. But this is not maple syrup turned to stone. Resin is generally not to be confused with sap, or latex, or gum, or other chemically different viscous liquids that ooze out of trees. Structurally different from those other liquids, resin is a guardian: it protects a tree by repairing injuries from damage, insects, disease, and fire.[4]

H. protera wept out its resin in copious amounts over millions of years. Its volume may have stemmed from widespread, catastrophic damage to forests; or it might've been a slow but constant outflow. There are many other kinds of amber, including Baltic and Mexican amber, as well as Lebanon amber, the oldest of all ambers and thus home to the oldest specimens trapped in its embrace. All told, more than 160 large deposits of amber exist worldwide, and many more trace quantities have survived. Because of differences in locale, environmental conditions, formation, and types and distribution of trees, there is great variety in purity, density, and locality of amber.

Although fossils and amber are both chapters in nature's long notebook, they're from different volumes. Fossils need water to form because the minerals that replace organic elements in plant matter are carried by groundwater to fill the cellular spaces of dead plants and animals, taking on their precise shapes. Amber is different. When a tree produces resin, it's usually in the form of essential oils, or oleoresins. These oils are volatile; that is, they readily evaporate at what we, from our urbanized perches in the twenty-first century, might call "room temperature." As the oils evaporate, the resin polymerizes and turns into a substance called copal, becoming harder and more resistant to environmental forces, and then, over more time, under the weight of overlying sediment and lacking oxygen, it turns into what we call amber. Fossils are rare accidents, requiring ideal conditions that include a dead, undisturbed organism, the slow and steady arrival and continued presence of water, and then the accumulation of layers of sediment. Fossil creation is about being in the right place at the right time, and under the right conditions. Getting trapped in amber just requires being in the wrong place at the wrong time: one false move, a gust of wind, a drip of resin, and you're caught in a sticky substance from which you cannot escape.[5]

Because amber traps organisms in a blob of oxygen-free resin, the stilled life within is preserved with its components intact: chloroplasts, cell nuclei, pigments. The fidelity of insect details in particular astonishes. We can see a termite pollinating a flower; we can see flies having three-dimensional sex; we can view the flight muscles of a stingless bee; we can even observe the folded membranes of mitochondria.[6] As the science journalist Katharine Gammon noted, "Studying fossils in amber after studying fossils in rock is like switching from grainy black-and-white television to high-definition movies."[7] Put another way, fossils in rock whisper about the climate past, but amber speaks in a rich, clear voice. Life arrested in amber consists of four kinds: microbes, plants, invertebrates, and vertebrates. We're talking small-scale: no one has found a baby T. rex preserved in amber. Bigger insects can often wrestle free; the longest insects ever discovered in amber are about two and a half inches long. There exists what is sometimes called Lilliputian bias in amber fossils. If you were an alien who landed and began rooting through a museum's extensive collection of fossils in amber, you'd conclude that the Earth's past life was only made up of tiny animals. Because amber immediately enrobes its foreign contents in oxygen-free ooze, it preserves anatomy, soft parts, and feathers in three dimensions. As a bonus, most amber also contains compounds that inhibit bacterial growth, further keeping the specimen from decaying. Fossils in rock, by contrast, tend to be squashed, given that they're formed between layers of sediment.

Insects witnessed the rise and fall of the dinosaurs, and the cascading effects of humans coming into the world, and everything in between. The greatest percentage of life trapped in amber consists of arthropods: insects and spiders. (Most high school biology students will remind you that they're not the same: insects have three body parts and six legs; spiders have just two body parts, eight legs, and, usually, eight eyes.) There are about forty-five thousand known species of spiders. But they're completely outpaced by insects; entomologists have described more than a million species of insects worldwide, and these represent more than half of all known living organisms. There may be as many as ten million insect species, and in their totality these might constitute over 90 percent of animal life on Earth. Understanding this corpus of bugs lets paleoentomologists align the present with the past, fitting newly described species of amberized insects into locations on the tree of life that constitutes the enormous, complex puzzle of diversification.

But the numbers of insects are less significant than their effects on the natural world. For eons, they have been a central part of the food web for organisms around the globe. They provide nutrition for hundreds of thousands of other species, including humans; they pollinate many of our fruits, vegetables, and flowers. They offer us honey, silk, and beeswax, and are masterful decomposers, breaking down and getting rid of wastes, dead animals and plants, and other detritus. Insects have been performing these functions since they appeared on the planet some 345 million years ago. Amber is the textbook of this ancient insect life from the deep past. Dominican amber is unusually transparent, rendering its contents legible—a very useful quality if you're looking for the remains of trapped life. But for scientists, our Dominican tree's amber has another key quality: it tends to have more embedded life than other kinds of amber. This density has allowed scientists to not just identify individual critters frozen in time, but to reconstruct the ecosystem of a tropical forest from millions of years ago. Out of one substance—amber—worlds emerge. In the same way that the French anatomist Georges Cuvier could identify an entire animal from a single bone, so too does seeing the details in amber reveal a much wider interrelated world.

Insects in amber have many instructions about the future. What's past is prologue: amber lets us make sense of insects' contributions to biodiversity and diversification in deep time, and then allow for extrapolation for future scenarios. Researching insects from a long time ago can provide news about pest evolution, pollination, and even gigantism—the tendency for some prehistoric insects to grow to a very large size—as a result of climate change. Comparing prehistoric insects with modern relatives frequently uncovers secrets, or provokes important questions: what classes of insects were smaller then, and why; what has caused them to be larger, and what does that mean for our future relationships with insects? These are a scant handful of the investigations entomologists make. The effects of long-term environmental conditions and change are inscribed on evolved bodies. Museum collections around the world support these research efforts. These include the Smithsonian's collection of thirty-five million individual insects, the largest in the world, providing evidence of the scientific value of their study.

Insects in amber are especially useful for the inferences they help scientists draw about plants. Botanic matter appears in resin, including grasses, small flowers, seeds, and little leaves. It's clear from the presence of once-living organisms in these amber nuggets that the natural world was a wildly diverse, disruptive, and crowded place millions of years ago. We know that many classes of insects depend on specific types of flowers, fruits, or leaves that don't themselves occur in the amber, either because those plant parts are too large or don't grow in ecosystems sufficiently near to the trees. Figs are known to have been present in some places entirely because of the presence of certain kinds of wasps in amber. The wasps and the figs have formed a symbiotic relationship over the eons: the wasps pollinate the flowers, which in turn give the wasps a safe place for raising their wasp young. Another example is the presence of the palm bug (*Paleodoris lattini*) in amber. The bug implies the nearby presence of the palm; its flattened body lets it live between the palm's tightly closed fronds.[8]

Occasionally, amber captures a part of *H. protera*, the tree from which it was born. We can see the tree's winged seeds, which disperse on the wind; we can view its fine, delicate plant structures. These even include the stomata, or little pores, which have been used extensively to reconstruct ancient levels of CO_2 concentrations in the Earth's atmosphere. But while we have flattened fossil versions of those flowers and leaves, the amberized items provide new details about *H. protera*. Scientists love to partner with high-powered tools for studying amber, because of all they show and tell. The tree's fine details are so well preserved that scientists can study its ultrastructure—cellular and tissue details visible only through high-powered microscopes.

The wealth of arthropods found in Dominican amber is an entomophobe's nightmare: at least fifty different species of spiders, as well as scorpions, mites, ticks, winged ants, midges, termites, earwigs, bees, leafhoppers, leaf-cutters, and butterflies. Finds of insects in amber have provided a window into defensive and offensive mechanisms, social and mating behaviors, and bug sex, caught *in flagrante* (from the Latin for "in blazing fashion") for millennia. Acts of desperation abound: a leaf beetle blowing noxious bubbles in a last, frantic attempt to defend itself against the resin in which it's just been trapped; worker ants trying to carry their brood to safety—nature frozen in tooth and claw. Many flies reflexively lay eggs when they die, and there are many female flies in amber that have eggs trailing behind: a final effort to create life out of death.[9] A blood-filled tick has even appeared. It likely fell into the resin, fresh off its latest and last meal. And the blood cells are probably mammalian. After the arrival of humans on Hispaniola around six thousand years ago, but especially after the European invasion more than five hundred years ago, mammals almost disappeared.[10]

Liquids are especially important finds in amber because they're not found in fossils. The magic of permineralization can only go so far, and it won't preserve any bodily fluids, or any kind of soft, gelatinous material, or saliva—only stone traces of those liquids. Only in recent decades have we been able to identify even modern species from their blood. DNA can survive for up to about 1.5 million years, but not much longer. So efforts to harvest the much older DNA from amber specimens are only speculative. But if enough usable DNA were extractable from amber, it could pinpoint the particular animal from which the tick or other biting insect had taken its last meal.[11]

Every discipline needs its dean or doyenne, and the study of Dominican amber is no exception. George Poinar Jr., of Oregon State University, knows more than anyone alive about the amber, having made many discoveries over the long decades of his research and fieldwork. In 1987, Poinar described the first amphibian fossil in amber (and only the third vertebrate), a tiny frog found in the Dominican Republic, and again, from the La Toca mine. Understanding fossil species is not just about chronology but also biogeography—what plants and animals have lived in what areas—because if a species is found somewhere new and unexpected, it changes our understanding of their distribution, and thus of their ecosystems. The frog's anatomical details render it identifiable: it's a member of the *Eleutherodactylus* genus. Its skin and eyes are intact, and much of the skin has become transparent, which provides a window into the skeleton's fine details.

Poinar has also discovered a microinvertebrate locked in Dominican amber: *Sialomorpha dominicana*, an animal also known as a "mold pig" (not to be confused with the tardigrade, despite its similarity) and so named because it ate fungi and because it looks for all the world like a tiny pig. It was Poinar's 1982 research paper on the ultrastructure of this forty-million-year-old insect tissue that gave the author Michael Crichton the central idea for his book *Jurassic Park*: the preservation of cellular structure and soft tissues in an ancient organism. After the movie by the same name came out in 1993, there was an enormous surge of interest in amber and its organic cargo. Many paleontologists have objected to the movie's premise, however, because of the misconceptions it fueled: that dinosaur remains included viable DNA that could be extracted; and that de-extinction of dinosaur species was in the realm of possibility. But ugly opportunism arose when a team of researchers took advantage of the movie's popularity to promote the idea that recovering ancient DNA was possible, publishing an article on the day the movie appeared in theaters, writing about their work extracting and sequencing DNA from a 125-million-year-old ancient weevil in Lebanese amber. Poinar was one of the coauthors. Other scientists expressed skepticism; one study speculated that the weevil's DNA sequence was that of a fungal contamination, not the weevil itself.

Interest in amberized insects fell away after the cinematic hubbub died down. But by the twenty-first century, research had picked up again. In the last decade alone, paleobiologists and others have produced many hundreds of papers related to preserved finds within amber from around the world. As the paleontologist David Grimaldi, the amber curator at the American Museum of Natural History, remarked recently, "Right now we're in this frenzy, almost an orgy of scientific finds."[12]

Now in his late eighties, Poinar remains active. He's used the plants and animals in amber from *Hymenaea protera* to reconstruct an entire tropical forest on the island of Hispaniola, providing a snapshot of the colonies of insects, various plants, and many other rich finds dating to the same approximate era. He has made some unsettling discoveries. Analyzing some dried blood from a flea found in Dominican amber, Poinar was able to isolate what appears to have been a plague germ, possibly an ancestor of *Yersinia pestis*, the bacterium now known to have been responsible for the Black Death in Europe. Epidemiologists had thought this plague had appeared during humans' time on Earth, but the amber evidence suggests that it is very much older.[13]

The lessons seem limitless. Only recently has true structural color from ancient creatures been discovered in amber, and color can provide a bucketful of clues about an insect's behavior and ecology because of its role in camouflage, thermoregulation, and diverse communications strategies, including attracting mates. Some ancient insects caught in amber are purple, blue, and vibrant metallic green.

How has all of this amber come into human hands? A lot of it lies underground. Christopher Columbus mentioned it in late 1492, reporting that he took Dominican amber back home after he reached the island and saw amber beads decorating a pair of shoes given to him by a Taíno chief.[14] Almost all amber mines are in poor countries, and the work is difficult and dangerous. Miners crawl through claustrophobic, water-filled tunnels typically too low to stand up in, lying on their sides for hours, chipping away. Most of the amber is extracted through an inefficient but cheap technique called bell pitting—a dangerous undertaking because of the risk of tunnel collapse. Digging a bell pit involves sinking a shaft straight down, into which miners are lowered and raised in a bucket. The pits don't have drainage systems and are prone to crumble during flooding, and difficult to buttress. Digging a deep enough hole in the ground without supporting it makes gravity mad. The unreinforced walls of most tunnels and pit mines mean that collapse of the entire structure is a constant danger. Candles are often the only source of light, and humidity hovers at or near 100 percent.[15]

The rest of the world's amber has moved around the planet aboveground in an endless churn. If you look at maps of the planet's geographies and geologies over many millions of years, you will see that configurations have changed a lot. Climate warming and cooling cycles have caused much of this movement. Rivers appeared, then disappeared. Rowdy geologic activity has relocated amber as continents have slid away from each other. Water has flowed and pooled in areas that are now at thousands of feet of elevation; mountains have thrust up and slumped down; and oceans have covered vast areas of what is now dry land. Most amber floats, which means that water has swept much of it around the world, sending it down rivers where it eventually becomes stranded and concentrated along the banks or swept out to sea. But like innocent witches, a lot of fresh amber also sinks, depending on its density, which can vary greatly. Sometimes amber hunters extract it from shallow ocean waters, often by sucking up quantities of rocks from the bottoms of shorelines: a miner's approach to finding a kind of tree gold.

So how does the tardigrade survive extreme conditions? Scientists finally sorted it out several years ago, and it's a very neat multipart trick. When it senses that dry conditions are approaching, it pulls its head and limbs into its exoskeleton, stops moving, and waits for water. Tardigrades can stay in this dormant state for decades, popping back into motion when water returns. But desiccation isn't its only tool; other less hardy animals have the ability to live in a dried-out state for long periods of time, such as brine shrimp and nematode worms.

Those animals use a sugar known as trehalose to protect their cells from the damage that dehydration brings. Microbiologists speculated for a long time that trehalose was how the tardigrade protected itself. However, the process is completely different. As it dries out, the water bear, in a stunning feat of transformation, turns most of itself temporarily into glass, producing something called intrinsically disordered proteins. This glass coats the cell's molecules, protecting them. A tiny bit of water still remains in the most dried-out tardigrade, and in concert with these proteins—the exact mechanisms remain unknown—the tardigrade vitrifies and suspends itself from the rest of the world, waiting to be reborn: Sleeping Beauty awaiting a hydrating kiss.

But how does this particular protection against dryness keep ultraviolet radiation at bay? It doesn't, as it turns out; still other defense mechanisms are at work. A newly discovered species of tardigrade, *Hypsibius exemplaris*, might provide the key. Hiding beneath its skin are fluorescent pigments that turn ultraviolet radiation into harmless blue light. Further, tardigrades have exceptionally robust DNA repair mechanisms, which spin into action. We don't know whether tardigrades found in amber had the same survival skills, or completely different ones. Finding more specimens would help us understand their evolutionary histories, to help us further our futures.

Without *H. protera* and its amber, we'd be depauperate. It's so much easier to make sense of a tree still alive on the planet, because we have much greater density of information: photographs, maps, records of distribution, and direct access to the tree's own biology. But while a living tree can provide a denser record, it's also just a tiny dot on the line from then to now, compared to a tree that has taken the measure of evolution's vast and cumulative arc. Although the tree is long extinct, *H. protera* has provided us with a means to know about ecological interactions and evolution over a grand timescale. There are countless advices that the chronological deep dive into amber can provide about the resilience of plants and animals during long epochs of change. It appears that some classes of organisms were more resilient, while others were less so. Understanding which taxa survived a wide range of conditions may provide a model for focusing conservation resources on plants that have had a shorter evolutionary life, or on larger families of plants with a high percentage of extinctions across species. Amber's contents also show us that some ecosystems have been surprisingly protective of the individual species found therein, while others were not. These are the kinds of research topics paleo-botanists, paleoclimatologists, and paleoecologists pursue, working in concert with conservation biologists studying the living plants of today. Extinction isn't necessarily a suffocating blanket that smothers the future of all organisms. There is longevity and hope in these trees and their residues over deep time.[16]

CHAPTER 5

Understory Alliance: The Longleaf Pine and Its Fiery Partners

"Fire to the longleaf is like rain to the rainforest; it's part of the system. Pull it out, and the whole system collapses."

—Jesse Wimberley

Lightning strikes our planet more than two billion times a year. Ground-based sensors and satellites detect these electrical charges, which hammer every square mile on Earth. Lightning—a giant spark that can take place inside a cloud, or between a cloud and the ground—is a complex dance involving the collision of ice particles, the buildup of an electrical charge, and the release of what's called a stepped leader: the hot, jagged stripe of electricity that blasts toward the ground. That strike can reach an astonishing fifty thousand degrees Fahrenheit, five times hotter than the surface of the sun. When lightning hits a tree, it can cause it to explode. The heat frequently also starts a fire. This fire is—seemingly paradoxically—a lifeline for *Pinus palustris*, the longleaf pine.

Regal, with greenery distributed across most of the upper two-thirds of the tree, the longleaf has reddish, scaly bark, and small but lush bundles of long, green pine needles, hence its name. The most ancient of these conifers are at least five hundred years old, reaching about 120 feet. They grow ramrod-straight, naturally pruning their

own lower branches, which fall off as the tree grows. A cohort of
canopy specialists and tree scientists tend to study redwoods for their
football field–long upper regions. But most of the ecological study of
the longleaf concerns its bottom six feet. This is where fire blossoms,
and in doing so renews the longleaf's ecosystem. Fire in longleaf
forests "is not about the trees. It's the grasses, the forbs [flowering
plants], the birds. It is the bottom six feet that's important to wilderness," noted Robert Abernathy, president of the Longleaf Alliance,
the country's largest longleaf conservation group. Or to shorten it
further, as a Nature Conservancy manager observed, "In the longleaf
forest, the diversity is from the knees down."[1] The longleaf understory is one of the most diverse habitats in North America. And tend-
ing to these habitats involves a ground truth: traveling among the
trees in the forest and setting fires, in the form of controlled burns.

These burns are essential to the health of the land and the tree for
numerous reasons, but chief among them is that fire reduces the fuel
load in a forest, so that when fire does come along, the entire forest
doesn't burn to the ground. Before settlement by humans, lightning
caused the fires, so they would occur in a window roughly between
April and July. Because the tree has evolved with fire, it holds back its
reproduction cycle to get in sync with the fire cycle. Longleaf can't
even germinate without fire. In the forest, every tree you can see,
looking down vast sight lines, has evolved with a fire cycle. But after
a century of vigorous fire suppression, the land needs more well-
controlled fires, not fewer, if it is to survive.

Much about this fire-breathing tree has changed over its long,
crackling past. More than ninety million acres of longleaf pine once
stretched across southern North America. The botanist William Bar-
tram, whose works on American trees are the botanical equivalent
of John James Audubon's works on birds, described the landscape of
the coastal plains in the southern United States as "a vast forest of
the most stately pine trees that can be imagined." The now-vanished
green blanket of longleaf pine forest that ran from Virginia south to
Florida and west to Texas may have been the largest ecosystem that

ever existed in the United States. The longleaf's dramatic decline has surpassed even the losses of old-growth Douglas fir forests of the Pacific Northwest. The tree has receded from its Bartramian numbers by 97 percent, among the most severe retreats of any ecosystem on the planet. The surviving acreage of longleaf is somewhere around five million acres—an area about the size of New Jersey.[2]

To compound its risks, longleaf has no federal legal protections. Regional organizations have stepped in to preserve the tree, although federal agencies have also dug in to help with its restoration—a mea culpa after the federal government declared fire evil in the twentieth century. Despite its decline, the tree is still abundant enough that it is not considered endangered by federal standards, and hence is not protected by the Endangered Species Act (ESA). But this lack of protection doesn't change the fact that many of its residents—plants and animals that live in and among the trees—are under threat.

Just as the longleaf pine's ecology is a story of life from the ground up, so too has been the most effective conservation approach to its survival: a grassroots solution, starting with private landowners, rather than through dictates by political entities. The Longleaf Alliance (LLA), based in Andalusia, Alabama, has about thirty staff members. It began in 1995 to serve as an informational clearinghouse for training and educational opportunities, and to facilitate partnerships. Conserving the tree means not just protecting its current numbers but increasing them, and the group has planted more than a billion longleaf seedlings since its founding. The LLA provides everything from seedlings for planting, to education and outreach, to tax tips for forest landowners. They have also begun work on a massive geodatabase to track the location and status of every known longleaf. In the process, they've identified some 250,000 acres of the tree that had not been previously mapped. Its members work on so many fronts that it's hard to imagine a more comprehensive species-specific undertaking for tree protection and proliferation. The late Harvard biologist E. O. Wilson called the LLA the point of the spear for longleaf conservation efforts.

But the LLA doesn't labor alone, working with partners across several states and federal agencies in the Southeast. This convergence of interests sounds as if it might be inherently haphazard, given the number of participants and the crossing of federal, state, and regional land interests, but it's a good approach. Longleaf conservation organizations each have different emphases and skills. Working together means that they're able to deploy broad and deep talent, as well as provide sufficient numbers of workers to confront the challenges of preserving a tree that's spread across the American South, encompassing rural, urban, and mixed-use land. Unlike the coast redwoods, almost all of which are on public lands, the longleaf pine is found primarily in nonindustrial, private locales: farms, smallholders' properties, and residences with small, fragmented acreages of the tree. Because of this high private ownership of longleaf pine lands, the trees have been broken into pine "islands" that are often isolated from other tracts. Nearly 90 percent of forest land in the American South is privately owned, dramatically higher than in other parts of the country, especially in the American West, where forested lands are largely under the aegis of federal and state governments.

A collective of citizens works in the woods to maintain the trees' health and restore its ecosystems. The legendary North Carolina burner Jesse Wimberley wrangles hundreds of these citizens; most own land covered in longleaf. Wimberley runs the North Carolina Sandhills Prescribed Burn Association (SPBA). One of his main jobs is to educate private landowners about the utility of prescribed burning—putting fire on the land—and training people how to do it safely and effectively, for the long-term health of the forest and the trees. Prescribed burning is a common practice on the East Coast, and a key management tool to aid in ecosystems processes. Slow, careful burning helps to restore ground cover, enhance wildlife habitat, restore vegetation structure, and reduce fuel loads. It's also intended to mimic natural fire regimes thousands of years old.

I go along on a burn in North Carolina on a cold, clear March afternoon in 2020, on the front edge of a global pandemic, to see for myself. We're here on a private landowner's property to learn about community burning on longleaf pine land. Wimberley, overseeing the day's work, is a fourth-generation burner, part Lumbee Indian, born and raised in the area more than sixty years ago. A burn like this is known as an Rx fire, as in, it's what the doctor ordered for the health of the forest. It's an intentionally set fire, designed to reduce fuels that lead to bigger and worse fires: a little hair of the dog. We are ankle-deep in pine needles. There are eight or nine of us, and as we stand around, Wimberley takes us through a preview of the burn. This is where the art of fire comes in. Fire, he says, is like a live animal at 20 percent humidity. It might be counterintuitive, but you want to start your burn closest to a human-built structure, and then burn away from it. One of our party then steps forward with a drip torch—a piece of equipment designed to seep burning kerosene onto the ground—and lights the field on fire.

Restoration ecology is not an exact science, because life is dynamic and unpredictable. The particulars of restoration work are correspondingly inexact. Combine the relative lack of precision in restoring habitat with the personality of fire, and you have a mix that requires the closest of attention. For Wimberley, fire is always on the move. It has to be. For it to clear underbrush, or to continue to burn, it needs to be in motion. As Wimberley talks, gunfire keeps sounding off in the distance. No one pays any attention; this is, after all, a land of hunters and target practice. He explains that everything is a variable: the slope of the land; the water features, however minor, running through the land; the ways the trees are grouped; the density of the material on the ground; the distance from structures; the temperature and humidity; the time of day. All are part of the considerations for a safe and effective prescribed burn. Burns can proceed in tiny parts: a small, problematic region burned before a bigger burn the next day.[3]

"Pinestraw is designed to ignite, and designed to carry fire," he tells our little group in his southern drawl. "It's resinous, and it's pyrophytic"—adapted to fire. "It *wants* fire. An oak tree doesn't want fire and will succumb." He talks about the parameters of the property: where it dips or rises, the location of the nearest river, the density of pines. "Fire wants to go uphill, and it certainly wants to go with the wind." He demarcates the lines for the burn from a specific start to an end location.

The complexities of longleaf pine ecosystems are deceptive. The landscape looks simple, with widely spaced pine trees, and grasses on the ground—nothing like the dark, clotted forests found elsewhere in moister regions. But many species of plants thrive amid longleaf, including sedges, carnivorous plants, and orchids. The forests are home to gopher tortoises, keystone species that dig burrows that in turn provide habitat for hundreds of other species known as commensals: organisms that make use of the tree. These tortoises, which build extensive burrows, are the only land tortoises native to the American Southeast, resident in the forests for the last sixty million years. Meanwhile, the commensals find refuge, food, and other benefits. These commensals include both vertebrates (snakes, mice, frogs) and invertebrates (moths, beetles, flies, crickets). The gopher tortoise rove beetle (*Philonthus gopheri*) is found nowhere else besides gopher tortoise burrows, removing dung from the tunnels and reducing the parasite load.

Other reptiles and amphibians are intimately involved with the tree. The tiny Florida bog frog (*Lithobates okaloosae*), a threatened species measuring less than two inches from snout to vent, lives in seepage streams, low-volume rivulets that ooze water out of nearby wetlands. The streams create bogs of shallow water full of carnivorous plants, herbaceous species, mosses, and other hydrophytes. The frogs, which are sensitive to minute changes in environmental conditions, sit in breeding pools to attract females, and live in sluggish backwaters and seepages, the muckier the better.[4]

Because these ground-dwelling species evolved with the tree, they have incorporated strategies to survive when fire arrives, and they do poorly when fire is absent. The bog frog, for example, needs the kind of plant environment that successive fires bring. Some plants and animals among the longleaf lie dormant until activated by fire; others return to the forest from further afield after a blaze, drawn to the burned land and its new niches.

While prescriptive burns work to reduce the fuel load on the ground, they also control ticks and chiggers, release nutrients, and increase soil fertility. And because the land is cleared down to the soil, the controlled burns prepare the seedbed to germinate new seedlings, giving them a chance to generate without having to compete with other plants growing on the forest floor. Restoration through fire doesn't just maintain good habitat for the older trees, it also prepares younger trees to grow well. And new trees mean new opportunities for carbon storage. All of the burning of grasses and shrubs does release some sequestered carbon into the atmosphere. But the longleaf's deep root system means that the biomass below ground level is seven times greater than the aboveground materials consumed by fire. Carbon is stored in roots as well as in the trunks and leaves, and those roots are a carbon sink. Growing trees stash more carbon away everywhere, bottom to top. So burning the longleaf aids the restoration of an endangered ecosystem, encourages a diversity of species, and helps to blunt climate change.[5]

Wimberley identifies himself as a community organizer. His SPBA, which he started in 2015, is a leaderless organization. The structure of the organization or, more properly, its lack of structure, perplexes people. The SPBA doesn't even have members. You can show up and get some exhaustive, and sometimes exhausting, training, learning how to burn safely. The neighbor-helping-neighbor approach has educated thousands of North Carolina residents about fire's place in forest restoration.

Wimberley has certified about thirty burners, and trained thousands, since the group's inception. He notes that relying on busy farmers and landowners to run the organization hasn't worked well. He tried different approaches to bring landowners together in person, but all failed due to attrition. Busy people didn't want to sit in a meeting. So he simplified, assigning a small steering committee: two landowners from each of the counties they work in, who serve as ambassadors for the SPBA. "There's really not a lot of decision-making," Wimberley noted. "When there's a burn coming up, we'll let you know." The SPBA offers workshops that range from how to thin your land to how to handle a drip torch. Ultimately, the group's simplicity is what gives it strength.[6]

But what caused the decline of the longleaf in the first place? Maybe there was so much of the tree that it simply didn't register with us, like the passenger pigeon of the nineteenth century—so abundant, and so integrated into perceptions of the natural world, that its presence was predictable, unremarkable, inevitable, and its absence unimaginable.[7] The trees began to disappear to feed the need for lumber and timber in the South. But war accelerated its decline during the American Revolution, when shipbuilders began to extract sap for what were known as naval stores. These included turpentine, pitch, rosin, and tar, all used to patch and maintain ships and their riggings. Doctors also used tar to cauterize bleeding and sterilize wounds. It was easy enough to extract pine tar out of cut wood, building tar kilns and roasting the wood to extract the gooey substance. Some trees survived in situ sap extraction, but most died, green casualties alongside the human ones.

Another factor in the trees' drop in numbers in the eighteenth century was the adaptation of the copper whiskey still to refine turpentine, used as a solvent and medicinal elixir. This relatively fast and effective distillation method ramped up production, and led to widespread destruction of longleaf forests. A wave of deforestation swept south, and then west along the gulf, topping out in Texas at the turn of the nineteenth century. The increased use of water-powered sawmills sped up the conversion of logs to lumber, much of it then floated down waterways to port cities, helping to fill America's bottomless need for building materials. The remaining 3 percent of the original longleaf acreage has survived partly due to dumb luck, or because stands were located in distant or inaccessible areas or on tightly controlled private lands whose owners wanted to maintain the aesthetic of the forest.

Wimberley presses his foot into the ground at the base of a tree. "This tree is probably eighty or ninety years old." He rakes his hand down the trunk, dislodging bits. "Since fire's never been here, all this bark and limbs and stuff have fallen off and landed here, and created a huge buildup of what we call duff." The leading causes of mortality for longleaf are duff fires. People talk about eighty-year-old trees, but here they also speak of eighty-year-old duff. Some older trees have massive duff aggregations at their base. If that duff ignites, the fire could kill the tree, despite its love of fire. Wimberley picks up a handful of the duff. "If this stuff came up dry," he says, "we would just shut down; we would not burn. Because [landowners] Kim and Bruce? I like 'em. And they would really not like Wimberley anymore if I killed their eighty-year-old longleaf." The space between life and death seems slender here: not enough fire, and the trees continue to be endangered by an overly heavy fuel load; too much fire, and the tree dies. "We never burn unless we can feel moisture," Wimberley notes. "And especially"—and his voice drops to almost a whisper—"this is where the RH comes into the puzzle." Relative humidity is the most important marker of all for a proper burn, and any burn plan must note the RH at which a burn will, or won't, proceed.

Listening to Wimberley talk about the role of fire among the longleaf, I realize that one of the difficulties with promoting prescribed burning is simply that it's a scary proposition. Our fire language signals danger: Conflagration. Holocaust. Inferno. Incendiary. Humans have probably always had an innate fear of fire, because it's generally something we've tried to avoid. We burn ourselves in the kitchen, we lie out in the sun too long, we tell our kids not to play with matches. I don't have a good track record with fire. When I was a kid, we did our own controlled burning of a sort. In the rural Hawaiʻi of my youth, you could do pretty much anything on private land. For years we burned our paper trash in a fifty-five-gallon drum, rusted to rich shades of brown, in a corner of our property. In my hometown of Hilo, the rainiest city in the United States, a runaway fire was a near impossibility. But one day, emptying a wooden trash can full of paper into the burning drum, I dropped it. It was made of teak, thin, elegant, and slippery. In a frantic effort to rescue what I'd come to think of as a family treasure, I braced my right hand against the big drum while I reached over the top with my left hand and fished out the wastepaper basket, but at a cost. The drum had been burning debris for a couple of hours, and it was so hot that when I braced my hand against it, it stuck. I screamed and yanked my hand back, minus a lot of skin, and ran inside crying. Fire hurts, and we try to avoid it, and it's only when we can understand how it's used as a tool that we can tamp down those deep instincts that tell us fire is bad.

Millennia ago, native peoples in the American South, including the Clovis people and Paleo-Indians, as well as Wimberley's Lumbee ancestors, used fire for hunting, collecting nuts, and encouraging the arrival of new plant species onto fire-cleared land. Natives undertook frequent low-intensity burns among the longleaf specifically to create and maintain the forest's viability and to reduce lightning-caused fires. Their prescriptive burns apparently worked well enough that Europeans adopted the practice as the decades passed.[8]

But fire practices have changed in the American South in the past century. Congress established the US Forest Service in 1905, but the fire suppression movement had already begun, starting in the late 1890s. Fire control became the central task of the Forest Service, which had concluded that fires of any kind were destructive. An immense blaze in 1910 scorched more than three million acres of forest across the northern Rocky Mountains, hardening the Forest Service's antifire leanings into militant ideology. This didn't stop everyone, because in more remote areas, people still burned regularly on their own property, understanding its benefits. Then a popular film came out that portrayed southerners as crazy people out in the woods with lighters setting the forest on fire. According to Wimberley, the Service even recruited a psychiatrist to figure out just what it was about people in the South that caused them to light blazes. As the decades passed, the Service took up the public relations challenge with renewed vigor. Out of those efforts came the Smokey Bear campaign, with its cheerful, jeans-wearing, ready-to-get-the-job-done mascot—the most fire-suppressive government program ever launched, and one with terrible consequences.

In recent decades, the federal government has strongly supported longleaf restoration. The US Department of Agriculture, through its Natural Resources Conservation Service (NRCS), has provided extensive funding and resources, issuing a four-year implementation strategy in 2020 for longleaf ecosystem restoration. Aiming to increase the five million acres of extant longleaf to eight million acres, the NRCS has precise conservation goals: vegetation management, prescribed fire, establishing new longleaf growth, and protecting existing forestland from encroachment and development. The NRCS also offers farm bill programs to provide incentives and technical assistance to agricultural producers and forest landowners, along with a robust stewardship program. The federal government's backing provides a huge benefit to private landowners, to private organizations like Wimberley's SPBA, to regional partnerships, and to local universities and private contractors who can use geospatial data to map the trees' density, location, age, and other factors involved in protection and restoration.

While organizations on the Eastern Seaboard have worked to regularize and institutionalize prescribed burning, the American West—in many places comprised of tens of thousands of acres of arid forested regions—has been slower to respond. The reasons for the West's lag are complex, but there are important differences between the two geographies. Plant species in the West are more flammable than those in moister deciduous forests in the East. Although wild-fires occur in the eastern United States, they are much more influential in the West. Strong regional winds, called the Santa Anas, can move a fire through a dry landscape with shocking speed. Less rainfall and higher temperatures mean more dead trees, which burst into flame with little provocation. But most important, the historic fire suppression in almost all of the American West means that the fuel loads across many thousands of acres are often many decades old, primed to burn like hell.

Prescribed burns are not without their own hazards. One of the biggest issues related to these prescribed burns is smoke, which can affect livestock and poultry, as well as people downwind. As the property owner with a burn plan, Kim has to list, for the Forest Service, all the adjacent smoke-sensitive areas, and describe what allowable wind direction she'll burn in. She notes that today, the mixing height is low: the atmospheric ceiling that keeps your smoke at a certain elevation. With a high ceiling, oxygen can pull the fire upward, making it less predictable. The smoke is often a bigger concern than the fire. At some point, wind direction on the ground becomes irrelevant, because when smoke pulls up high it can go anywhere, at the whims of winds hundreds of feet from the ground. And as it cools, smoke drops and can follow a drainage like water, running onto a highway and causing an accident.

We're ready for the burn to begin. Several members of the team fire up large, loud leaf blowers, intended not to move leaves but to aim a fire in a particular direction. Wimberley starts talking about the all-important gear, but the leaf blowers drown him out. "We have water, we have a blower, we have drip torches," he shouts. Drip torches are simple, and Wimberley's participants use a ratio of three parts diesel to one part gasoline. "It's the diesel that's the fuel," he reminds the team. The torches they're using look like gizmos fabricated by farmers during the Great Depression: irregular, banged-up metal cylinders with a big metal handle welded on, and a curly spout ending in a wick. "Once you get this thing lit, do not put your face anywhere close to it," Wimberley adds unnecessarily.

The main job today is to get the landowner some real-world prac-tice, with a big support team, lighting a safe, slow-moving fire on her property. Quite literally, it's a trial by fire. We troop down a gravel road along the property line, a ragged crew of women and men, a few of the latter with a great deal of facial hair in different configura-tions, and spanning maybe three generations, armed with drip torches and blowers, along with rakes and other long-handled implements. It looks apocalyptic, like we're about to run someone out of town. Fire often has that characteristic. It's got a reputation as a rogue in the wilderness, as a touch out of control.

Kim starts off gingerly, lighting a clump of grass at one of the corners of her property, bounded by a gravel road. This is a test burn: a bit of practice for her, and to suss out the wind and humidity con-ditions. It burns slowly and steadily, gradually expanding out beyond the line of original diesel dripped on the ground. The fire is mes-merizing. It's leisurely, blackening the land, and marching along. If fire on the loose in a forest could be described as peaceful, this was it. "We're increasing the size of our fire break," Wimberley notes, reminding us about the fire triangle: air, fuel, heat. Now that the fuel is burned in this area, it will then stop fire coming from another direc-tion, since there's nothing else to burn.

The flames lick up against some longleaf seedlings. The duff has been here a long time; it's knee-deep in places. The flames aren't any-where near intense enough to do any damage other than to the small pieces of duff. The leaf blower pushes fire in specific directions, keep-ing it burning if it falters. Without air moving, the fire wants to go out. But wind turns it from friend into foe; more dangerous than any fire is the wind that can spring up as an uncertain opponent. "Fire is a good servant, but a bad master," as an old saying goes. Someone with a water dispenser strapped on like a backpack occasionally squirts water at what must be strategic locations on the ground, but there's a bigger, more robust water vehicle at the ready for more serious fire extinguishing if needed.

As the flames pick up, another shiver runs through the crowd: for the moment, at least, fire is fun. You can see it in people's smiles, the snap in their steps, the enthusiasm of their shouts. As we talk by the side of the road, something shifts, the wind kicks up, and the fire starts to burn even more vigorously, and more raggedly. Now a good portion of the field is on fire, and the flames are converging on each other. "Fire is attracted to fire," Wimberley shouts above the noise of the forest floor burning. The more superheated the air gets, the more readily the material ignites: the third part of the triangle.

There is another factor here, too: confidence. I was never good at geometry, but it seems a sort of fourth side of the air-fuel-heat triangle, or perhaps its center. To make the fire work, you need to control for the variables of confidence and its parts: desire, self-possession, experience. It's about learning the proper procedure and feeling sure you know what could happen at any given time.

But it's not all rah-rah-longleaf in the American South, and not everyone is a fan. A number of cleavages exist within the longleaf pine's political ecosystem. Although the tree is not federally protected, one of its most common residents is: the red-cockaded woodpecker, a smallish bird with typical woodpecker black and white stripes, a black cap and neck, and white cheeks, along with small patches of red on either side of the cap, visible only when the bird is defending its territory. This woodpecker, often called the RCW, is found year-round in its only habitat: the old pines of the American Southeast, ranging from Texas to Florida. Overlay a map of the bird's range with that of the longleaf, and the commonalities are obvious. The red-cockaded woodpecker has been protected by the ESA since its inception in 1973, and although approximately a hundred different bird species use longleaf pine forests, it is one of only two woodpeckers with federal protection.[9]

The RCW is also the only woodpecker that makes a nest in a living tree, although there are a couple of twists to that approach. The bird typically forages on pines that are more than thirty years old, and often much older. Its survival depends on the trees' decline, for although it takes up residence in living pines, not dead ones, its host trees are typically infected with a disease called red heart fungus, which softens the heartwood and makes it possible for the bird to dig sufficiently into the tree to make a secure lodging. As a bonus, the tree produces sap when injured, and the birds have learned to create small holes around the entrance to their nests. This causes sap to flow down and deter tree-climbing snakes, which are common in the South and are always eager for a meal in the form of a bird's egg or two. The birds create a tunnel into the tree, and then excavate a circular cavity either upward or downward from the tunnel, but this tunneling ties them intimately to the tree's architecture: they have to follow the idiosyncratic path of the heartrot, because they can only excavate rotted wood within the living tree. Even then, it's unhurried work, and can take months or even years to complete. So the birds' tenancy among the trees is long.

In some circumstances, it's difficult to tell a crisis from an opportunity, and in the Anthropocene, both conditions can coexist within a tree's ecosystem. The commercial extraction of naval stores that denuded much of the longleaf across its range has also made the trees more attractive to birds. Many trees survived being slashed to create the notches from which the turpentine would flow. But cutting up the bark made the tree more susceptible to invasion by fungi, which helped the woodpecker get into the heartwood, and also made it easier to extract bugs from the tree for food. So slicing up the longleaf weakened the trees, and along came the woodpeckers to meet the moment. And as the twenty-first century dawned, we've ended up with trees that lack federal protection, but which nevertheless cannot be disturbed or altered, to protect the woodpecker.

The restrictions against harming the trees are specific and numerous. You can't clear-cut your lot without a permit, although you are allowed to cut other hardwood trees on your property. You also can't use insecticides on any standing pine trees, build roads or utility rights-of-way within a cluster of trees, store construction equipment or construction material within the clusters, or build any structures—no campgrounds, residences, commercial properties, sheds, or shacks. You also can't plant any other species that will exceed seven feet in height within fifty feet of either active or inactive cavity trees.

That the woodpecker has restricted a wide swath of landowners' rights has infuriated some. Drawn in its starkest form, it's a case of landowners' rights versus the federally mandated preservation of the woodpeckers' habitat. In the little city of Boiling Spring Lakes in North Carolina, with about six thousand residents, a conflict in 2006 between landowners and environmentalists made the national news. "What's black and white and dreaded all over?" opined a *Washington Post* article about the fight.[10] The city is home to one of the few relatively dense populations of the bird, which outnumbers the townspeople by about two to one, with about six thousand clusters housing maybe fifteen thousand birds. The birds, trees, and townspeople all got along fine until some building permits risked violating the ESA. The US Fish & Wildlife Service (FWS), which enforces the act, warned the landowners, and the ill will spread. The town wanted to build new homes on private land, while the FWS was required to protect the birds. The city's boundaries happen to include a healthy population of longleaf pines, and it was one of the few places on private lands where the woodpecker was thriving.

The bird's presence and the resulting restrictions meant a tangible loss of property value and a slowdown of new development. To avoid the costs of mitigation, Boiling Spring Lakes landowners began to cut down uninhabited trees before the woodpeckers even showed up. The *New York Times* trumpeted, "Rare Woodpecker Sends a Town Running for its Chainsaws." No wood, no woodpeckers; you can't violate the Endangered Species Act if the endangered species in question isn't present. And it was easy to saw the trees up for firewood, sending any evidence it might've ever housed a woodpecker up in smoke. "It's ruined the beauty of our city," the mayor bemoaned. To stop the cutting, the city issued a moratorium on all permits for clearing residents' lots.[11]

This community conflict, and others, have put the US Fish & Wildlife Service in a difficult position. These tensions aren't new, because for many decades, the Service has had to balance the political realities of development with protection of wildlife. One of its founding principles was to provide land on which timber could be grown, and it has a long history of conducting timber sales, hitting twelve billion board feet annually between the 1970s and 1990s. Susan Miller, a wildlife biologist with the FWS in North Carolina, told me that if the landowner is requesting removal of an active cavity tree, they'll work with them on a solution. Still, there's a hard stop, in favor of the bird: "We do everything we can to protect marked cavity trees since they are a limiting resource," she noted, in the cautious language of the federal government.

These interactions between landowners and bureaucrats can lead to a complex calculus. Landowners (and the FWS) need to determine whether there's still enough habitat available for birds if the trees are to be removed. If there are significant removals of active cavity trees, plus the presence of more than eight or ten large-diameter pine trees, and the activity (road, building, or other disturbance) takes place within a half mile of the woodpecker cluster, an environmental consultant needs to work out a solution. But in the best of American community spirit, the most successful outcomes for everyone involve compromise.[12] Although the federal government is often vilified as the dampener of economic engines because of ESA restrictions, the FWS works very hard to make terms acceptable to all parties. The goal is to motivate people to take proper action, rather than punish them for improper action, offering so-called safe harbor agreements, which say that if private landowners promise, in effect, to voluntarily manage and protect the endangered species on their land, the government will assure landowners that they'll face no future additional restrictions. One critique of the ESA is that it isn't aimed at protecting ecosystems but only individual species. That protecting the birds has extended the act's effects to protect the longleaf pine by proxy

demonstrates, in a small but indelible way, just how intertwined
our fortunes are.[13]

The federal government has taken other steps to protect the tree, contributing abundantly to its conservation and survival. It's been in their
best interests to do so; land owned by the Department of Defense
includes more than 730,000 acres of longleaf across the American
South, and forests are important training grounds for troop move-
ments and other activities. The longleaf has also offered a somewhat
unsettling benefit related to training: the trees' resistance to low-
intensity flames meant that tracer bullets, fired at night so they could
be easily seen, often started small fires, and it was the government's
habit, if not its policy, to just let those fires burn unattended. This
habit continued for decades in southern military installations, and
ironically, these random, low-grade fires were the closest we got to
natural fire in the twentieth century.

Fort Bragg (recently renamed Fort Liberty) in North Carolina
maintains one of the largest surviving longleaf pine forests.[14] The
immense fort occupies more than 250 square miles, and more than
half of its 161,000 acres contain longleaf. The trees are scattered
about the base, which takes a good hour to drive through. Conservation and the US military have a vexed history; there is a long
rap sheet of environmental abuse by the armed forces, including
dumping plutonium, Agent Orange, and other chemicals around the
Pacific; abandoning lead-contaminated ammo in Alaska; spraying
military herbicides in Vietnam; and trashing much of Okinawa and
other islands with discarded military hardware. The US military
also is the world's largest institutional consumer of petroleum, and,
correspondingly, the single largest institutional producer of greenhouse gases in the world.

Coupled with the training opportunities they provide, forests
have gifted the military with benefits that trees everywhere provide: cooling, erosion safeguards, and drought mediation. Fort

Bragg has been committed to the longleaf, and has involved itself in the RCW's protection. But in 1990, although Bragg's forest managers thought they were doing a fine job of administering the woodpeckers' tenancy in the trees, the FWS disagreed and issued what's known as a "jeopardy opinion," a regulatory opinion that was an order to be more diligent about the woodpeckers' habitat. The fort redesigned some training sites, modified their training activities, closed some shooting ranges, and took other actions. But many up the chain of command resisted this. Finally, the Department of Defense—more specifically, the secretary of the army, in charge of Fort Bragg—and the secretary of the Interior got together to craft a workable policy. The agencies are government partners, ostensibly on the same team, but they're not equals in influence. The Department of the Interior supports over a million jobs and supports some $400 billion in economic activity. The army has some equivalencies: there are just over a million US soldiers, and it in turn contributes billions of dollars to 420 military installations in all fifty states and several territories. As with the much smaller-scale dustup in Boiling Spring Lakes, both branches of government had an interest in cooperating, and the staffs of the two agencies worked out a strategy that both supported and protected the bird and let the army continue effectively training its troops. It was fortunate that the open-understory nature of longleaf was ideal for military drills: no slogging through vines and other dense growth, and decent light to be able to see because of the trees' open canopies.

But other problems arose. Over the years, more private landholders pressed up against the perimeter of the fort's massive property. Homeowners complained about the noise from military actions, and the woodpeckers, which flew between protected and unprotected land, remained at risk on these margins of the fort. What to do? The fort created a conservation easement, buying up adjacent properties, and worked with The Nature Conservancy (TNC), a global environmental nonprofit, to forge a buffer zone. TNC had a history of working with the Department of Defense, and the two agencies, working with the FWS, created the Fort Bragg Private Lands Initiative. Fort Bragg now has its own Endangered Species Branch, and an extensive ecosystem management program. A 2013 report issued by the fort noted longleaf was likely to increase in range to encompass a greater percentage of Fort Bragg land by 2050.

In the face of a changing climate, widespread species tend to survive more than rare ones, so simply running up the numbers of individual longleaf trees, and expanding their range, will serve as one buffer against decline. Even on Kim and Bruce's relatively small property, the trees are everywhere you turn, as far as you can see. The burn begins to wrap up, as the fire has consumed almost all the target vegetation. We talk about spot-overs, when flames jump over a road or come toward an existing fire. Still another landowner takes a turn with the drip torch. There's not much smoke until the fire starts to go out as it exhausts the fuel on the ground; then it's a coughy, murky mess. My clothes smell like an extinguished campfire. There are still a few more spots remaining, and Wimberley turns them into small-group practice sessions. But no one relaxes completely. "I'm terrified," mutters one of the landowners when her turn comes. But she takes hold of the drip torch and, like a pro, is soon working away.

For now, the longleaf thrives. Throughout our time during the prescribed burn, the tall trees around us remained essential sentinels: topped with green, looking healthy under a cobalt-blue sky. As you walk out of the forest's shadow, it's easier to see that longleaf's resurrection is a twin story of adaptation: first, the tree's magnificent integration into its landscape; and second, people's abilities to grow solutions to protect it. No longer can we rely on lightning to do the work the tree evolved to need.

Jack Kerouac wrote, "I have lots of things to teach you now, in case we ever meet, concerning the message that was transmitted to me under a pine tree in North Carolina on a cold winter moonlit night."[15] Trees continue to school us, even as we help them. If the longleaf could speak, it would ask us to be patient, to accommodate, to value our communities. It would also tell us fire isn't always a horrible scourge, and that sometimes, the best thing to do is to start a fire.

CHAPTER 6

Making Folk Medicine Modern: The Road of the East Indian Sandalwood Tree

"I wondered a little bit about what life would do all by itself. Afterwards a richness like every perfume gathered by some alchemist and brewed into a benediction ointment came upon me and behold, the Seer held his hand for a cup against the tree he leaned upon and it gave forth of its deep core small drops of oil. And he anointed me and I rose up and went on my way bearing a knowledge of eternal peace and covenanted to heal and not destroy."

—Zamin Ki Dost, *Incense of Sandalwood* (1904)

If you're looking for a magical grove of trees, you can't do much better than spending a few hours in the Marayoor Sandalwood Forest, spread across about thirty-five square miles in southern India's Kerala state. Within the forest borders, you'll find the world's last remaining naturally occurring East Indian sandalwood trees (*Santalum album*), grown huge. Monkeys and spotted deer cavort, and the occasional bison visits. It's a beautiful, dreamy landscape, often shrouded in mist.

But it's not an unsullied experience. In the highly regulated and protected reserve, each tree is numbered with a reflective sticker and a metal plate. Groups of trees are fenced. You can only view them from a distance. Tampering with them is a serious offense, and stiff fines and prison time are the usual outcomes. Prominent signs offer up phone numbers so visitors can report anyone stealing sandalwood to the local authorities. Every few years, the Kerala government counts every tree, a process that takes six months. In 2019, it tallied about thirty-five thousand trees greater than one foot in diameter—an attempt to keep track of what trees might've disappeared from poaching or fallen from natural causes.

The sandalwood tree has been revered for millennia as the most favored tree of the gods: a part of cosmic mysteries, ritual, the divine, and humans' relationships with plant remedies. But modernity has made sandalwood ugly at the same time that it's helped millions through both folk and modern medicine. As users celebrate the tree and its oil on the Asian subcontinent, the government manages the tree's growth and harvesting with a steely grip. There's just not enough sandalwood to go around. Poachers, most of whom hover on the edge of poverty, account for about 30 percent of the tree's loss. Location influences tree inventory, because it's much easier to poach sandalwood trees from nearby roads and settlements.[1] The scented wood is second in cost only to ivory for its uses as intricately carved objects, but the oil cloaked beneath its bark is even more desirable.[2] Individuals were banned from growing the tree under any circumstances until 2002, and can rarely do their own cutting and harvesting. To violate laws about who can grow and harvest the tree, and where, can even get you killed. In 2015, police murdered a group of twenty suspected sandalwood poachers after being confronted with arrows and axes. But even authorities responsible for overseeing trade practices get their hands dirty, creating the occasional forged certificate for sandalwood export.

The state's right to monopolize the forests and their care, use, and preservation has been a guiding principle in Indian conservation since rulers took formal forest management steps in the nineteenth century. These efforts, though, have not been about preserving the tree but about monetizing it, and, more generally, exercising control.[3] Tipu Sultan, the ruler of Mysore, declared sandalwood to be a sacred tree in 1792, and an often repeated but apocryphal story claims the punishment for stealing the wood was amputation of a hand. Through long tradition, sandalwood has been the king's property, an arrangement that has colored governmental entitlement to the present day.

It's not illegal everywhere in India for private entities to farm the tree (although every tree has to be registered with the government). But small farms typically can't invest in security fencing, security staff, or other protective means, leaving them prey to poachers. Some trees are wrapped in barbed wire. The supply chain also needs attention: the government still doesn't do a very good job of ensuring that harvesting is sustainable and ethical, and that exports are quantified and certified. Some of the southern states have now legalized bigger commercial enterprises, but growing sandalwood is a tough task if you're an entrepreneur wanting to take advantage of the tree's immense value. When a farmer has approval to harvest, a government official must come in person to uproot the entire tree.[4]

Ranked by the International Union for Conservation of Nature (IUCN) as Vulnerable, the East Indian sandalwood is threatened with extinction across much of its range because of these intense pressures. Indian laws aren't concerned solely with harvesting the wood. They also dictate particulars of subsequent possession, sale, and purchase— a persistent form of control that artisans find crippling. But while the government has pressed hard, and often struggled, to regulate the trees, controlling the threats resulting from climate change has proven much more difficult. The sandalwood's climate future is also bound up with the workers who harvest it. Agricultural labor drives a high percentage of local economies in India, and poor residents have fewer buffers against a changing climate: less disposable income to relocate, or to improve living conditions in the face of hotter days and nights. They also have fewer resources to manage changes to their immediate surroundings: bridges to accommodate more swollen streams, for instance. The twin challenges of regulating the wood and combating

climate change are unequal, for the tree is a relatively small governmental challenge within a much bigger crisis. But climate policies, and
the changing climate itself, imperil the tree's future.[5]

The sandalwood tree was probably present in Indonesia before
it arrived in India, and artisans and tradespeople have trafficked it
across South Asia, Indonesia, and the Pacific and Indian Oceans, and
used it for different cultural purposes around the world. There are
about eighteen species of sandalwood in total, perhaps a quarter of
them found in the Hawaiian archipelago, where they almost certainly
predate humans' arrival. (I say "perhaps" because of the constant taxonomic shuffling, and the attendant arguments among biologists as to
whether a plant deserves recognition as a full species, rather than as
a subspecies or variety.)[6] The Hawaiian Kingdom's first written law
was a sandalwood tax, issued in 1826, requiring every adult man to
deliver sixty-six pounds of the wood to the governor of the district to
which he belonged, or, in lieu of sandalwood, a cash payment.

In line with its international past, *S. album* is grown in Sri Lanka
and continues its long residency in Indonesia. It's also farmed in
Australia, where harvesting and processing it privately won't get
you fined or arrested. A substantial patch grew in the Hughenden-
Cloncurry region in Australia, providing enough wood to produce
four tons for Gandhi's funeral pyre, which was lit on the banks of the
Jumna River in India. Various eyewitness accounts confirmed the use
of the Australian sandalwood in the pyre, but it remains a mystery as
to why Indians used sandalwood from another country to honor an
Indian icon.[7]

The sandal tree has had its most intense cultural presence in India,
having been domesticated there for the past twenty-three centuries.
It's widely used for ceremonial purposes, especially as a central element in cremations, where the aroma of the wood is thought to help
carry the soul to its next destination. Most Hindus wear a small mark
of sandal paste on their foreheads, to keep the pituitary gland cool,

and in some settings with pigments added to serve as a marker of caste status.

But more than any other aspect, it's the sandalwood's oil that shapes its conservation status, cultural life, and future. It is a beautifully scented, sweet, and slightly viscous liquid, stored in the tree's heartwood. Revered Hindu texts from antiquity speak of the fragrant oil, which has been used to reduce inflammations or other "heatings" of body and mind.[8] Practitioners of traditional Asian medicine have used it as an antimicrobial, antioxidant, antispasmodic, diuretic, and expectorant—to treat the common cold, various inflammations, psoriasis, bronchitis, and gallbladder complaints.

None of the oil comes easily to market. Sandalwood is worth about a hundred dollars per pound when it's sold in India—a lot of money, considering the average salary of a sandalwood laborer in the region reaches a maximum of fifty dollars a month. After harvesting, the local forestry department sells the sandalwood at auction to factories, who take it from there. There are numerous classes of sandalwood, all carefully described and quantified by the government entities selling them. These classes are based on the color, texture, and fragrance of the sandalwood. Although all are the same species, there is great variation from tree to tree.

Stripping the outer lighter sapwood away to get at the darker heartwood containing most of the oil is an almost completely manual process, even in the largest factories. Its oil is an "essential" oil: a concentrated liquid that doesn't mix well with water and contains volatile—meaning easily evaporated—chemical compounds from plants. It's essential in that it's the essence of the tree's fragrance: an olfactory standard-bearer. A lot of oils from plants are not essential; they're diluted or cut with other substances. After the hand-cutting, the heartwood is then chipped by a machine and turned into a powder. A long steam distillation process follows. It takes a week to distill about one metric ton of the oil. After the oil is extracted, what's left is a brown, powdery residue that is turned into incense, used in religious rituals. A famous brand of sandalwood soap, Mysore Sandal, has been sold by a government-run company for more than a century.

By the time oil reaches end consumers, it's very costly. I bought a glass container of five milliliters, and if you scale up what I paid, it would cost eleven thousand dollars for an eight-ounce cup of the oil. The wood from which it comes is also the second-most expensive on the planet, lagging only behind African blackwood (*Dalbergia melanoxylon*). The intense, concentrated qualities of sandalwood oil and its manual extraction mean that compared to the economics of other trees' by-products, it's a small-scale operation, albeit one with an outsized significance. Companies working under British rule in India only harvested about sixty tons of the wood in the first decade of the twentieth century, and it has never gotten any higher than about fourteen hundred tons in any year since. At the same time, acreage has declined 20 percent annually since 1995 up to the present day, for the sandalwood's long roots degrade soil to a substantial degree, and pulling up trees leaves the ground deplenished.[9]

The quantity of oil varies from tree to tree, but less rain usually means more oil, and faster growth often equals less oil. The older the tree, the more oil it produces, which creates a conservation hazard, since the oldest trees (which sequester the most carbon) are the most desirable. The inequities between supply and demand for East Indian sandalwood oil (frequently written today as "EISO" in the broad medical and pharmacological literature) have led, naturally enough, to ever-increasing prices.

Evolutionary forces work in the tree's favor at the same time that commercial factors imperil it. Sandalwood, known in India as *chandan*, is parasitic, meaning that it gets some of its nutrition from another living plant. It's what botanists call an obligate parasite, because it cannot live, at least as a juvenile, without a host. About 1 percent of angiosperms—flowering plants—are parasitic. Like all parasitic plants, members of the sandalwood family have developed structures on their roots called haustoria, which penetrate the roots of other plants, from which they acquire moisture as well as nutrients. Sandalwood can parasitize more than three hundred species, from grasses to other sandalwood species. This strategy often involves an underground struggle. Opportunism can be hard work, for the sandalwood has to overcome a number of obstacles to parasitize another plant: distance, for starters, and then it has to breach the host's defenses, which vary. The sandalwood's roots excel at seeking out nutrients, moisture, and hosts, running up to ninety feet from its base.[10]

Understanding the tree's geography helps to make its climatic challenges more legible. It takes moderate rainfall, substantial sun, and long spells of dry weather for the tree to thrive. It mostly exists in its natural state in open forests, widely scattered. Two southern Indian states, Karnataka and Tamil Nadu, account for 90 percent of the country's sandalwood trees. Sandalwood is spottily distributed around the Indian subcontinent, but its primary indigenous range is the deciduous forests of the Deccan region of peninsular India, where the Marayoor Sandalwood Forest lives. Southern and northern regions have different weather—wetter in the north and drier in the south—and across the country, temperatures have risen over the past quarter century, but with increasingly greater variation between north and south. Climatologists have proposed various theories to account for this north-south dichotomy, such as variations in cloud cover, the role of airborne dust, and other factors that influence agriculture and human health, but no one can say with any confidence why the regions' climates are diverging from each other so quickly, and meteorologists' understandings of these differences are somewhat conjectural.

These climatic changes now shape the pace and density of sandalwood growth. In turn, they may lead to numerous ripple effects: changes in the government's ability to regulate and oversee growth in more remote parts of the country; a different time frame for harvesting trees in wetter parts of the region; unpredictable outcomes due to labor forces molded by climate; and other effects that we won't understand until younger trees are mature enough for harvesting. The sandalwood tree is also relatively short-lived, not growing past about a century, so its oil is often not viable for decades, sometimes only reaching commercial maturity around the half-century mark. Its wood doesn't even develop any odor until a decade in the ground has passed.[11]

In its liquid form, though, the scent of the oil is the first quality you notice. Modern studies of the value of aromatherapy have assessed sandalwood oil's odor effects. A 2016 study in a leading pain research journal found that aromatherapy substantially reduced pain. These results indicate that aromatherapy should be considered a safe addition to current pain management procedures, and the article noted that the cost of aromatherapy was far less than that of standard pain management treatment.[12] Aromatherapy even eased severe pain, including pain management in burn patients.

Smells are powerful, and can summon memory more effectively than any other stimuli, lighting up the amygdala and hippocampal regions of the brain. In one study using MRI brain scans, researchers asked five female participants to identify a perfume from their past whose sight and scent elicited a particular pleasant memory. The researchers then bought the perfumes as stipulated by their test subjects (Royal Secret, Opium for Women, Juniper Breeze, and White Musk). These five women's triggered memories conclusively demonstrated the scientific basis for the emotional potency of odor-evoked memory.[13]

Not every plant smells good. Some are renowned for their stinkiness, such as the corpse flower (*Amorphophallus titanum*), which sits at the opposite end of the appealing-smell scale. The plant is described in some quarters as smelling like a rotting body. In August 1999, the Huntington Gardens produced a blooming example of *A. titanum* in captivity for the first time. Normally, it's not possible for the plant to self-pollinate, but we hand-pollinated one with its own ground-up pollen, and it survived, and then bloomed in spectacular fashion, briefly becoming a national phenomenon for a few weeks. I had been traveling that week, and returned at the zenith of public interest to find the largest crowds ever to visit the Huntington. The line to see the flower stretched for a good half mile, snaking around the grounds. People love extremes, and smelling bad can be a kind of attractive extreme. Why else would you stand in line for hours on a hot day to get a whiff of a smelly plant? I did get my own whiff, and it wasn't terrible: akin to lifting up a dumpster lid and getting a blast of unsavory trash.

By contrast, people don't queue up for great smells. I've never seen a line of hundreds of people eager to sample, say, the brand-new fragrance of a recently hybridized rose. Taking in good smells is a private activity. And the scent of the sandalwood oil is heavenly: warm, balsamic, woody, and sweet. I obtained the purest sample of the oil I could find, to smell for myself. It reminds me of my dad's woodworking shop, or a cedar chest. In its purest form, not mixed with any kind of binder or perfume, it's quite sharp, bright, fresh, clean. It's the odor equivalent of being carried around the room on the shoulders of your friends; the thought of a corpse couldn't be further from your mind. There's also a modern intersection of the smell of sandalwood and men's grooming products. The smell is often associated with a soft-edged masculinity, present in innumerable beard and shaving concoctions, shaving creams, and lotions.

Mario Molina, a physician who is also a historian of medicine with a deep contextual knowledge of medicine and its past, helped me understand how modern medicine has received claims from traditional communities. Molina noted that it probably took a long time for humans to gain a working understanding of a plant's curative properties, a study known as pharmacognosy. The first native discoveries would've happened by accident, and then after that probably by lengthy trial and error. From there, more widespread native use would have followed, and anthropologists who learned the languages of native communities would have gleaned the medical uses. Papers would then have appeared in anthropological and scientific journals.

Pharmacognosy has been around for a long time. At the end of the eighteenth century and into the nineteenth century, as chemistry became increasingly sophisticated, the era of so-called modern drugs began. In 1785, the British botanist William Withering first described the remarkable effects of digitalis, a drug derived from the foxglove plant, as a treatment for heart conditions. Plants had evolved and diversified over millions of years, offering deep chemical diversity and novel mechanisms. In 1805 Friedrich Sertürner, a young German pharmacist, isolated morphine from the opium plant. Other chemical transmutations followed; in 1820, the French chemist Pierre-Joseph Pelletier isolated the active ingredient in quinine, used to treat malaria, from the bark of a cinchona tree. The Quechua people in South America had known of its medicinal properties for centuries beforehand, and it was also known to the indigenous Cañari and the Chimú peoples who inhabited what is now Peru, Bolivia, and Ecuador before the Spanish arrived. But isolating these plants' active ingredients and understanding their chemical effects created more effective remedies. Eager to monetize these opportunities with new products, pharmaceutical companies began to explore botany in the wild with their own scientific teams.

By the last third of the nineteenth century, organic chemists had learned how to not only identify the mechanisms at work, but also synthesize the active ingredients in plants that held potential medical value. By the second half of the twentieth century, more than half of anticancer drugs had emerged from natural products. Only a tiny sliver of the total number of existing plant species have ever been researched for bioactivity. Pharmacognosy is big business. The American anthropologist and biologist Darrell Posey estimated that by 1990, pharmaceutical companies were making about $85 billion annually from plants that were first known to indigenous peoples for their healing properties.[14]

The ability to synthesize medicines has also been important for a number of conservation reasons. First, it's prevented the destruction that inevitably comes along with large-scale harvesting of the plants.

The chemotherapy medication paclitaxel, first isolated from the Pacific yew tree (*Taxus brevifolia*) in 1971, has been used with great efficacy to treat numerous kinds of cancers, including ovarian, breast, lung, cervical, and pancreatic. The problem was that the Pacific yew tree is a slow-growing plant native to the Pacific Northwest in the United States, and by the 1990s the tree was becoming scarce due to its use in paclitaxel. By 2003, researchers had developed a semisynthetic version from extracts of cultivated yews of other species, synthesizing it into a highly effective set of compounds and reducing pressure on native populations.

Could isolating an active ingredient inadvertently leave out a compound in the plant that we hadn't realized had its own therapeutic role in native uses? Molina noted that missing some key ingredient was, and continues to be, a possibility, but an unlikely one. He pointed out the science community's work with marijuana. "It contains not only THC [tetrahydrocannabinol, the psychoactive substance that makes you high]," he observed, "but it also includes a whole bunch of other cannabinols—oils that have different properties." These were not necessarily known to early smokers of weed, and their effects weren't known until they were synthesized and the components tested. Some of these have proved useful in unexpected ways, such as in treating seizures.[15]

Isolating the active ingredient in a plant with medicinal properties also allows for proper dosing. It came to researchers' attention that getting stoned might help hospitalized patients who suffered from cachexia, a common condition marked by a lack of appetite and body wasting. "People talk about how marijuana gives you the munchies," Molina noted. "We can harness that to someone who is cachectic and losing weight and won't eat; maybe we can make them stronger and help them get through their chemotherapy." But as he pointed out, you wouldn't want someone smoking a joint in the hospital, in part because it would set off smoke detectors and risk contact highs for anyone in the vicinity—but also because you take in all sorts of oxidized debris when you inhale a burning plant wrapped in paper. Smoking drugs is not an ideal way to deliver them. But even if smoking in a hospital were an acceptable idea, you might have to smoke three joints to achieve the effect that you'd get from a single joint derived from a different, more potent strain. The same problem would apply to edibles: the risk of huge variations in potency and efficacy. There are at least 779 different strains of marijuana. So extracting, regularizing, and, often, synthesizing the active ingredients makes a dosage more reliable, makes moderating its intensity more consistent, and makes for a more effective medical therapy.[16]

Effectively synthesizing the active ingredients in EISO has proven elusive, because the molecules are complex. The synthesis process can also be environmentally harmful. While a truly functional synthetic version of EISO will probably appear eventually, current biotechnology research has focused on interventions with the tree to modify the oil's properties more naturally. Through investigations published in multiple refereed scientific journals by different authors from around the world, findings about EISO's modern medical benefits are beyond startling. It has been reliably demonstrated to treat two of the herpes simplex viruses; reduce insulin resistance in diabetes patients; improve skin diseases and conditions; provide neuroprotections against strokes; and guard against metastasizing cells in cancers. Most cancers require their own treatments, medications, and remediations. But sandalwood oil seems to have some effect on a variety of cancers, ranging from melanoma and nonmelanoma to leukemia, breast, bladder, and prostate cancer.[17]

EISO is bound by chemical and botanical standards of quality, defined not by the pharmaceutical industry but by the International Organization for Standardization (ISO). ISO standards are like passports to global trade: necessary if you're going to convince people that your item is of high, consistent quality and can safely cross geopolitical, economic, and cultural borders. You've almost certainly run across an item with an ISO number in your daily life. Some are large and complex standards with multiple parts. There are standards for information security management, occupational health and safety, camera film speed, child seats for cars, date and time formats, medical devices, and antibribery management systems. And there's also an ISO standard for EISO. The East Indian sandalwood oil standard is ISO 3518:2002, specifying the qualities you'd want for medical consistency: the purity of the two key active ingredients, α-santalol and β-santalol; and also its odor, color, and consistency. People are opportunists, and fake or adulterated EISO abounds—sometimes with risks to users, and the ISO standard keeps people on the chemical straight and narrow.

In one recent study, only one of six brands of EISO even came close to meeting the ISO standard. It's not that difficult to reproduce the smell with other herbs, or to approximate its color and viscosity. Analysis and rigorous chemical testing of the oils is key, because medical entities need to get the most accurate and efficacious oil. If you're suffering from ailments ranging from eczema to cancer, you and your doctor want some confidence that you're getting the proper treatment.

Scarcity in the face of demand usually breeds crisis, and increasing the yield of sandalwood in India would help with many of the tree's difficulties. There is now a useful body of knowledge about what works and doesn't work when trying to plant sandalwood in new places. Selecting seeds from productive groves could lead to more productive trees. Pretreating seeds to speed up germination, through scarification (nicking or otherwise weakening the seed coating) or soaking in certain kinds of acid, is also a promising means of ensuring successful germination. Botanists have also suggested using a dual-host system, starting with a seedling in a pot with a primary host. This pairing allows the sandalwood to leech resources from the other tree, in a sort of fostering situation. Growers then plant the seedling in a field with a longer-lived secondary host that's planted nearby. This is a bit like having a tree sidle up to another tree to see whether it might be interested in some kind of botanical tango, but it has had good results in tests in Indonesia. In Nepal, one of the recognized hosts for *S. album* is a tree known as *Acacia catechu*, and not only does it occur naturally but it could serve a secondary support role: providing shade and protection from animals browsing, because it has thorns.

Still another successful approach to protecting the tree from predators involves poisoning some of the tree's seeds—enough to deter hungry animals but not enough to kill the seeds. Pretreated seed is dribbled into the ground in areas that have potential hosts nearby. After decades of close scrutiny, the tree's biology is well-known: its rainfall and temperature requirements, the appropriate soil (fairly moist, fertile, and iron-rich), and the great benefit of having a host. Careful attention to the most viable regions to grow sandalwood, with lots of them growing across a broad swath of land in different environments, could help assure the tree's chances for survival.

The species also gets a boost from its natural distribution network. Throughout its life, regardless of climate, sandalwood fruits year-round, albeit at different rates. This fruiting attracts a host of endemic bird species in India. In one study in Tamil Nadu, 217 birds from eight different species took sandalwood fruits away over several days of observation: bulbuls, mynas, parrots, barbets, hornbills, and other fruit-loving fliers. These actions mean that the fruits are well distributed and will grow, in messy, non-government-sanctioned fashion, wherever the birds' poop lands.[18] The dispersing ways of nature can almost always confound the restricting ways of officialdom.

Having a plan to manage successful commercial endeavors with the sandalwood tree is only a partial solution. Nature is green in tooth and claw, to paraphrase Alfred, Lord Tennyson. A variety of threats to sandalwood have proliferated. Phytoplasmas, which can infect more than seven hundred species of plants, are bacterial parasites carried by insects. One of these phytoplasmas causes sandalwood spike disease

(SSD), or "spike" in the shorthand argot of botanists. The disease has been prevalent for more than a century, and more than a million sandalwood trees were removed in India due to spike in the first two decades of the twentieth century. Strangely, creating in vitro cultivations of phytoplasmas has proven practically impossible, which means it can't be manipulated in a lab. With spike, leaves shrink and stiffen, creating a spiky appearance (hence the name), and trees die a year or two after symptoms first appear. Spike has been by far the most substantial disease threat to sandalwood. The pathogen that causes it has now shown up in every major sandalwood-growing state in India, although it isn't yet a serious threat to other populations elsewhere on the planet. There is still no effective control mechanism for spike, and the only recourse is to cut down and remove the infected tree.[19]

For the East Indian sandalwood tree, the best conservation prescription might be one that may not be ideal for other trees, in other settings: to expand its range through explicitly commercial strategies. This would allow the tree to expand and to provide its pharmacological benefits, and its happy oils, for people everywhere. More trees would also eventually mean that the government might simply throw up its collective hands, understanding that it will take an enormous village, outside of its control, to create a resource like sandalwood in equally enormous quantities.

The Marayoor Forest is a beautiful and brooding place. Cryptic, prehistoric rock art is etched in deep caverns along its hillsides. Some of these ancient markings depict trees, with humans walking among them. Also scattered around Marayoor are dolmens—single-chamber stone tombs—where ancient peoples are believed to be buried, as part of some ritual not yet deciphered. At the same time that the dolmens are evidence of all of our mortality, the forest still overflows with wildlife, solemnity, and beauty, and the scent from the big trees still wafts up and past the wired fences, warning signs, and metal tags, liberated, an olfactory sign of their ability to help heal the world.

CHAPTER 7

A Lawful Lot of Wood:
Central African Forest Ebony

*"We've lost so much. We might lose more. But for now
I can sit here, under the trees and sky, and pull music
from the strings."*

—Emma Trevayne, *Coda*

Musicians, cabinetmakers, chess players, and pool hustlers have lusted for centuries after the wood of the ebony tree, primarily exploited on the African continent. One botanist has described the wood as the tree world's equivalent of the blood diamonds of Africa.[1] The hardwood has stunning characteristics: dense enough to sink in water, and breathtakingly gorgeous in its polished form. Buyers and sellers have used it as a form of global currency, dating back to ancient Egypt. Despite its long use, the wood also retains its mysteries, for scientists still aren't sure just what dictates the color of ebony, and we still have only a rudimentary grasp of its biology.[2]

Desire can cut different ways: it can move people to protect trees, but at the same time, it can bring waste and loss. People lose their minds trying to achieve their heart's desires. Acting on lust without contemplating consequences often triggers bad behavior: corruption, a lack of cooperation, and looking the other way when the right way isn't far around the corner. Ebony's intense appeal has made it a mighty commodity.

One of the most desirable of these woods is *Diospyros crassiflora*, known as Central African forest ebony, but also called Gabon ebony, West African ebony, and a few other common names. The tree has a fluted base, tapering upward as it rises, reaching about seventy-five feet in height and a bit more than three feet in diameter. Native to the forests of the Congo basin, *D. crassiflora* is widespread across the region but has probably never been abundant. The most recent estimates suggest a surviving population of fewer than thirty million individual trees above ten centimeters in diameter.[3] It lives among a vast cohort of other tree species, all hard at work: Congo basin forests across six countries sequester forty billion tons of carbon, more than any other part of the world and surpassing even the Amazon basin. Nature produces ebony very slowly: the trees take around sixty years to get to a harvestable size when they're planted in a sunny location, and many centuries to reach maturity when they're under the shade of deep forest canopy.

The Congo basin is a magical place, but a foreboding one. Its forests are ancient, rich, and complex in their ecological workings, bristling with biodiversity, an imperial past, and various dangers. Joseph Conrad's novelistic descriptions of the region, based on his travel journals while serving as a boat captain up the Congo River in 1890, sketch out the region's ambiguities as well as the sheer awesomeness of the forest. "The sky was a benign immensity of unstained light," he wrote in *Heart of Darkness*, his critique of European colonial rule in Africa. "Going up that river was like traveling back to the earliest beginnings of the world, when vegetation rioted on the earth and the big trees were kings. An empty stream, a great silence, and an impenetrable forest. The air was warm, thick, heavy, sluggish . . . It was the stillness of an implacable force brooding over an inscrutable intention."

Northwest of the river, hugging the South Atlantic Ocean and butted against Equatorial Guinea, lies Cameroon. The country's forest estate covers 21.6 million hectares, including wild, lush landscapes that have summoned explorers for centuries. Distributed across southern Cameroon and into Gabon, and farther east and more sparsely into the Democratic Republic of the Congo, the nearly thirty million individuals of *D. crassiflora* might sound like an abundance, but it's not. To put this number in perspective: in 2019, in a burst of national civic and environmental duty, Ethiopia, on the eastern side of the continent, planted more than ten times that number of trees—more than 350 million seedlings, in a single *day*, closing schools and government offices so everyone could join in the planting work.

But putting a tree to work takes a lot more than just planting it in the ground. The current count of individual ebony trees is also deceptive, because the majority of the big, carbon-sequestering examples have been logged, and of the surviving trees, only 190,000 have a diameter at breast height (DBH, a standard tree measurement) of more than sixty centimeters. That diameter, about two feet across in English units, is the minimum size for legal tree harvesting across much of Africa. Coincidentally, this is also the diameter at which the ebony tree begins to have enough black wood to be commercially viable.[4]

The tree's heartwood is the source of the dark wood, living below its cloak of cambium and sapwood. Because of its hardness and finely pored structure, ebony can be polished to a beguiling sheen. The wood is embedded in the planet's cultural life. The French term for "cabinetmaker" is *ébéniste*, but ebony has also been used for furniture inlays; sculptures; carvings; the handles of doors, umbrellas, and walking canes; lots and lots of pool cues (about a thousand cubic meters' worth in a single year around 1910); the tips and handles of weapons ancient and modern; doorknobs; piano keys; chess pieces; parts of bagpipes; organ-stops; and guitar fingerboards and bridges by the linear mile. *D. crassiflora* has unique acoustic properties, and musicians have desired it over the centuries for use in musical instruments. It shows up as the wood of choice for tuning pegs on orchestral stringed instruments in all of their flavors, small to big: violas, violins, cellos, and double basses.[5] Violins, which are only slightly less popular than guitars, have their own specific intersections with ebony. One story, seemingly impossible to confirm, claims that ebony became an especially desirable wood for violins in the eighteenth century when shaving became increasingly common and the use of dark ebony provided a form of camouflage—the oily, sweaty, bare chins of players made far less noticeable marks on the dark ebony butt ends of their violins. There is also the embarrassment of violin hickey. That's its common name; dermatologists call it "acne mechanica." Some people are allergic to ebony, along with other woods, and prolonged playing can leave a mark where the violin nestles; it's also sometimes called "fiddler's neck."[6]

But regardless of its uses, musical or otherwise, not all ebony is alike. The seemingly simple term "ebony" (along with other generic names such as rosewood or mahogany) causes confusion in the realms of regulation, legislation, trafficking, enforcement, the gathering of statistics, and other metrics that are vital to tracking the ways that wood is transported and used around the world. Proper identification tightly circumscribes how commercial and environmental groups use and respond to scarcity and abundance. One species of ebony might be legal for importation, but another with a very similar common name might be prohibited. The tree is part of a big, shaggy family—the Ebenaceae, a clade of flowering plants, containing nearly eight hundred species of trees and shrubs. Witness the persimmon, the best-known tree in the group. All persimmons are in the same genus as *D. crassiflora*. In 2018, the planet produced more than 4.7 million tons of persimmon fruits, most of them for eating, and the majority of those being from *Diospyros kaki*.[7] Persimmon wood is used for woodworking, and musical instruments too, like other species of true ebony. The American persimmon is also called American ebony, as its heartwood ranges from brown to black, or has variegated color, as does *D. crassiflora*.

There are one billion people in Africa, and that number will probably quadruple by the end of the twenty-first century, putting ever-greater pressure on the land. Central African forest ebony faces two of the same threats as tropical forest trees elsewhere: illegal logging, and deforestation through rapid conversion of forests into agricultural and grazing land. The first process removes individual trees from the forests, and the second scrubs them from the Earth in an untidy roar, caught up in the wholesale destruction of vast acreages of other trees. The landscape is grim. Cameroon has one of the highest concentrations of forest-cover degradation in the Congo basin; forest cover declined by about 1 percent per year between 1990 and 2015.[8] Removing trees monetizes land, but when done for short-term agricultural subsistence purposes, it's ultimately self-defeating, for renewing the land takes much longer than tearing it down. Blunting and reducing the wholesale felling of forests requires a dance between local, national, and international actors, brimming with ambiguities and contradictions. The warming climate also continues to work its murky magic: recent World Bank data from 2022 shows that climate change increasingly drives forest loss in Africa by creating more intense and prolonged exposure to fires, storms, droughts, and insect infestations. Some two million people—about 9 percent of Cameroon's population—live in drought-affected areas. Forests cover nearly 40 percent of the country, and they provide eight million rural residents with a variety of traditional staples, including fuel, food, medicine, and building materials. To risk the forests' lives is to risk those of Cameroonians.

The tree has experienced a long slide. The first large-scale logging of *D. crassiflora* began around 1840, well before the wood had been scientifically described. Foreign investment and interest have long driven logging in Cameroon, and illegal cutting of trees has been supremely easy in tropical Africa for centuries. Cut down the trees in remote areas, far from prying eyes, send off the logs or mill them locally and then send them abroad, and never bother to replace them with a new tree in the ground.[9]

Lumber companies large and small have undertaken a great deal of legal harvesting of forest trees, but these efforts aren't entirely ethical.

Although forestry in Cameroon is profitable, it's mostly to the benefit of the countries to which the wood is exported.[10] Total exports of ebony to China from Cameroon between 2009 and 2014 consisted of about a million cubic meters of ebony of all kinds. That's a lot of wood, far more than the quantity used in stringed instruments worldwide. Craftspeople use almost all of the exported wood in furniture, buildings, and other larger projects, while guitar makers typically only use small pieces of Central African forest ebony. But ebony has an outsized presence in the music world. It's beautiful, it's adored by musicians, and it's seen by millions of fans who watch professionals playing onstage. Musicians play guitars, with their ebony-modified sounds, for film and television, around campfires, in dorm rooms, on farms, in the biggest penthouses and the poorest barrios, and in many other places where people gather.

You can't just do anything you want with wood from other countries, even in tiny quantities. For hundreds of years, almost any action involving wood was acceptable. Just a generation ago, there were no laws of substance governing the forest products trade. But that's all changing. In crafting laws to prevent unlawful or unethical action, you want uniform solutions, not ones rejiggered to fit particular circumstances. That's because small incidents of illegal action, easily condoned and readily overlooked, have a way of becoming larger and more impactful. In the United States, conservation measures have been in place for a long time, most significantly in the form of the Lacey Act, a piece of American environmental legislation. Named after Congressman John Lacey of Iowa upon its creation in 1900, the act remains a cornerstone of American conservation law. Lacey crafted the law to stop the illegal trafficking of wildlife across any state line in the United States or its territories. Congress voted to revise the law in 2008 to extend its protection to include a broad range of plants and plant products, bringing trees into the international conservation equation. Social and economic justice figured into the new dress for the act: corporations were making many millions of dollars importing and selling valuable forest products, undermining the US lumber industry, but the illegal logging was also costing developing nations—where most of the wood was grown—nearly $10 billion annually due to lost revenue and diminishing assets. The scope and scale of illegal logging in Africa is breathtaking. According to the Congressional Research Service, in 2019 illegal logging in Cameroon made up between 50 and 65 percent of all logging activity in the country.[11]

In 2009, FBI agents raided Gibson, one of the United States' largest guitar makers, because of its purported importation and use of ebony and rosewood from Madagascar. After the raids, the company became a cause célèbre among the conservative Tea Party group, which considered the act government overreach. Their CEO, Henry Juszkiewicz, launched himself onto the talk show circuit and started using the hashtag #thiswillnotstand—ironic, given that the whole dustup was about a crime related to felling trees.[12] The company ultimately paid a $300,000 fine as well as agreeing to a $50,000 payment to the National Fish and Wildlife Foundation to promote conservation activities related to protected trees used in the musical instrument industry.

A few years later another guitar company, the California-based Taylor Guitars, purchased a dilapidated ebony mill in the city of Yaoundé in Cameroon, and soon became a leading driver of change in the guitar industry, leading a conservation charge to transform the growth, harvesting, and replanting of *D. crassiflora*. The sawmill's name, Crelicam, is apparently a portmanteau of the previous Spanish owner's making—a business providing credit for companies that buy books. It's hard to shake the book-and-tree metaphor. *Cre* (credit), plus *li*, as in *libros*, or books, and *cam*, for Cameroon. The name lives on with its new owners and has become more generic. Guitar salespeople and musicians simply call the wood "Crelicam ebony,"

sidestepping nomenclatural vagaries. The mill allowed Taylor to take direct control of a traditionally used species in a complicated region of the world.

Yaoundé is the capital of Cameroon, established by the Germans 130 years ago. It has some 2.8 million residents; if it were in the United States it would be the third-largest metropolis, wedged between Chicago and Los Angeles in population size. Vincent Deblauwe, the world authority on *D. crassiflora*, described it to me as a conglomeration of neighborhoods that have fused in a continuous alternation of administrative buildings, uphill residential areas, slums in the periodically flooded valley bottoms, and markets on dirt roads, often muddy from the rains. Traffic congestion abounds; few large thoroughfares cross the city, and the ones that do exist are often clogged with street sellers, motorbikes, and taxis. A car left in the middle of a road after an engine failure is a common sight. Unemployment is low, but the average annual income in the city proper is less than nine hundred dollars annually, in a region with many urbanized professional niches, including banking and white-collar commerce. The difficulty in earning a living wage means that opportunities to make money often skirt ethical considerations when it comes to putting food on the table.

Despite its grit and poverty, Yaoundé is the center of other conservation activities. The Congo Basin Institute (CBI) maintains offices there, leading a multinational effort to model partnerships in building conservation capacity in Cameroon. The CBI's presence in the capital city is important in part because it helps to keep residents who have gone overseas for training tethered to their home country. Only 20 percent of those who leave for education as ecologists and biologists elsewhere ever return to Cameroon, so providing them with local opportunities to do sophisticated science, and train in partnership with people from developed countries, helps to keep them around. The city also houses the International Institute of Tropical Agriculture (IITA), a nonprofit geared toward innovations in reducing malnutrition, poverty, and the degradation of natural resources.

Crelicam provides the raw material for fingerboards and headplate veneers for electric and acoustic guitars, along with violins and cellos—all of which are cumulatively some of the world's most popular instruments. Aficionados note that the worst day of a guitar's life is the first day it's taken home and played, when its wood is the newest, the least seasoned, and as far from its potential as it will ever be. (Just what is it about the passage of time that seasons a musical instrument? Oddly, no one has a very precise idea about why this is so.) Nevertheless, people crave guitars. In 2013, the music industry in the United States peddled nearly 1.4 million acoustic guitars (all of Taylor's guitars are acoustic; they accounted for a bit more than 10 percent of this total), and more than a million electric ones. They're popular in other countries as well; China imported more than ten million guitars that year. *Diospyros crassiflora* has been used in almost every instrument Taylor Guitars has made. With a crush strength of more than eleven thousand pounds per square inch, its extraordinary hardness means that all of the handling that goes into playing a wooden stringed instrument won't easily wear it down or change its shape.[13]

But getting the finished ebony in responsible and ethical fashion is difficult. There's a long supply chain involved with commercial wood, and lots of room for mischief and misunderstanding along the way. Illegalities in the forest products trade can take many forms, such as intentionally mislabeling one species as another; moving wood out of the country without paying any tariffs or taxes; harvesting it illegally from private forests; cutting trees before they're of legal size; cutting down a larger percentage of trees in a region than the law allows; or violating any number of other regulations and decrees. To combat these crimes, a host of entities have taken up the charge with potent tools. The power of legal agreements and consortia efforts, including the stipulations of the Lacey Act and other international agreements, has helped a great deal. TRAFFIC, an NGO international wildlife monitoring network, allied with the World Wildlife Fund and the International Union for Conservation of Nature (IUCN), not only monitors but makes conservation recommendations. It might not be easy or even possible to stop a country's illegal logging practices, but it is possible to control the flow of illegal wood into other countries. As with the Lacey Act, other countries or blocs of countries have entered into strict requirements for importers to make their work legal. The European Union Timber Regulation (EUTR) outlines the obligations of operators and traders who place timber on the market.

Regulations such as the EUTR and the Lacey Act are designed to reduce illegal logging worldwide, but attempts at local solutions have met with mixed success. Cameroon passed a forestry law in 1994, designed to decentralize forests so that their management could be undertaken more locally. But the role of numerous participants was not clearly defined, costs have proven exorbitant, and traditional African law has been largely ignored.[14]

There are many other participants who have published documents stipulating proper practice in Cameroonian forestry. Trees don't hew to geopolitical boundaries, and other countries on the African continent have crafted international consensus. African nations worked to alleviate deforestation issues across the Congo basin through a 1999 agreement, the Yaoundé Declaration, signed by Cameroon, Equatorial Guinea, the Republic of the Congo, Chad, Gabon, and the Central African Republic. Together, these six nations formed a consortium, known as COMIFAC (the Commission des Forêts d'Afrique Centrale, or Commission of Central African Forests), to harmonize and coordinate the fight against deforestation. For countries emerging from the long fog of colonial rule, even decades later, issues of self-determination are challenging but essential. Within Cameroon there exists the Ministère des Forêts et de la Faune—MINFOF, or the Ministry of Forests and Fauna, another member in the large rumble of regulatory bodies. But nobody rides for free, and it's the rare entity that has a hand in timber regulation and does not also have a related financial interest. Still, these efforts help to bring forestry processes into the brighter light of day.

These regulations pushed Taylor into obtaining ebony legally. Companies typically think of corporate social responsibility (CSR) as a voluntary initiative, rather than mandated or motivated by law. But legal organizations and conservation groups have started a trend to legalize CSR, to prod companies to act ethically.[15] Relying on ethical impulses alone has not been sufficient to protect trees. Law, along with its close cousin public policy, might appear bloodless, and far removed from the forest, but like nature, law evolves, and in its refinements has become a central organizing principle for environmental protection. Other laws in the United States besides the Lacey Act address the illegal trade of plants and animals. These include the Endangered Species Act of 1973, which now includes protection against illegal import of some species of wood; and CITES (the Convention on International Trade in Endangered Species of Wild Fauna and Flora), an international treaty to protect endangered species. These are well-known protective laws. But other, much less known pieces of legislation are also in place. Foremost among these is the Tropical Forest Conservation Act (TFCA), first enacted in 1998 by the United States. The TFCA addresses illegal logging not through prosecution but by authorizing debt-for-nature transactions. If a country has debt held by the United States, that debt can be restructured in eligible countries, paid toward local grant-making efforts rather than to the United States. The act supports programs in those countries to conserve tropical forests, a powerful form of self-regulation.

Other regulatory efforts have fallen short. Cameroon still lacks a comprehensive legal framework to achieve its decarbonization goals; as of this writing, there is no law in place that requires public institutions to manage climate change. But individual pieces of legislation provide a superstructure with which to manage human behavior, and misbehavior. The 2008 amendment to the Lacey Act had two main parts: first, it made it illegal to import plants that harvesters had taken in violation of national or local law in the country of origin; and second, it required that importers in the United States provide the scientific name for the plant. This nomenclatural necessity has been important, given the deep confusion at times over the importation of look-alike species. Importers are also now required to quantify the import further, noting the value, quantity, and country of harvest origin. And under the terms of the act, you don't even need to know you're violating the act to get into trouble for violating it, motivating US importers to have a clear and close understanding of the law.[16] With the act's passage, American companies suddenly had a legal obligation to get any wood imported into the country in an ethical and more sustainable way, including making detailed disclosures about the wood being imported, as well as understanding other countries' laws related to wood harvesting.

The co-owner of the Crelicam mill is Vidal de Teresa, the CEO of Madinter, a Madrid-based company whose exclusive province is the sale of wood for musical instruments. Vidal, a former veterinarian, had established a distribution company that supplied tonewoods for instrument builders around the world. The Lacey Act's 2008 revisions, and similar laws being considered in other countries, prompted him to take greater responsibility for the wood he sourced, and perhaps persuaded him to partner with Taylor Guitars to purchase the Crelicam mill. In October 2011, as they were contemplating the purchase, Bob Taylor and Vidal visited Cameroon—an exciting journey for both men. But they were naive, and problems arose. Some of those involved people who needed to be paid under the table. This didn't fit the men's standards, and they ended up with a substantial ethical problem. During a pivotal moment in Cameroon, sitting in their hotel room on the eve of making a decision about the mill, Bob said to Vidal, "We have to agree tonight that if we don't buy Crelicam, neither one of us would ever use ebony again. Because we could never buy ebony from a company that had those problems."[17]

Cameroon distributes ebony in a convoluted and intensely regulated fashion, in recent years issuing permits for about 3,000 tons per year for export—tiny potatoes. In 2020, Crelicam exported 1,200 of those tons of *D. crassiflora*, and the next-largest permitted amount for other companies has ranged between 250 and 850 tons. Taylor

Guitars has gotten some special dispensations after a long tenancy in Cameroon. Scott Paul, Taylor's Director of Natural Resource Sustainability, confirmed what Vidal had told me: Bob Taylor bought the mill because in Cameroon, and only in Cameroon, ebony is governed by a specific law to control ebony exploitation. Government officials don't allow anyone to cut ebony in Cameroon, even large forest concession holders, without a permit. In 2020 the government gave out just eight permits, including one to Crelicam, and Taylor is allowed to harvest a fixed tonnage of ebony per year.

Fixed tonnage, quotas, permits, sustainability, rules, and regulations: these aspects of the story have the unfortunate effect of masking Cameroon's vibrant musical tradition, which has included instrumental innovations, complex rhythms, and the popularization of frenetic, lively bikutsi music, a local musical genre. Among his countrymen, the Cameroonian guitarist and musician Vince Nguini has had the largest international reputation, working for decades with the American singer-songwriter Paul Simon, first on his 1990 album, *The Rhythm of the Saints*, and then in later collaborations, going on to record with artists Peter Gabriel and Jimmy Buffett, and establishing his own label, Nguini Records.

The popularity of acoustic guitars has worked out for Taylor Guitars from a financial standpoint, but they have reason to be proud of their leadership in what they call the Ebony Project: an integrative partnership where business, communities, and researchers work together to protect a valuable timber species, reforest degraded land, and improve rural livelihoods. From its earliest days, the organizers have designed the project as a pilot for larger-scale rainforest restoration efforts for the Congo basin.

The undertaking caught the attention of the US government, and in January 2014, the company won an Award for Corporate Excellence from the State Department. Secretary of State John Kerry noted that Bob and Taylor Guitars had fundamentally changed the entire ebony trade. In 2017, the company partnered with the Congo Basin Institute to conduct basic ecological research and plant ebony trees.

Since then, one Cameroonian student has earned her PhD and two gained master's degrees through the project.

"I'm not saying this to diminish our ethical or moral responsibilities," Scott told me, "but guitar makers typically use less than one percent of the global trade in any given species of wood used in their guitars." This despite the fact that acoustic guitars are almost entirely made out of wood. A huge swath of Cameroon's forests is open for business, with a total of 15.7 million hectares designated for production. Taylor Guitars accounts for what amounts to a sliver—a splinter—of that total, although famous musicians use their instruments (Taylor Swift plays a Taylor guitar, naturally; so do Eric Clapton, Shawn Mendes, and John Legend).[18] Harvesters collect the wood solely from narrow bands along roads, in temporary forest estates where villages are located and where farmers clear the forest for small-scale agriculture. I asked Scott whether the supply process was transparent to company executives. "It's not," he admitted. "There's no way to know for sure if you'll receive your requested quota each year. Some years we get what we ask for, and others, less than we ask for."

But Vidal noted that Cameroon is the only place in Africa that he knows of that has a dedicated and separate system to regulate ebony. This was a selling point to him and Bob Taylor. It meant that there was a protective framework of some kind in place to regularize the process. "In other countries, you can buy ebony, but it's not common, so it's difficult to get, and you don't usually know who you're buying it from."

Economists and sociologists have extensively studied corruption in sub-Saharan Africa. A 2010 World Bank report noted that nearly 78 percent of firms in Cameroon expected to make informal payments to public officials to lubricate the machinery of business; half of companies planned on giving gifts to secure an operating license, and fully 85 percent expected to give gifts to secure a government contract.

Yet only 52 percent of firms in the country identified corruption as a major constraint. Living within a particular system regularizes the system and makes it seem downright routine.[19]

But Cameroon, emerging out of a long history of political patronage and influence after its independence from France in 1960, continues to make strides in placing the country's forests at the service of its economy, its people, and the environment. Subsequent democratization and decentralization have led to a host of forest policy reforms. Cameroon has never had a huge timber export presence, so the relative smallness of their forest operations has made them easier for government entities and NGOs to observe, regulate, and repair.[20]

This is not to say that it's easy now. Vidal likened it to a daily battle, with new government issues arising constantly. Only rarely now is corruption a problem for Taylor Guitars; more often, the difficulty is with new taxes the government tries to impose. These taxes are legal, but they require changing the business plan. For example, a few years ago, one of the taxes Taylor pays on every kilo of ebony was raised by 1,000 percent.

Vidal observed that after a decade, the administration in Cameroon knows how Crelicam does business, and understands that they're highly competent at it, and to the benefit of the local populace. But he pointed out that corruption still exists in pockets outside of governmental control, and it uses time as leverage, because for business endeavors, time is money. Containers at the port waiting to leave, documents waiting to be paid, extra documents that need to be filled out. "You have no time," Vidal observed, "but they have the time. Corruption works like this: if you're on your way to work in Cameroon, the police (or others claiming to be police) can stop you and ask for your papers; they can wait you out, until you pay them off, and you can be on your way."

Crelicam is an island of sorts. Although the mill's parent companies are bound by the realities of doing business in the city, and the country, Taylor Guitars and Madinter help in the daily lives of workers. They provide continuous and extensive machinery training, pay well, offer health benefits, give workers free lunches, hand out work clothing, and provide upward mobility at the mill. It has changed the lives of some employees, whose newfound work stability has allowed them to start families. The mill's operations also provide workers with a path to increasing responsibility through more sophisticated jobs at the mill and elsewhere, and generally provide meaningful careers.

Controlling the trees' own journeys from ground to guitar has also led to greater efficiencies and less potential for corruption. The company uses GPS traceability for every tree extracted so that they're able to maintain chain-of-custody transparency, using mobile devices in the field. Every stump gets a chalked ID number and an inscription noting its exact latitude and longitude, which is recorded and then accompanies the tree on its journey to the lumber mill and beyond. Taylor staff assess more than the wood's provenance; they also examine their supply chain to evaluate risks of human trafficking and slavery. Sometimes they give advance notice to vendors to let them know they're coming, and sometimes they arrive unannounced.

But there's another twist to the story of *D. crassiflora* and Taylor Guitars. One of the discoveries that most shocked Bob and Vidal upon arriving in Cameroon was that the dark ebony heartwood only made up a relatively small percentage of most trees. The fixed tonnage involved a lot of unused wood: because the dark wood was the most desirable part of the tree, the remainder of the wood— the variegated outer sapwood, a splotchy mix of light and dark wood (thus colored for reasons botanists are still working to understand)— was wasted and often left to rot on the forest floor. About 10 percent of each tree was usable. Bob Taylor hit upon the idea of changing guitar players' hearts and minds, to make them find the mottled wood at least as interesting as the black ebony heartwood. After all, the tonal qualities were identical: the wood's hardness, density, and ability to take a finish were all the same. So Taylor started using the striped wood on the company's priciest guitars, making it a desirable element rather than a waste product.[21]

Scott also observed that beyond the ethical reasons for taking advantage of the tree's striped wood, a much more efficient use of the wood is better for the company's bottom line. If half of the wood they bring into the factory is striped, and it doesn't get used, half of their permitted tonnage would disappear as waste. For corporations, the bottom line remains the biggest line. But Taylor has noble and ambitious goals in the country. "This is a huge statement," Scott told me, "but we're hoping to try to build a middle class in Cameroon."

Not only does Taylor use more of the tree, and much more efficiently, it also replants ebony and fruit trees with local communities that buffer the Dja Reserve, a UNESCO World Heritage site, to the tune of 27,810 trees in 2022. Although these plantings seem like a relatively small-scale effort, it's an admirable exemplar of a long-term investment, as it might be closing in on the twenty-second century by the time the trees are mature enough to harvest.

The successes of Taylor Guitars—which Scott insists aren't financial but environmental and legislative—have hinged on numerous forces outside their control, including the many legal pressures on the company that obligate them to act responsibly in importing wood. Vertical integration cuts out the middleman and lessens the odds that corruption can take hold within their supply chain, reducing the chances that the company will land in hot water with the Cameroonian government as well as with agencies in the United States that keep an eye on illegal importations. But I appreciate Taylor's ethical stance as a relatively enlightened corporation. In 2021, Taylor Guitars transferred complete ownership of the company to its nearly twelve hundred employees. This new ownership structure does not extend to the employees of Crelicam, which is technically a joint venture with Madinter, and is based in a country that prohibits employees from participating in employee stock ownership plans.

As of this writing, Crelicam still survives despite the structural difficulties of working in Cameroon. Large-scale land conversion to agriculture is the biggest difficulty for the integrity of the forest, but illegal logging and small-scale slash-and-burn tactics have been a major source of deforestation in the country.[22] The stereotype about slash-and-burn agriculture is one of localized villainy: native people wantonly destroying precious resources. But a long tradition of land-clearing survives, one started many decades ago via a determined attempt by colonial settlers, not natives, to make way for their big farms, followed by a reliance on livestock. Annual deforestation rates of moist closed-canopy forest in Cameroon have been estimated at about 108,000 hectares, most of this done to plant profitable crops of oil palms, cocoa, cassava, and plantain. Now these modified lands contribute a great deal to food assistance in a very poor country, where more than 2.6 million people suffer from acute levels of food insecurity. This pits the country's intense need for local food solutions against the imperative to prevent deforestation.

Cutting down legions of trees mutes biological diversity and increases disease, food insecurity, military and civilian conflicts, and the loss of cultural identities. The mechanisms in place to regulate logging on the continent, though, are moving in the right direction. The World Bank has funded a framework known as REDD+, which seeks to reduce emissions from deforestation and to support businesses to sustainably manage forests. But what can be done to mitigate deforestation resulting from attempts to clear land entirely for other uses? It's a hyperlocalized problem: a subsistence farmer needs to clear land to grow crops to feed his family, so he lights a fire. Communal living and land tenure systems in Africa don't provide incentives to individuals to resist deforestation activities. Population pressures also mean that humans need open land on which to live. Even documenting deforestation involves difficulties, because there's no consensus on just how to define the term.

Any solutions offered here will seem pat, so I can only offer up some synthesized suggestions. First, formal rules and foreign aid can help but also harm efforts to stanch the flow of deforestation. The most recent and most enlightened thinking suggests that Africans must look to one another for solutions. There is also a chronic failure to recognize that conservation is only possible under very limited, specific conditions. Rather than asserting themselves as guardians of the forests, local and national leaders could try to "see like a farmer" and emphasize local community. Extensive surveys of communities show that state rules are much more commonly broken than community ones. Hybrid systems of rules emerge out of repeated interactions among local governmental, private, and state actors, and the existence of rules, per se, is less important than the context in which these rules are promoted and put into action. When you know your neighbors, you're more likely to listen to their arguments, and when you trust your community leaders, you're more likely to comply.

There are also often deep spiritual issues in play in Africa that affect attitudes about trees. It's a widespread belief that the spirits of people's ancestors live in forests, and it's easier to sidestep sanctions for breaking state rules than for violating community norms, because negotiating with spirits and avoiding their anger is more difficult, and the outcomes less certain, than paying a bribe or a fine to the state. Cultural values and beliefs matter; people fear the retribution of spirits, and these beliefs govern their behavior. As a rule, forest management prescriptions that focus only on purely economic concerns will not work well. Ultimately, it takes rules to constrain behavior, but the ways in which those rules are understood, implemented, and succeed need to take local motivations, fears, and intentions into account.[23]

Researchers still struggle to understand the ecology of West African ebony. Because of the large size of the tree's seeds (about two inches in length), the ebony's distribution requires a decent-sized mammal capable of swallowing those seeds. Although this detail has yet to show up in the scientific literature, Vincent Deblauwe found many seeds in elephant dung, and seeds produced by a close cousin of *D. crassiflora* are recorded in gorilla poop, and in the stomachs of duikers, a class of small brown antelopes resident in heavily wooded regions in sub-Saharan Africa.[24] But despite the fact that fruit remnants have been found in the stomachs or dung of these animals (a means of dispersal that biologists call endozoochory), the tree's dispersal lines aren't well mapped or well understood. Most of the large mammals in the western Congo region are endangered, and as the mammalian dispersers start to decline from poaching or hunting, the distribution of a tree's seeds to new locations, and a new life, also diminishes.

The causes of the wood's greatest attraction—its black color—also remain a mystery. It was once thought that the black or dark compounds in the wood were due to insoluble tannin-iron compounds. But as it turns out, there are no tannins in the wood, either in its heartwood or in its sapwood, which wraps the core.[25] Although its coloration mechanisms are far from well understood, darker areas are often associated with knots, branch stubs, decay, insect holes, or other injuries and insults. Some evidence suggests that an injury to a tree's roots can lead to black heartwood.[26] So *D. crassiflora*'s unique coloration might be the result of a clash: an attack by fungi, followed by a protective response, or some other kind of biological arms race. Deblauwe confirmed that he's seen that the wood is always blackened around holes made by insects. He noted that ebony cutters in Cameroon have reported that rocky soils favor black wood, but that wet soils do not.[27]

What does it mean for the future of the tree to say that there are nearly thirty million trees left? The IUCN ranks *D. crassiflora* as Vulnerable, which means that it is likely to become endangered unless the circumstances that have caused it to be in decline can be arrested or reversed. We still don't have an accurate fix on the genus's vulnerabilities. IUCN guidelines recommend the conservation status of a species be reassessed every five years, but some 70 percent of existing *Diospyros* assessments are already five or more years old. The IUCN's thousands of scientists fight a noble fight to undertake these assessments, but without financial support on a par with a national military budget, it's difficult to stay current. Conservation biologists point to habitat loss as the primary reason for the decline of vulnerable species, be they plant or animal. The IUCN expects that in the next century, despite aggressive planting and conservation efforts, the tree's numbers will decline more than 30 percent. Whether or not these numbers can change, in the face of efforts of corporations and other NGOs, as well as government entities, remains to be seen.[28] "We are but a moment's sunlight, fading in the grass," as Jesse Colin Young of the Youngbloods sang in 1969, on their album *Elephant Mountain*. Decline and atrophy are the way of the world.

The mighty struggle continues to keep *D. crassiflora* viable, pushing up toward the sky, still on the planet. Conservationists point out that we need to think about life at the species level, more than the individual level. Of course, saving the individuals means saving the species. In *Heart of Darkness*, Joseph Conrad's critique of colonialism in the Congo taps the dark heart of humans: our tendencies toward self-endangering corruptibility. When we have a chance to act inappropriately or self-destructively, we often do. But music is a stupendous cultural force, and a lever of great power, and *D. crassiflora* has played its part in the symphony. As Plato noted, music is a moral law. It's generated not from the material but from the heart. The ties between West African ebony and guitars run deeper than the simple wood. Musical instruments act as portals, prompting us to reflect on the connections between physical objects and people. Keeping time is a deep human desire and need. Even the poorest of communities usually have music: a drum, or a drummer, or a singer, and often someone strumming on a guitar, and it can help close the gaps between otherwise unbridgeable chasms.

CHAPTER 8

Belonging and Beyond: The Blue Gum Eucalyptus

"Humans are strange that way, full of contradictions. It's as if they need to hate and exclude as much as they need to love and embrace. Their hearts close tightly, then open at full stretch, only to clench again, like an undecided fist."

—Elif Shafak, *The Island of Missing Trees*

The blue gum eucalyptus (*Eucalyptus globulus*) has an image problem. Also known as the Tasmanian blue gum, it's an evergreen broadleaf tree native to southeastern Australia but now found worldwide. The eucs can make big messes, and catch fire like gasoline in a match factory. Fire crews and urban planners loathe its dangerously flammable ways. Lumbermen hate its warped wood. In the United States, it's been called the nation's largest weed. In California, where the eucalyptus has taken up broad residency across the state, many of its detractors consider it an invasive species.

The eucalyptus' detractors have also often reflexively equated the arrival of undesirable plants with the influx of undesirable humans. California has a long history of exclusion of foreigners, limiting the presence of both Chinese and Mexican laborers since statehood in 1850 up to the present. People in power around the planet have claimed these associations between humans from overseas with undesirable flora and fauna for centuries. In the late nineteenth century, people spoke of sparrows arriving on American shores as "dirty immigrants," echoing nationalist and isolationist language common to that era, and, alas, to every era in America, to a greater or lesser degree. The blue gum has been subjected to the same whiff of nativism. "Californians . . . ransack the world for exotic trees with which to beautify their homes," noted an 1890 editorial in the Harvard-based journal *Garden and Forest*. "California valleys are fast becoming converted into groves of Eucalyptus . . . while one looks in vain outside the rapidly disappearing forests for the native trees, which are world-wide wonders, and which ought to be the pride of every true Californian." This is not just a nineteenth-century notion. A member of the public, writing in 1970 in support of the removal of the trees from Angel Island, a state park in San Francisco Bay, remarked, "Anyone who's had to live with blue gum and other related over-sized eucalyptus trees know that they just don't belong. They are non-native, dirty, and dangerous."[1] Angel Island, where more than a million Asian immigrants were detained and examined under the terms of the Chinese Exclusion Act of 1882, had a long and vexed relationship with race and ethnicity, and such comments, especially in the context of an immigration station, have only served to agitate anti-immigrant sentiment.

Refracted through a different lens, though, the tree is a beautiful, richly scented, wind-blocking resident of the state, vital to the survival of migratory butterflies and other natives, and now an integral part of the landscape of California, loved by generations of residents up and down the state. The fast-growing eucalyptus is now the most common nonnative tree in California. Is it at risk because of perceptions of its villainy, and if so, do we care? Does it belong? What we should and can do about it, for it, and to it, if anything, remain open questions. Eucalyptus trees provide a useful way to think about belonging not just in coastal California, where they are ubiquitous, but across the world. Along with trees growing wild, there are enormous, commercially farmed plantations of the eucalyptuses in Brazil, Southeast Asia, and portions of Europe. They are also omnipresent in their original range in southeastern Australia. The tree has changed in its tenancy in California too, after nearly two hundred years: it now gets much bigger, probably because it has been treated to much richer soil than it has in relatively nutrient-poor Australian land.

The eucalyptuses comprise a big genus of more than seven hundred species. They come from common ancestors, as do humans, as do all living beings. But we don't privilege them all the same way. Curse one family's relative but praise another. The quiet cousin, the rowdy daughter, the bookish aunt, the brash sister. Some are short and busy; others tall, quiet, and stately. A few prefer wet conditions to dry ones. And with the blue gum eucs in particular, we encounter qualities that work both for and against the tree's reputation, such as the ability to grow in very dry conditions—great for arid inland Southern California, where they grow with grace and beauty, and potentially disastrous when clustered together in dense urban settings. In 1991, blue gum eucalyptuses helped fuel a disastrous two-day fire in the Oakland Hills, an event that seared their long-term undesirability into the region's consciousness.

The tree is also messy, which can't have helped dampen its fiery reputation, as it sheds its shaggy bark in large, extravagant ribbons, along with other bits of its detritus. This shedding can be spectacular; in some species of eucalyptuses, but especially in *Eucalyptus deglupta*, native to Asia but found worldwide, the peeling bark reveals magnificent shades of reds, greens, oranges, and grays. Bark cells are also able to photosynthesize, making fuel from carbon dioxide and water, a job usually done by leaves alone. This adaptation gives the blue gum an extra survival advantage. The bark's messiness might not only be a consequence of its rapid growth but serve as an evolutionary survival strategy: the understories around large stands of the trees become so densely covered with the shed bark that it's difficult for any other trees to grow, preventing other species from crowding it out. The quantity of debris fall at blue gum trees' bases can reach thirty tons or more per acre in some places in Northern California.[2]

The blue gum can grow up to eighty feet in its first twenty years, and adds between a half inch and an inch in diameter annually. The tallest specimens of the tree are crowding three hundred feet tall, second only to the coast redwood. It also has immense economic importance in temperate parts of the world, serving as the primary pulpwood species for paper products. Its fibers are slender but have thick cellular walls that impart strength, making for a light, strong, and smooth paper. Native to disjunct areas in Tasmania and southern Victoria, the tree grows in many kinds of soils, and outside of Australia, it tolerates both higher and lower rainfall than it receives in its original home. It's a tree on the move, readily adapting to new homes.[3]

Blue gums are pretty, with smooth olive-green trunks and bright blue juvenile foliage. They provide wind protection, firewood, healthful oils, elegant foliage, and a beautiful scent. As the British historian Peter Coates has noted, "For some Californians, the redwood is their green icon. For others, California without eucalypts is not California."[4]

But sometimes, eucalyptuses and their brittle wood cause troubles for humans, and in many cases, hot weather has been anecdotally blamed, through a phenomenon called summer branch drop. Some Los Angeles foresters have claimed that hot weather can pop a branch right off, and examples of this show up elsewhere in the enormous global literature on the tree over the past several centuries. One LA news article noted that in the early 1960s, a branch fell out of every eucalyptus tree on a particular street in a single summer afternoon. In May 1947, a foreman in the City Forestry office in Los Angeles died when a branch on a fifty-foot-tall euc he was trimming fell and "cracked his skull." In the summer of 1983, four-year-old Frieda Williams was similarly killed by a relatively small branch two inches in diameter that fell about twenty feet, landing on the little girl at the San Diego Zoo. The bereaved father didn't blame the tree, or anyone. "I don't have no harsh feelings toward nobody," noted her father. "That won't bring my baby back." A half dozen other examples have been documented, almost all involving kids playing on or beneath the tree. But the blue gum's popularity has usually won out. The trees fill the sprawling Scripps Ranch neighborhood in San Diego; it's even on the community's logo. The president of a homeowners association was asked whether he'd ever switch to a smaller, less troublesome tree. "Never," he replied.[5]

For the minority of people outraged by the blue gum, I suggest a long look in the mirror. Our daily lives belie our intentions. We each breathe out nearly a million tons of carbon dioxide in an average lifetime.[6] We consume about thirty thousand gallons of water during that same span. We are resource users, the most hypocritical of organisms, ranting about invasive species while not confronting our own invasive ways. Disposable diapers use some 715 pounds of plastic per kid, and pulp from more than four trees. Each of us will eat an average of 2.5 tons of beef in a lifetime. And any one of our ubiquitous computers will require at least 530 pounds of fossil fuel to manufacture.[7] And we speak in the same way that we act; we can hardly help ourselves. As the narrator in the Daniel Quinn novel *Ishmael* remarked, "I mean, you hear this fifty times a day. People talk about *our* environment, *our* seas, *our* solar system. I've even heard people talk about *our* wildlife."[8]

Although the blue gum is native to Australia, it didn't take off on its own. A voyage into the obscure pages of history extracts the person responsible for the tree's earliest peregrinations. Key in its expansion was Ferdinand von Mueller, a German-Australian government botanist in the then colony of Victoria, and later director of the Royal Botanical Gardens in Melbourne. In a burst of international enthusiasm in the middle of the nineteenth century, he introduced *E. globulus*

to southern Europe, the African continent, California, and large areas of South America.

As one of Mueller's contemporaries noted, "In the history of the future naturalization of the Eucalyptus, Mueller is the savant who justly calculated the future of the tree, traced it to its prospective itineracy, and predicted its destiny."[9] Australians loved their blue gums. In the 1880s, Melbourne residents wrote to the city council pleading for the tree to be planted to "absorb bad gasses" coming from a nearby manure depot.[10]

The blue gum likely arrived in California in early 1856 from Australia. Later that year, the Shell Mound Nurseries and Fruit Garden, probably east of the Oakland Auditorium, and not far from the site of the deadly 1991 fire, was selling Australian gum trees for five dollars apiece.[11]

The blue gum arrived in the Bay Area along with a vast, heterogeneous wash of newcomers from around the world in the last years of the California Gold Rush. Farmers and arborists planted the tree in great quantities between its arrival and the 1930s, buying it mostly as seeds from nurseries. Gold miners in the Golden State found the wood useful as mine props, to hold up ceilings in tunnels. Spreading to the north and south, the adaptable and fragrant tree provided fast-growing greenery and shade to large swaths of California. Before the blue gum arrived, large regions were treeless; the Central Valley—that gigantic lozenge of flat land running down the spine of California from the Klamath Mountains to the Transverse Ranges in Southern California—was decidedly untreed, despite beautiful rivers and wetlands. As the second half of the nineteenth century unfolded, the eucalyptus tree transformed these otherwise featureless landscapes.[12] One of its anticipated uses, when the expansion of railroads started to stitch together the enormous American West, was for railroad ties. The wood held promise as timber; it was heavy, solid, and an attractive yellow-brown color. But it proved to have no value in finished structures, nor in any setting that required precision; the larger pieces cracked and checked badly when dried. This behavior disappointed both railroad builders and real estate developers, given the demands for building materials. But it was still popular as fuel, and even more for aesthetics. To settlers from the east and Europe, "California didn't look right," the tree historian Jared Farmer observed. "It looked unfinished. A land blessed with so much sunshine, warmth and fertility demanded more greenery, flowers, and shade . . . Where nature erred, settlers meant to repair."[13]

The tree also got a solid cultural push from artists and promotional literature. "California at its Best!" crowed the cover of *Pasadena* magazine in the 1920s, showing a grove of eucs dominating the image of a Spanish-style home behind it. Various other eucalypt artworks depicted the tree embedded in the California landscape. Activists helped keep the trees in the public's mind. On the first Earth Day in 1970, a group of fifty students from Moorpark College in Ventura circled a stretch of trees to stop the destruction of a cluster of fifty-five blue gums and pepper trees by a bulldozer in the Simi Valley, alongside a roadway slated for widening. Although the trees were felled, the students won a temporary victory with a judge's stay, and Moorpark College's president made a pledge to plant two trees on the campus for every one lost because of the street widening.[14] Other choices embedded the tree further into the state's consciousness. There are some 306 streets (and avenues, and ways, and courts, and drives, and roads, and lanes) in California with the word "Eucalyptus" in them, many named by developers and city planners during the big building booms following World War II.

A 1910 city directory for Los Angeles notes eucalyptus investments, eucalyptus lands, and even eucalyptus novelties for sale. A lot of it was hype. A 1974 *Los Angeles Times* article called the blue gum "the beloved failure" in the region because it was ineffective as a source of lumber and then adored for its aesthetic virtues. The tree also acted as a windbreak that could provide a little pocket of calm and a haven of cool, scented quietness: "peace, even within a few yards of an agonized freeway," as the *Times* remarked. And for a time near the end of the twentieth century, the tree generated renewed excitement as a possible fuel ("eucfuel," it was sometimes called, in an awful portmanteau). But as a commercial product, it was only good for firewood, and even then, who wanted to burn more wood in a region beset by some of the worst smog in the nation? The tree, however, was an important export during early statehood: short on coal reserves and dependent on energy exports from afar, California traded the tree's wood for coal.[15]

One reason the blue gum makes such great firewood is that it's flammable. This quality is fine if you're talking about a region of the world that's only lightly populated. In denser urban environments, though, fire is a brute. Besides its shedding qualities, the bark also has a pyromaniacal aspect: in fire conditions, which are usually accompanied by wind, the bark will catch fire, curl up, and fly off the tree and up into the air, to be borne away—a glowing bad-luck charm, the perfect fire-starter wherever it lands. In greater concentrations, clusters of the tree can carry an enormous fuel load. The 1991 Oakland conflagration killed twenty-five people, destroyed nearly three thousand homes, and caused $1.5 billion in property damage. At the fire's height, it consumed a house every eleven seconds.

The *San Francisco Examiner* observed, "The air was filled with the crackling sound of blazing pine and eucalyptus trees . . . gas lines ejecting 15-foot-long jets of flame and frequent explosions of propane tanks, trees and electrical transformers."[16] The *Press-Democrat*, in nearby Santa Rosa, remarked that by eight o'clock Sunday night, in the hills above Piedmont, "the eucalyptus trees of Mountain View Cemetery just to the north were burning like giant candles." The *Los Angeles Times* noted, "Even the eucalyptus trees that festoon the hills conspired. Eucalyptus, for all their leafy calmness, are not indigenous to North America and are extremely susceptible to drought. Dry or dead, they explode when fire strikes. They, along with pine trees, sent torches of flame soaring from tree to tree and from house to house."[17]

The *Modesto Bee* remarked, "Many of the hills are dotted with blue gum eucalyptus, a tall Australian tree that provides shade, a rich aroma and a gentle rush in the breeze. But in a severe fire, the trees tend to become torches because their oily sap causes them to explode like the tips of matchsticks."[18]

In the aftermath of the fire, Oakland's urban planners grasped the confluence of events that caused the disaster: warm, high winds raking an existing brush fire over a land where the density of trees pressed up against urban development; an inadequate water supply; and a dozen other contributing factors over the two days of the fire, including poor planning; too-quick growth; crowded, curving streets high in the hills; and more. I found not a word bemoaning the fate of the trees themselves, which were, of course, not the villains. For how could they be? They did not decide to plant themselves there. We did. As Mark Twain wrote, "Nature knows no indecencies; man invents them."

News accounts predating the Oakland fire reinforced the trees' reputation for flammability, so it wasn't as though city planners couldn't have known about the issue. The fear of fire seemed inordinate at times, and wartime only made people's sense of panic worse. During World War II, the California town of Inglewood had cut its eucalyptus trees to one-third of their height, fearing that antiaircraft guns situated near the coast could somehow set nearby trees on fire. As the town's mayor remarked, "If a shell so much as hits a leaf, it's supposed to explode."[19]

More than thirty years after the Oakland Hills fire, people still disagree as to whether the trees are a fire threat. Municipalities in the region have continued their thinning and removal efforts on a large scale. But some knowledgeable fire personnel believe that removing the trees could give fire more room to spread through dry grass. Some think that eliminating more trees also heats up the atmosphere by increasing the albedo effect—the degree of reflection of sunlight from lighter surfaces (like trees) back into space, or the absorption of it by darker surfaces (say, soil). It also removes their role as windbreakers.[20] Those in the love-the-eucs camp continue to be as passionate about the trees' right to survive as those in the hate-the-eucs camp are about wanting to eradicate them. In 2015, the trees, and the region where the 1991 fires occurred, came back into public view when the Federal Emergency Management Agency (FEMA) allocated $5.7 million to the California Office of Emergency Services for a euc-clearing program in the East Bay Hills. This plan was not popular in some quarters. One news headline from the era reads, "Berkeley Protesters Get Naked to Save Eucalpytus Trees." Artfully edited photos show men, women, and children in the buff hugging up against a grove of the trees on the Berkeley campus.

But the trees are threatened by more than fire. One traditional characteristic of an invasive species is that it lacks natural predators that can control its density and distribution. But the euc has enemies, if you care to characterize them as such. Beetles have wreaked havoc on the tree. Nurserymen in Southern California spotted a particularly pernicious one, the Eucalyptus longhorn borer (*Phoracantha semipunctata*), in the fall of 1984, and it spread across the region. To co-opt Sigmund Freud, biology is destiny. It's easy to imagine a bio-invasion of eucalyptus-loving insects running through an entire species like— well, like wildfire. Another invasive species, a gall wasp, *Selitrichodes globulus*, threatens the tree. It's attacking a species that's already invasive. Is the enemy of my enemy my friend? How do we position organisms like this wasp, not to mention the tree, in our calculus of belonging? It becomes difficult to assess just what belongs, and who gets to decide. It's been suggested the eucalyptus should get a green card, or environmental amnesty.

Conservationists have long understood how fast an insect or a fungus can decimate a tree's population across a large range. The spongy moth (*Lymantria dispar*) arrived in New England in 1869 from Europe, and began spreading south and west. The airborne larvae means that the insects can disperse widely; they find a home in many common trees, including oaks, aspen, apple, birch, poplar, and willow. The moth defoliated more than eighty million acres in the United States between 1970 and 2010.[21] That's a lot of tree habitat. The classic fungal examples are chestnut blight and the beetle-vectored Dutch elm disease (often appropriately used in its acronymic form—DED—and named not for anything known as an elm of Dutch origin but for the two Dutch phytopathologists who discovered it). DED has constituted one of the most destructive diseases of woody plants ever known.

The decline of the elm tree serves as a warning for the eucalyptus, for it involves the diminution of a common tree down to almost none. The insect that attacks elm trees can be one of several different species of beetles; they kill the elms by distributing a microfungus. Several species of elm bark beetles were introduced into the United States at different points in the first half of the twentieth century, but one—*Hylurgopinus rufipes*—is native to the United States. So it's not only invasive species that can upset the lives of natives, but ones that have lived in the same place for millennia. A seemingly minor evolutionary change, or a change in a species' range, facilitated by climate change, can amplify an organism's ability to establish a beachhead in a new tree. The little *H. rufipes*, a scant inch long, eradicated at least 95 percent of the gigantic, iconic American elms. And it's an irony, given the tree's hardy qualities; it can withstand temperatures down to minus forty-four degrees Fahrenheit, lives for hundreds of years, and has had a hold on the American literary imagination for centuries. Henry David Thoreau wrote of the elms that "some are so lifted up in the horizon that they seem like portions of the earth detached and floating off by themselves."[22] Yet a tiny native beetle, and its much tinier microfungal freight, which can't even be seen with the naked eye, has helped to bring a once hyperabundant tree to its knees. (Elms in their great variety still survive, though, and extensive breeding programs that are now decades in the making have produced many DED-resistant cultivars.)

There's no fixed reason why such a decline could not happen to the blue gum eucalyptus. Insect invasions large and small, potential and actual, threaten more than half of US forests. But the blue gum has naturalized in dozens of different countries. Its widespread distribution provides both threat and benefit. This might sound like a contradiction, but more trees in existence means more trees might be destroyed. At the same time, the trees' far-flung distribution enhances the species' chance for survival. Many of the populations live in isolation from one another and continue to evolve in diverse locations. Pathogens would have to hop from cluster to cluster to take them all down.

Modifying trees to be more resistant to pests and pathogens provides a promising pathway to survival. Sometimes those modifications involve creating cultivars, grafting plants to more resistant strains. Sometimes they involve direct genetic manipulation. A technique called induced resistance (IR) has come along, full of restorative hope. Plants' defensive mechanisms can be stimulated by infecting a small portion of the plant with pathogens that can resist viruses, bacteria, fungi, and other threats. The blue gum provides a good target for induced resistance, as it's an ecologically friendly approach that activates a tree's own genetically programmed defense mechanisms. Plant pathologists tested IR at the close of the twentieth century on crops such as tomatoes and rice, short-lived perennials, melons, beans, and potatoes, and it could work well for crop protection and improvement. Trees are different from most crops; they're usually much larger and longer-lived, have a much bigger ecological footprint per tree, and face many different pressures. Still, the technique shows promise.[23] For centuries, humans have tasked one life-form with trying to control another one. Sometimes, biocontrol has worked quite well. At other times, though, it's been disastrous. IR removes the unanticipated threats that arrive with insects or other life-forms whose ways we can't predict. Trees aren't helpless. But sometimes they need help, and this help has grown sophisticated.

But the tree also has plenty of its own defenses against different threats. Hailing from the hot and dry climates of Australasia, where fire has been a regular team player over millions of years, eucalypts have developed the ability to resprout from buds lying dormant under their bark. They also can regrow from lignotubers—swellings of the wood at the root crown, at ground level—when pressured by drought or fire. Lignotubers also can store nutrients for a tree in the absence of photosynthesis. They show up in coast redwoods proportionally sized, like gigantic muffins.

Understanding the species' deeper gene pool also provides geneticists with a potential map for survival. Plants evolve as a result of random mutations, selective pressures, and subsequent genetic modification and adaptation, and the eucs are no exception. Genetic material gets passed around constantly within a species, and even across allied species. As it spread across the globe in large numbers, *E. globulus* changed in response to conditions such as harsher frosts and drought, and through beneficial mutations and artificial selection. The genus's gene pool is more like a gene ocean. The fire historian Steve Pyne summarizes the immensity of the trees' variety and presence on the planet: "Eucalyptus had exploded so widely that it is considered by some authorities as less a genus than an alliance composed of three suballiances, ten subgenera, and over six hundred species," he noted in his 1991 book, *Burning Bush: A Fire History of Australia.* "The plasticity of the genus is extraordinary. Hybrids are common within subgenera, juvenile habits persist into adulthood, and even phantom species have been identified." It's hard to imagine a more flexible tree.

Plantations have especially contributed to the tree's genetic diversity. You might find this counterintuitive, thinking that trees grown on huge farms would be genetically homogenous. These trees make up the great bulk of the world's sheer blue gum biomass because of their commercial pulpwood uses. But the farmed blue gums, called landrace plants, are grown from seeds that typically aren't selected or marketed by breeders or seed companies. They come to farms from a variety of sources and are genetically diverse as a result, originating from many thousands of different trees and numerous regions of the world. In Europe, *E. globulus* grows primarily on the Iberian

Peninsula, where it occupies 1.3 million hectares (more than five thousand square miles), mostly on plantations. There may be between 3.2 and 5 million hectares planted by farmers worldwide. When I asked Jim Folsom, then the Huntington's Director of the Botanical Gardens, what he found most interesting about the tree's plantation future, he responded, "The curious issues to me are whether or not the trees are escaping into wild areas across the globe, and therefore establishing new populations that are allowed to persist. Are the plantation farmers content to accept the wide variation of seed-grown trees, or will there be selection over time for seed from superior specimens?"

Despite the great genetic variety present in this enormous worldwide body of blue gums, there is still room for genetic manipulation of the blue gum—artificial selection, which in 1859 Darwin made famous in the opening chapter of *On the Origin of Species*, where he gently winds up his natural selection pitch by talking about how humans have been modifying pigeons for centuries. Darwin was doing his best to disarm his readership with the most basic, irrefutable examples about pressures that could modify the most basic qualities of organisms. Humans can change genetic outcomes through artificial selection very quickly by selecting genetic variants that please us, or provide ecosystem services, to cultivate rose hybrids and countless other plant forms. So selective breeding of the eucalyptus to be less fire-prone might be possible, although the topic has received scant attention.[24]

But always, there are other offerings a tree can make. I propose that one of the eucalyptus's primary ecological contributions has been as a windbreak around the world, but especially in more arid, developing countries where soil viability is low and ground cover less abundant. The scouring effects of winds present one of the biggest obstacles to crop growth and viability around the world. A broad range of recent studies confirms a number of older, more anecdotal observations to show that the blue gums combine to form superb windbreaks.

Although fragmented regionally and internationally, these wind-breaks have provided a stupendous cumulative benefit across the planet, helping other organisms, including humans, to survive. Eucs are even present on Rapa Nui, successful immigrants that have been part of the long efforts to reforest the island with hardy, wind-resistant species that can help prevent soil erosion.

To be fair, not everyone has had positive feelings about the tree's role as a shelter from the wind. "A single eucalyptus will ruin the fairest landscape," noted the Scottish author Norman Douglas. "No plant on earth rustles in such a horribly metallic fashion when the wind blows through those everlastingly withered branches; the noise chills one to the marrow; it is like the sibilant chattering of ghosts."[25]

Besides helping to prevent soil erosion and crop damage, wind-breaks also can lessen the windchill factor, preventing frosts and freezes in colder areas. When Southern California surged as an agricultural mecca at the dawn of the twentieth century, eucs were frequently planted across vast acreages to protect orange groves from cold snaps and damage. Greater Los Angeles was the largest citrus-producing region in the world in the first third of the twenti-eth century, accounting for about three-quarters of US production of oranges, with millions of individual trees producing Valencia and navel varieties. Uncountable rows of blue gums bordered those groves. Citrus farmers considered the blue gum superior to other potential windbreaks. "My windbreaks are about 450 feet apart, and are so effective that one does not feel the wind at all among the orange trees," reported the citrus magnate Nathan Blanchard of Santa Paula about his eucs. "Neither is my fruit in the least impaired by the wind, however strong it may grow up or down the valley." Growers of grains also benefited. A Santa Barbara farmer observed that "in the immediate vicinity of the groves of Eucalypti there was a much heavier crop and taller straw. Near the ocean, where the trees protected the grain from sharp sea wind, there was certainly more than twice as much grain and twice as much straw."[26]

Other regions where the trees grow include Patagonia in South

America, portions of Central Asia, and the western United States. These are all BWk climates, as they're described in the widely used global climate classification system known as the Köppen climate classification: cold and dry. The Köppen climate classification was the innovation of the obscure German-born and Russian-trained meteorologist Wladimir Köppen. A fascinating figure in nineteenth-century science, Köppen was a polymath who created the first cloud atlas, translated some of his publications into Esperanto, published hundreds of scientific articles, and thought big global climate thoughts, many of which were prescient, and wind-related. One fundamental of his climate system is the way it unites climate and world vegetation. Köppen also had a particular fondness for trees and their growth. Within these BWk climates, eucalyptuses are omnipresent. Is persistence, diversity, and relentless botanical drive a crime or a shining virtue? As usual, it depends.[27]

Blue gums are a full-service tree. Beyond serving as windbreaks for human activities, they also capture airborne particulates: wind-driven dirt, dust, powdered chemicals, and other tiny bits, sometimes contaminated with heavy metals. The Berkeley grove where protesters disrobed is also one of the largest and most densely packed plantings of blue gum eucs in California. Planted in 1877, not long after the university's founding, the clumpy grove was ostensibly planted to provide a windbreak for the adjacent cinder running track to keep pieces of grit from getting into runners' eyes.

The blue gum is also a conservation warrior for its protection of an endangered species—the monarch butterfly (*Danaus plexippus*), a long-haul voyager that endures an annual trip of up to twenty-five hundred miles from its breeding grounds in the United States and Canada, down to forests in central Mexico. The monarch evolved in North America over two million years and has the most highly evolved migratory pattern of any butterfly. But monarch populations are declining, and *D. plexippus* has recently been ranked for the first time by the IUCN as Endangered. The milkweed plant provides the only food source for monarchs, and entomologists determined that these declines have been substantially due to the loss of milkweed across their migratory route, where the distance from clump to clump of milkweed makes the journey more perilous.

One key culprit in the monarch's decline appears to be the extensive agricultural use of glyphosate herbicide, the active ingredient in Monsanto's Roundup weed killer, which has come under scrutiny for its potential hazards to humans. Roundup is bad for both butterflies and blue gums. We used a lot of Roundup in Hawai'i. As a kid, I was pretty sure that Roundup was magical, as my dad extolled its virtues as a necessary tool in fighting unwanted weeds and plants in the tropics. It's not that magical. The International Agency for Research on Cancer (IARC) categorizes glyphosate as a probable carcinogen for humans, although other studies have reached conflicting conclusions. It's been used a lot to kill eucs. FEMA's recent plans to remove Northern California specimens calls for twenty-five hundred gallons of glyphosate, or approximately 2.5 gallons per acre, to be applied to stumps to prevent regrowth. Most bugs can't tolerate Roundup, as it inhibits the production of melanin, which insects use as part of their immune system's defenses against parasites and bacteria.[28]

But the eucalyptus trees are a part of the evolutionary battle for survival by providing windbreaks for nonhumans, too—not from flying cinders, but from winter storms that affect the butterflies as they flutter by. To survive, monarchs must have suitable microclimates, with trees having a range of sunlight from full sun to filtered light. These are services provided by exotic trees such as the euc, not natives. Monarchs rest in eucalyptus groves at about 75 percent of the state's overwintering sites, which are necessary stopping points during a journey that grows more risky with each passing year. There are endless instances in the scientific literature of nonnatives across taxa that provide ecological services not offered up by natives, and the monarch-eucalyptus pairing is a prime example. As a 2020 article in *California Fish and Wildlife* noted, nearly all California monarch overwintering groves require nonnative trees.[29] This news is music to the ears of many California gardeners, who understand that while milkweed provides nourishment and habitat for the monarchs, their beloved eucalyptus offers safe haven.

The music industry has also come up with uses for the blue gum. Bob Taylor, of Taylor Guitars, has worked out a process to steam euc wood to modify its color by using ammonia, an old-world dyeing technique. Tannins in wood react with ammonia gas, and this shifts the naturally light tan eucalyptus color to a beautiful rosewood hue. In the smaller pieces used in guitars, the wood is perfectly compliant, not subject to the cracking inherent in larger pieces.[30]

In Australia, aboriginals use the tree to make didgeridoos, traditional wind instruments that are long, skinny, and slightly conical. The tree and its insect inhabitants make key decisions about the didgeridoo: when the aboriginals cut down the deadwood of a eucalyptus trunk, it can only be used if it has grown in a suitable shape and configuration.[31] The insides of these termite-bored instruments are necessarily irregular, and musically, that pulls them away from nonharmonic frequencies: sounds our ears aren't accustomed to hearing and which can sound dissonant. The players' own lips and breath can modify these tonalities substantially. These qualities all give the instrument great range, complexity, and subtlety, thanks in large part to the euc-loving termites, whose erratic eating varies the sound across individual instruments.

Finally, eucalyptus oil has an important therapeutic function, offering widely touted health benefits. *E. globulus* is the primary producer of these therapeutic oils, which healers have used for centuries to treat colds, bronchitis, influenza, dysentery, scabies, tonsillitis, and much else. Modern medicine has concluded that the oils have unambiguously antiseptic, expectorant, and mucolytic (mucus-thinning) properties, along with other broad beneficial effects. However, I'm allergic to the euc oil. Even a brief sniff of it puts me in danger of going into anaphylactic shock. My sinuses close up, my eyes water, and I feel lousy. I could find no evidence to support my own difficulties, which I have no burning interest in trying to reconstruct. I'm apparently at the far end of the bell curve. The oil's therapeutic properties are otherwise almost all good news.

Does a tree's ubiquity make it bad? Anything can be turned into a difficulty, in the same way that, say, eight billion people on the planet make them problematic as a class. Love the sinner, hate the sin, you could say about the entire human population and its destabilizing effects on our only home. It's not just that species' survival can swiftly turn upside down, going from abundant to goodbye in shockingly short time frames. It's also that life can fade by different degrees—for individuals, for classes of all kinds. Some thrive, others weaken, still others die.

Many people knowledgeable about trees, including conservation biologists, often speak about trees' utility or reception or place in the landscape as an all-or-nothing proposition. This doesn't make sense to me. All life is complex. It's true that for humans, at least, one bad act can ruin a reputation, or a life. But it takes courage to summon compassion, and the blue gum is much more than a potentially deadly neighbor. Put simply, the tree has caused problems for humans by growing in our wrong places at our wrong times. It's also possible to loathe and love at the same time.

We need to take the idea of belonging down to its studs and rebuild our understandings of the term and its contexts. Nativeness, and belonging, aren't about the desires of those who judge those qualities. We get to decide for ourselves where we belong, who and what our communities are. Nonnative plants and animals don't have the same option. So what do we do in the face of species that come to our shores, and how do we assess their fitness to be here? And should we even do so? Conservation biologists often make claims about ecosystem "integrity," or "health," but those are difficult metrics to apply to any particular region. It's a sliding scale. We recognize depauperate ecosystems by their relative lack of biodiversity. People fret about the eucalyptus's effects on abundance. To turn back to the toromiro, and its Rapa Nuian environment in the middle of the Pacific, lacking forests and mostly populated by relatively recent arrivals from elsewhere, the little three-cornered island seems distinctly denuded. But compare Rapa Nui to, say, a spit of black lava emerging from the ocean to create new land, or to the Arctic biome, or geothermal fields in Ethiopia that are unable to support even microorganisms, and "diversity" gains a different meaning, and a new competence. Rapa Nui contains about 150 extant plant species, including 50 indigenous ones. Hawks (introduced from Chile to control rodents) fly overhead. Is endemism your religion as a biologist? Then maybe it's time to think about worshipping a new god. And even by indigenous standards, Rapa Nui surprises, as do so many other places that we've written off as denuded and destroyed. The invertebrate marine fauna of Rapa Nui, living in the coastal waters around the island, contains what one researcher called "a remarkably high percentage of endemic species for such a small and geologically young landmass."[32]

We have brought, and continue to bring, organisms from around the world in staggering numbers, dislocating them from their native ranges. Sometimes they cause problems for the species that brought them there: *Homo sapiens*, of course. Even what constitutes a "native" range is increasingly less meaningful as we modify those ranges through climate change and other anthropogenic actions. The passage of time makes the meaning of nativeness more ambiguous, and harder to quantify, both culturally and biologically.[33]

You might have personal or professional reasons to not like them, but all trees are good. Every last one of them, every species and every individual tree on this planet. Even the ones with atrocious thorns, even the ones that catch fire in spectacular, crackling orange blooms and ravage the landscape. And even the ones with more direct effects: trees that end up in places where they weren't born, as it were, these so-called invasive species that seem to crowd out native plants, and whose ways confound and preoccupy humans. *Homo sapiens* has a puny track record as a species: a measly three hundred thousand years.

Most species of trees, including those we consider highly invasive, have been around very much longer than that, evolving and surviving. We're the newcomers, not they. But trees are also good beyond their relationships with humans. They are active entities, with their own lives, their own rights, their own histories, each an ecosystem unto itself, providing a bulwark against a changing climate, offering nourishment, rest, and sustenance for other species, and space and quiet in their midst. They are the heartbeat of the world. Trees are Earth's reporters, chronicling life and change over the long, elastic curve of history. All we need to do is listen up.

CHAPTER 9

Slippery Slopes: The Olive Tree and Its Fruit and Oil

"The olive tree is surely the richest gift of Heaven."
—Thomas Jefferson, *Papers of Thomas Jefferson*[1]

Y ou will not find the olive tree (*Olea europaea*) on every continent. But olives, and olive oil, *are* found on every continent, including Antarctica. To confirm their presence there, I wrote to Tom Senty, who manages the provisioning of the food for McMurdo Station in the Antarctic. McMurdo is the largest year-round human settlement on the continent. The olive oil flows like wine there: in the course of a year, the station's commissary uses more than 180 gallons. McMurdo's population, highly transient, ranges from between 150 and 900 people, depending on the time of year. When you're stuck in a vast, tree-free tract of wind-driven ice and snow, you need good olives and their oil. Green, black, and Kalamata olives are the three varieties usually on hand. Olive oil and olives are also a staple for their pizza station, which bakes up sixteen thousand to eighteen thousand pizzas annually.

A cargo vessel arrives just once a year with the goods. The federal government procures and ships the food to California in the fall, which then arrives in Antarctica in January or February. It's a long journey, and the oil comes from a single supplier. Typically, this olive oil will have made its way through at least three continents before consumption: Europe, North America, then a short port call in Oceania (New Zealand). From there, the supply ship follows an icebreaker opening a channel through ice-clogged McMurdo Sound, and thence into Winter Quarters Bay at McMurdo. Olives and their oil are everywhere, but they have often taken long journeys.[2]

Despite the reach of its products into every nook and niche on the planet, the olive tree grows best where it's dry and sunny in the summers, and cooler and wetter in the winters. This environment constitutes the so-called Mediterranean climate, one of the major climate types within the Köppen climate classification system. Olive trees grow in these kinds of conditions around the world, including Southern California, which now grows the most olives outside of Europe. But the trees are most widely cultivated in a ring around the Mediterranean basin, serving as not only economic staples but cultural icons. Even Hawai'i has had a long, albeit limited, relationship with olive trees, though no one would describe the archipelago's climate as "Mediterranean." On Kaua'i, a Mr. Bush planted a grove of hundreds of trees in the 1880s, and the fruit has grown well on different islands over the years, including at the Hawaiian Ostrich and Egg Farm in Kapiolani Park in Honolulu.[3]

The olive tree doesn't get big, reaching between ten and forty feet, but it's recognizable in its numerous settings, both rural and urban. Odds are good that you've walked by one in a downtown area, with its lance-shaped leaves, dark green on one side and silvery on the other. Its textured and gnarly trunk is also a hallmark of mature trees. Although it's a single species, *O. europaea* exists in hundreds of varieties, cultivated for the different olives they produce. The olive tree's white, feather-like flowers are small, unperfumed, and usually ignored by bees, birds, and other pollinators. Rather, the olive tree relies on the wind to reproduce, at least in the wild. The flowers emit large quantities of light, airy pollen, and their stamens and stigmas (the parts of a flower that turn into fruits) are exposed to air currents that distribute that pollen far and wide.

Olive orchards are among the most important agroecosystems in the world. Olive trees are the oldest cultivated fruit tree, probably dating back to the earliest days of plant use, and certainly back to the Copper Age. The tree, its fruit, and its oil were well rooted into the land and the culture of the Mediterranean region in Europe by the eighth century BCE, and at a volume that suggests ubiquitous use. A single oil mill discovered in Ekron, Israel, from the seventh century BCE had the capacity to produce a half million liters of olive oil annually. Olives' flesh can contain up to 30 percent liquid oil. The tree is tethered to its fruit, and the fruit, in turn, is defined largely by its oil. The generic word for "oil" in English is derived from the ancient Greek word ἔλαιον, which means "olive oil."[4]

About 10 percent of olives are used for eating. The rest are used to make olive oil. The varieties of olives range from the big black ones kids stick on their fingers at meals, to the briny Kalamata, to the green ones you drop into your martini, and many cultivars designed for their flavor profiles. Olives show up in toppings, breads, salads, stews, and other expected and unexpected places on our plates. The ubiquitous desire for these olives and their oil means that the olive tree is so plentiful, and its by-products so desirable, that it drives entire economies. With its geographically sprawling influences, its long historical arc, and even its often shadowy, oily past, O. europaea may be more entangled with culture and cuisine than any other tree.

Olives are fruits, not vegetables. The proof is in the pit: the stone is the seed for the tree. Olives are known as drupes, or stone fruits, a category that includes cherries, apricots, mangos, dates, plums, avocados, and peaches. Like most other fruit, olives mature at different times: they're green and yellow at the start of their ripening cycle, and then purple and black at the end. The green olive at the salad bar was picked while unripe, and then cured to make it soft, palatable, and delicious. But a key difference between olives and most other fruits is that consumers don't really love fruit unless it's ripe. The hard avocado, the unripe mango, the crunchy peach: not delectable. Olives, by contrast, can be picked, cured, and eaten at almost any stage. But you can't just pluck an olive from a tree and consume it; it's a bitter and unpalatable fruit before it's brined.

So what makes olive oil extra-virgin? It's a bit of a tangle, perhaps akin to being a little pregnant, or half-alive. Virgin olive oil—not extra-virgin—is the unicorn of American supermarkets. Try to find an oil by that name on your supermarket shelf; you will not. But it does have its own definition. Most important, the juice of the olive has to be extracted from the fruit by mechanically crushing, pressing, or centrifuging. It's never heated above 27°C (80.6°F) during the extraction process; no steam, no heating, no solvents, no chemical interventions. But then we pivot to extra-virgin olive oil, and more limitations come into play. (It's typically written "EVOO," or, worse, "extra-VOO," as it's frequently called in the large and heterogeneous literature about olive oil, and which sounds like a Dr. Seuss character.) Some people claim that extra-virgin is the term used for oil from olives pressed within twenty-four hours of being harvested, but there's no law to that effect. Tracking which olives were removed from what trees and when would make measuring this timing well-nigh impossible.

The International Olive Council, or IOC, provides a different and more concise definition: if it is to be classified as extra-virgin, it cannot have more than 0.8 grams of oleic acid per 100 grams of oil—a measure of the acidity of the liquid, or its FFA (free fatty acidity). The best producers aim for between 0.2 and 0.1 percent of oleic acid. Confoundingly, though, oleic acid doesn't have much, if any, effect on flavor. And here is where the real regulation and gatekeeping occurs: in that slippery and often subjective zone known as taste. After olive oil is subjected to these chemical analyses to determine its purity, human testers step up to the plate, quite literally. The IOC and other olive organizations have taste testers, and to bestow their seal of approval, these organizations will typically have no fewer than eight highly trained testers sample each oil in a blind taste test. Given that there are more than seven hundred varieties of olives, and that each year brings a fresh harvest, there is a correspondingly huge variety of flavors of the oil extracted from the fruit.[5]

The IOC was founded in 1959 in Madrid and engages in serious business. It has eighteen member countries, as well as the European Union, and those countries account for more than 98 percent of the world's olive production. Only countries can join, not companies or individuals. A Women in Olive Oil group also exists and provides a support network for some two thousand women working in the olive oil industry, from more than forty countries. When it comes to governing bodies, there are two distinct sets of regulations for olive oil: those that are driven by European standards, where most of the global supply of olive oil is produced, and those driven by specifications in the United States. California, with its Mediterranean climate, produces about 95 percent of the country's olive oil and has its own regulatory strictures.

The sensory evaluation expert Orietta Gianjorio, a native of Italy, has certifications in four different food arenas: wine, olive oil, chocolate, and honey, and has been an integral part of the olive oil scene for some years. Gianjorio is also one of just two people in the United States qualified as a honey sensory evaluation expert. Full of Italian sparkle and flair, she has gained extensive knowledge, and accompanying credentials, in the olive and wine businesses, but especially as a taster. She was involved in the creation of the Olive Oil Commission of California (OOCC), the California government entity, and through her efforts and those of others, the extra-virgin appellation, and the standards it requires, were mandated by state law in 2015. As with European testing groups, the commission recruits eight tasters per panel, and if all eight people agree that there is a taste defect—usually rancidity—in the oil, it doesn't pass.

Gianjorio observed that the tasting and judging work comes with a great sense of responsibility, for tasters hold the livelihoods of many small farmers in their hands, or mouths. If tasters determine an oil is not extra-virgin in quality, that has a major impact on sales, and thus on farmers' livelihoods. Gianjorio has always approached the work and the responsibility it brings with humility. On the flip side, it's satisfying to have an impact on protecting consumers.

Olive oil tasters are different from wine tasters. There is no universal standard in the wine world as to what wine should taste like, but it's usually hard to miss when a wine has become corked, and thus unpalatable. Usually, though, people speak of wine's sensory qualities in rhapsodic language, and it's great fun. Here's a review from *Wine Advocate* of a 2016 vintage of Massolino Barolo, a big red from northern Italy: "linear and tight, with an arsenal of important Nebbiolo aromas ranging from red cherry and cassis to spice, smoke, licorice, dried ginger, rusty nail and blood orange." I'm not sure what appeals about rusty nail, or what it might actually taste like, but there you have it.[6] Wine tasters speak of their beverage as light-struck, dumb, slutty.

Olive oil, too, is spoken of in terms that are more than ordinary, but they don't get anywhere as atmospheric as wine. Olive oil experts describe the best oils as bright and peppery, or with hints of freshly cut grass, or with a subtle hint of green banana, or punchy, or grassy. Olive oils can contain many flavor variants, created by including natural additives to the oil to impart the flavor of lemons (in one version, the lemons and olives are crushed simultaneously to best integrate the essences), or garlic, or chili, or rosemary.

Tastings are often done during competitions, where the more hedonistic aspects of oil lie. The competitions mean that you're tasting between sixty and eighty olive oils in a four-hour stretch. As Gianjorio noted, "It's a lot! It's a job, to stay fresh, and to stay on point, and to stay alive, and keep your palate receptive to what you're tasting. But I'm very appreciative, and don't complain about what I have to do throughout the day."[7]

For those who taste-test olive oil for certification purposes, such as the IOC and the OOCC, there's an official scoring sheet that lets tasters rank just three positive qualities, each of which sounds quite subjective: fruity, bitter, and pungent—along with seven defects (fusty, musty, vinegary, muddy, metallic, rancid, and "other," the Seven Dwarfs of olive oil). As with wine, there are markers for greatness, or at least goodness. While wine tasters might swirl, slosh, swish, and spit their beverage to absorb its flavors, olive oil consumers have different bodily responses. As Claude Weiller, the VP for sales and marketing at the California Olive Ranch, notes about the Koroneiki olive oil, "I like to rate the pungency of our extra virgin olive oils by how many times people cough when they swallow the oil during a tasting. I tell people our Koroneiki olive oil is a 'two or three cougher.'"[8]

This Koroneiki olive, the most common olive for oil production, has some other non-taste qualities to recommend it. It's one of the most effective of all cultivars in its ability to combat disease.[9] This salutary aspect of Koroneiki oil might account in part for the success of the so-called Mediterranean diet in the lives of exceptionally healthy populations of people in France, Spain, Greece, and Italy. The Koroneiki is an olive cultivar from Greece, well suited to growing in dense groves, producing large quantities of olives, and their oil. The Koroneiki occupies more than half of the olive-growing land in Greece.

I also talked with Arden Kremer, who works as an olive oil producer and was a longtime member of the tasting panel for the California Olive Oil Council (COOC)—very similar-sounding to the OOCC, but a trade association rather than a regulatory body. Arden noted that to be an olive-oil taster, you have to take a series of organoleptic and olfactory tests, to see whether you have the aptitude to discern different flavors. Organoleptic testing covers not just flavor and odor but appearance and mouthfeel as well. Although there are machines that can test components and make determinations about acidity, sweetness, and so on, nothing comes close to humans' sensitivity with taste and smell.

If you have the olfactory equivalent of face blindness, you're out. Short-term difficulties can also impede successful tasting; people sometimes show up with colds and other compromised sinus conditions. "We do this little test, where you put a red jelly bean in your mouth, and hold your nose, so you can't taste the jelly bean, then you let go of your nose, which is really where all of the tasting actually occurs," Kremer noted. When it comes to taste, your nose knows more than your mouth. All of the tastings are done blind, with the oil served up in identical squat dark blue glasses, so even the color of the oil isn't identifiable to the taster.

Oil and wine are both ancient, life-affirming liquids that have great variety and subtlety, and both are considered good for you in moderation. There is depth and satisfaction in being an aficionado of either one, and a lifetime of possibilities to explore. The two liquids, though, have different expiration dates. Age embraces wine, its metaphorical arm thrown over wine's shoulders as they march through the years. Time, though, is olive oil's archenemy. As the months pass, olive oil begins to oxidize, producing free radicals. These are bad for you. Olive oil is freshest for its first several weeks, and then begins to turn rancid—very slowly, so that bottle sitting in your cupboard isn't likely to have an obvious defect in smell or taste for quite some time. But by about eighteen months, you should just toss it out. Fresh is best. Hoard your wine if you must, but unless you use copious quantities of it, don't hoard your olive oil.

Olive oil consumption in the United States has grown over the last few decades. Annual imports totaled 28,000 metric tons in 1980; forty years later, they hover around 390,000 metric tons. While Italy and Greece lead in production, the United States ranks second in the world in consumption, after the European Union. Production of the tree on American soil is also substantial. Because of the existence of a suitable growing climate in California, the state produces tens of thousands of metric tons of olives, comprising 95 percent of olive production in the United States.[10]

Before any of the testing and analysis takes place, the fruit takes a journey from tree to bottle. Olive farmers have taken a variety of approaches to get the olives to release their grasp on the trees. For centuries, laborers picked olives by hand. Then, before the rise of more automated methods, people used tools to assist in the olive picking: pickers took spiked implements and twirled them around in the tree, knocking olives to the ground in large quantities. There's now a modern version of this defruiting operation: a skip loader with an enormous skirt pulls up to a tree, and a slot in the middle lets the driver push the skirt up to surround the tree. Several workers with motorized rakes carry out a mechanized version of spinning sticks in trees to free the fruit. There are also handheld shakers that grip individual branches. A more extensive version of this shaking process involves using a truck with a giant pair of rubber pincers attached to the front. The vehicle drives up to a tree, grips its trunk firmly, and then shakes the entire tree violently. The olives land on a piece of fabric dozens of feet long that's placed around the bases of multiple trees, and the truck moves on to another tree while workers drag the netting up into bunches, transferring the olives by hand into more modular crates that can be stacked and carried off. Green olives make for the best oil, but those olives, being far from ripe, are more reluctant to let go of the tree, making the process of olive removal labor-intensive. The best olive oils are the most expensive, because slow, careful labor leads to better-quality fruit.

This meticulous picking of olives doesn't work well on large farms, which confront other difficulties. The more automated the process, the more likely that bycatch (a term for organisms unintentionally caught up in harvesting operations) will occur. Big olive operations use vacuuming techniques to pull olives from trees, working at night, because cool temperatures help to preserve the fruit's aromatic compounds. These highly automated harvesting machines unintentionally suck up millions of songbirds annually in Spain and Portugal—civilian casualties in the press of business. Roosting birds, blinded by spotlights and stunned by the machinery, are killed by this process. So slow-motion work not only makes for better olive oil but is better for the natural world.[11]

Olives used for olive oil are typically not pitted. Rather, processors use the entire olive. They separate the fruit from the leaves, stems, and debris that come along with the olives, and then macerate it—on many farms, they do so through the use of ancient techniques involving crushing the olives with granite stones, and then pressing the resulting slurry until oil seeps from the stone into a catchment system. Larger facilities use more modern equipment to crush the fruit. The remaining olive flesh is crushed by hammers, creating a paste. This paste is then centrifuged, separating more oil from the pomace—the skin, flesh, water, and pits left behind.

The Koroneiki isn't the only olive oil that's very good for you; a wide range of other olive cultivars have produced high-quality, healthy oils. An abundance of clinical, epidemiological, and experimental data has shown the Mediterranean diet to provide antiinflammatory and antioxidant protections. Researchers have had an extraordinarily difficult time coming to a fuller understanding of what specific olive compounds are beneficial. This was in large part because of the abundance of compounds in the simple olive. There are so many compounds that in 2018, two researchers created an organization called OliveNet to identify and document them. The comprehensive, curated library itemizes the fruit's nearly seven hundred compounds. Beyond understanding the constitution and identities of the beneficial compounds in olives, the work has resulted in important discoveries. European researchers have recently shown that oleacein, one of the olive's key chemical compounds, might provide protection against a variety of neuroinflammatory disorders, including multiple sclerosis.[12] And lest it be said that olive compound researchers focus only on olive compounds, OliveNet also publishes a chatty monthly newsletter (a recent issue notes the Molecule of the Month is hesperidin, one of the chemicals that gives olive oil its flavor, and includes Maialino's Olive Oil Cake as the Recipe of the Month).[13]

We still have a lot to learn about the effects of environmental change on the olive tree, which is especially sensitive to any fluctuations in climatic conditions: the proverbial *canarino in una miniera di carbone*. And the Mediterranean region is now a climate change hotspot. Future projections warn of substantial warming and drying trends.[14] Olive trees can also serve as bio-indicators of climate evolution in the Mediterranean basin. A recent study used palynology, or the study of ancient pollen grains and other spores, to glean insights into how the distribution of olive trees has changed over the centuries. The absence and presence of pollen from olive trees in different regions shows that they did not exist in areas now under cultivation. Their appearance in the fossil record also shows when and where they came to be cultivated; what droughts or severe winter temperatures occurred and thus caused areas of cultivation to shrink; and where grapevines, which are more resistant to cold temperatures, were planted in place of olives after they had failed to grow. The olive trees and their ranges thus serve, through this kind of analysis, as climate proxies, like the bristlecone pines: indicators of what climatic changes the region had experienced in deeper time.

But no tree rides for free, and the olive tree is no exception. Despite *O. europaea*'s abundance worldwide, the tree faces threats: the olive tree is at serious risk of attacks by insects and fungi. However, what seems like a liability in some of the tree's locations—limited and fragmented space to grow—has been a boon. Calabria, at the southern end of Italy's boot-shaped boundaries, accounts for a full third of the country's olive oil production, despite the region's high unemployment rates and economic difficulties. Calabria's steep hillsides have meant that plots of land are fragmented, and more so than in other Mediterranean growing regions. The production chain of olive oil in Italy consists of some 776,000 holdings, with an average size of just 1.3 hectares, a little more than three acres. (Spanish olive farms, by contrast, are more than five times that size, on average, and smaller farms in the United States, using agriculturally active Washington State as an example, run to about fifty acres, or twenty hectares.) Land fragmentation, it turns out, provides a key olive tree benefit. Italian smallholdings are just that—small—but small has proven to be good.

The smaller size of these farms, operating on tighter margins, means that their owners and managers are expert at conserving the natural resources in their regions. They preserve a larger percentage of their land as natural forest—some of it is unplantable—and to maximize resources, land managers tend to be better stewards of the soil, producing more olives organically by using less fertilizer or agrochemicals; using mulch and manure from existing farm operations; and adopting other integrative practices that tread more lightly on the planet. This less intensive management benefits other organisms, including bees, who benefit from the pollen as a food source.

Other aspects of olive farming enhance biodiversity in these small settings. In the hilly and irregular terrain in the southern Mediterranean basin, olive trees grow at varying elevations, rather than in large, flat tracts, as is the case with most bigger operations. Climatic impacts can be dramatic on the quality of a fruit, as even the most novice vintner would tell you. It's known by its French term, terroir, and is the characteristic taste imparted by a region to its products. It's a common term in wine, but olive oil also channels its origins, summoning up qualities affected by soil, water, climate, and region. As with grapes, olives grown even a few hundred yards apart can differ because of changes in microclimates, cumulative hours of sunlight, average temperatures, and other factors. This provides nuanced and wider varieties in flavors, for both the fruit and its oil. The various differences in taste might seem to be more of a culinary aspect than a conservation one, but creating a reputation for an olive oil makes it more prized and more valuable, and thus makes its soil likely to receive extra care and attention in the field.

Elevational differences like those found in Calabria and elsewhere in Italy also mean that genetic vigor is likely enhanced, because even minor differences in elevation can attract different populations of insects, fungi, birds, and other life. These elevational gradients enhance habitat diversity and species richness. There's also a benefit to erosion control provided by the trees' root systems on the commonly found steep slopes (between fourteen and twenty degrees of incline). Studies have shown that traditional olive groves are the most resilient agricultural systems around, having survived abandonment, resurrection, and a wide variety of local practices that apply selective pressures.

Every life-form is in the process of turning into a new form morphologically and genetically, through selective pressures and mutation, and moving so subtly that change can be difficult to detect. You see this rapidity most clearly in viruses, which can mutate in a matter of weeks to different, more vaccine-resistant forms. One advantage that olive-growing in the Mediterranean region provides over efforts in California is that the trees in the older region have experienced centuries of natural selection. Robustness rules: the heterogeneity of local variants, coupled with environmental conditions that have shaped the cultivation of *O. europaea* for a very long time to match the trees' needs for water, sunlight, and soil. Each of these smaller, more traditional landholdings might be no more than an oily speck on the huge map of olive production, but the total effect of hundreds upon hundreds of small farms adds up in terms of broader ecosystem and landscape health.[15]

Many organisms attack the olive tree, and some of them depend on the olive tree to survive. The olive fruit fly (*Bactrocera oleae*) has been the most pernicious pest in recent years. This bug was first discovered centuries ago as it laid waste to olive groves in Spain and Italy during the medieval period, but it remains a stubborn assailant, attacking both cultivated and wild trees. Although we have studied it extensively, we know little about some aspects of its life history and habits. We haven't yet determined its geographic origins, although Africa may have been its birthplace. From Africa, it would have been a short hop to the Mediterranean, and from there to other parts of the world. The fly's larvae eat the fruit pulp and take up residence, which leaves the olive fruit unfit for consumption, although oil can still be pressed from these damaged olives.

Insect pests can cause botanical destruction through two key mechanisms: either they consume enough of a tree or its parts to hinder its productivity, growth, or survival; or they carry other destructive payloads, like the microfungus that attacked the elm in America. Sometimes it's a bacterium borne by insects, including one especially damaging vector: the plant pathogen *Xylella fastidiosa*. First detected in the Puglia region in southern Italy in 2013, *X. fastidiosa* is also known as Pierce's disease in the form that attacks grapevines.[16] The pathogen was long thought to be a virus but later proven to be a bacterium, a discovery that allowed scientists to better understand the attack and defense mechanisms at work.

Plant-sucking insects of several genera spread the *fastidiosa*. The bacteria they transmit multiply inside vascular tissues and slow down the flow of sap within the tree, which kills off its extremities. These attacks are especially pernicious for olives, because those extremities hold the fruit. Although the bacteria have been documented to infect more than 350 host plants, they've been remarkably malevolent in olive groves in southern Italy, so much so that the infection has its own olive-related name: Olive Quick Decline Syndrome (OQDS), or Complesso del Disseccamento Rapido dell'Olivo. Known as CoDiRO in the global scientific literature, the syndrome currently threatens olive groves, and thus olive oil production, in all of the major olive-growing regions in Europe, as well as in California, Argentina, and Brazil. One model from 2020, that horrible first year of the global COVID-19 pandemic, predicted that the potential economic cost to Italy over a half century could range between two billion and nearly six billion euros.[17] Brian Duffy, a plant bacteriologist in Switzerland, noted that its devastating ability was almost beyond belief. He said that on the land that comprises the Salento peninsula, a world center of olive production, "it's like a bomb went off." A plant virologist on the peninsula described the scene as "an army of insects loaded with bullets."[18] Look at Google street views of groves that were healthy in 2011 and you'll see a shocking wasteland of dead trees four years later.

But as we've seen in multiple instances, humans are now a part of the tug and shove of evolution too, able to insert themselves into a problem with sophisticated solutions that can mitigate an organism's advance. Opportunities exist for biocontrol to help the olive tree by bringing in one organism to combat a perceived invader or pest. This approach has been fraught. Often, biocontrol works well, but there are too many variables to control for, and at times interspecies intentions have gone almost comically wrong. The sugar industry introduced mongooses to Hawai'i in 1883 to control rat populations, but the rats in question were nocturnal, while the mongooses were diurnal. They never crossed paths, and the mongooses ate baby birds and turtle eggs instead. The mosquito fish, prolific breeders introduced into parts of Illinois and Indiana to eat mosquito larvae, decided they'd rather eat native fish and frogs. The introduction of the cane toad to Australia in 1935 to control the grayback cane beetle proved catastrophic. The beetle usually feeds at the top of sugar cane stalks, a good fifteen to twenty feet high. But cane toads can't climb, or fly, or even jump very high, reaching only about two feet off the ground with their most enthusiastic hop. The beetle also tended to be diurnal, and the cane toad nocturnal. And they weren't typically even in the same places during the same times of year. The cane toads eat everything, and can outcompete native species for food and breeding sites. They also can lay up to thirty thousand eggs at a time, sometimes twice a year.

Biological controls are risky—genies uncorked from bottles to which they cannot be returned. For this reason, for many years toxic chemical defenses seemed to be the only approach that has reliably reduced insect populations without introducing new predators to a landscape. As is common with many insects, though, the little fly has evolved to develop insecticide resistance. Since about 1970, olive fruit flies have been managed by organophospate insecticides, and more recently by chemicals with fewer active ingredients. But conventional insecticides don't discriminate among harmful and beneficial insects, and can contaminate the olive's oil.

By 2020, Italian scientists had worked out a solution for the *X. fastidiosa* problem that didn't involve either living organisms or traditional insecticides: the use of a zinc, copper, and citric acid bio-complex, trademarked as Dentamet. The compound, which relieves but doesn't cure the infestations, has proven effective against three strains of the bacterium. And as it turns out, Dentamet is also effective against the brown marmorated stinkbug, another international pest. For now, the struggle has ended in a standoff. It's not feasible to eradicate the bacterium, simply because it's able to replicate itself in so many different plants. So the strategy has been to give the olive trees more resilience after being infected. Dentamet can also be sprayed on the bugs' eggs to kill the larvae. Scientists speak of using Dentamet as part of a general strategy that will allow for a cohabitation with the pathogen while still preserving the landscape in areas that have yet to be compromised by the bacteria. It's an uneasy détente.

There are more natural routes to protection and fecundity. One key to greater success and survivability for olive trees might lie in boosting their pollination. The self-pollination olive trees engage in is known as anemophily ("wind-liking," from its Latin roots). Botanists call pollinators that don't rely on birds or bees (or moths or ants or mosquitos, or lots of other pollinating insects) "self-compatible." The increasingly hot and dry weather resulting from global warming also messes with pollination: high temperatures can kill pollen and also dry out the female part of the flowers, drastically slowing or stopping pollination. Human help with pollination can increase the trees' ability to increase fruit yields in the hottest and driest olive-producing areas. This intervention has only been tried on a small scale, using a device to blow grains of pollen over flowers. Farmers have tested this approach in Argentina and Arizona, resulting in dramatic gains.[19]

In a curious and useful twist, it also turns out that olive flies are highly attracted to the color yellow, a fact that's been worked into sticky traps to capture and monitor the flies. Adding sex pheromones to the traps makes them even more attractive. Another proposed solution to the fly problem was to recruit some of its natural enemies, such as some parasitoid wasps—using a benign insect to attack a problematic one. But here we are back to biocontrols, whose ultimate effects are difficult to control or predict.[20]

Recent experiments have opened up still other avenues for investigation: green insecticides, with low toxicity. Several of these have promising potential. Another approach, which is being tried with other insect pests, is to find ways to stop them from reproducing. One strategy has been to raise thousands of the insects and render them sterile, through one of several approaches, including irradiation, and then release them into the wild, where they mate with female flies who generate no offspring. Still another clever study looked at a biomechanical issue: how well the fly was able to attach to the fruit's surface, which produces a substance called epicuticular wax. Different cultivars of the fruit provide different levels of traction for the fly. Mostly, this study showed that the fruit fly had a significantly different ability to land and take off from olives of different kinds: useful information on which future studies could build.

These investigations and interventions will continue in robust fashion, because the tree's future is on the line. Our labors to protect the tree demonstrate how much we value it and its product. The olive is not just a fruit, it's a ballad, and a way of life, and has been since antiquity. It's a functional food that works across cultural, geographic, and socioeconomic boundaries. Food pulls us closer, brings us joy, stitches together generations, sustains and nurtures us, makes us happy. We've all sat around a table, catching up, intertwining taste and talk and tapenade. If the bristlecone pine is like a book, the olive tree is like a song, blown from the hot and dry parts of the world, an aria that has reached all corners of the planet through the cultural, sensual delights of its fruit and oil. Let us continue working to ensure that the song remains strong.

CHAPTER 10

Elephantine: The African Baobab

"I pointed out to the little prince that baobabs were not little bushes, but, on the contrary, trees as big as castles; and that even if he took a whole herd of elephants away with him, the herd would not eat up one single baobab."

—Antoine de Saint-Exupéry, *The Little Prince*

Africa's most iconic tree, the African baobab, *Adansonia digitata*, is dying across the continent. Something is killing off the largest and oldest trees, and scientists want to know what, how, and why. Understanding the causes of a species' decline can teach us, in turn, about its lifelines for survival. In a corresponding vein, this story is about the workings of the IUCN, the International Union for Conservation of Nature, the world's largest and most diverse environmental network and the global authority on conservation in the natural world. Founded in 1948, the organization identifies at-risk species and the challenges they face; but unlike other conservation entities that focus on just one species, such as those supporting the longleaf pine, the IUCN and its sister organizations investigate and report across a broad landscape that includes many thousands of different organisms.

Making decisions about which species are endangered, and to what degree, is not a precise undertaking, although it is a complex one. Because plants and animals obey no geopolitical boundaries, and many species occur globally, efforts by local groups are often not effective in providing endangerment data beyond their relatively narrow purviews. The IUCN has taken on the work of providing a ranking of a species' endangerment status. Their Red List of Threatened Species, begun in 1964, is the world's most comprehensive accounting of the worldwide status of species. More than sixteen thousand volunteer experts and scientists, and another thousand full-time paid staff, sit on six different commissions that inform the organization's knowledge base, and do the work necessary to understand the survival status of species worldwide.

Despite its size, the IUCN can't manage every threat, because codifying and understanding species' conservation status is not just about concluding how precarious a species' survival is or is not, but also about projecting trees' survival routes into the future, a task that relies on imperfect data. There might be thousands of experts, but they operate in the face of the estimated 8.7 million species scientists think exist, many of which we haven't even discovered yet. I find it hard not to think of the Chinese philosopher Lao Tzu and his metaphorical ten thousand things—those human experts, fallible yet diligent and persistent and committed to the planet's long-term health—and to contrast those with what Lao Tzu called "the unnamed": all the rest of the natural world, the hidden, the mysterious, and the unknown. The struggle is not just one of survival but of assembling useful knowledge.

The bottle-shaped African baobab, a massively thick and long-lived tree, has been subjected to IUCN scrutiny, but it remains one with a highly incomplete accounting of its threats, which vary from region to region. It's one of eight species of baobabs, all in the genus *Adansonia*, and the only one found on the African continent. Evolutionarily speaking, it is the oldest of the baobabs; six of the other species are native to the island of Madagascar, and one is native to

Australia. Although its ancestral roots were a long-standing mystery, it's proven to be the only baobab that's native to the African continent. Scientists thought for decades that the continental African tree somehow split off from the Madagascar trees, but it was probably the other way around: the continental tree worked its way to the island of Madagascar, long ago, probably floating there.[1]

The tree on the African continent has long thrived in some of the driest territory in the world. It's one of a class of plants known as pachycauls, trees that have disproportionately thick trunks in relation to their height. That's a coincidental nomenclatural tie to pachyderms, some of which take great interest in the water stored in the tree—*pachy* meaning "stout," which applies to both baobabs and elephants. Ranging between about twenty and ninety feet tall, baobabs tend to grow in solitary fashion, rather than in groves. Like all baobabs, the African baobab is deciduous, shedding leaves in the dry season and remaining leafless for more than half the year. Famed not just for its bulbosity but for its eccentric, upside-down shape, the baobab has tangled rootlike branches that gave rise to folklore claims that the tree draws its strength from the sky. In elemental ways it does just that, drawing sustenance from sunlight and rain. The writer Richard Mabey calls the tree the "Rorschach tree," for its characteristic spidery limbs, looking for all the world like giant inkblots against the blue African sky.[2]

Many individual trees have long and rich cultural associations. Baobab products are used in rainmaking ceremonies, in fertility rituals, and as offerings to the sun. In Senegal, parents protect their babies from evil by bathing them in water that contains flour from baobab seeds. The genus was named for the eighteenth-century French explorer and botanist Michel Adanson, who was the first westerner to observe the tree, in Senegal, although he was not the first westerner to happen upon it. The trunk of one big baobab bears the carvings of passing sailors, dating to 1444 and 1555. Another large African baobab, on the bank of the Zambezi in Mozambique, was known as the

Livingstone tree. The legendary African explorer David Livingstone discovered the tree in 1858, entered through a narrow opening, and carved his name on the walls of its inner cavity. Livingstone described the cavity as being naturally "hollowed out into a good-sized hut." The space inside was approximately nine feet in diameter and twenty-five feet high; bats lived inside, and the tree's idiosyncratic internal bark structure was noticeable to the adventurer and his men.[3] Livingstone was quite taken by the "burly baobab," as he called it, throughout his travels in Africa, and when his "brave, good, English wife" died of malaria in 1862 on one of their trips there, she was buried under the branches of a great baobab.[4] The hollows in the trees have been ancient spaces for burials, used as tombs in Senegal and elsewhere, as a place where a body denied underground interment can be mummified so the body does not pollute the earth. The people not allowed normal burial who end up in the tree hollows are the griots, a caste that includes poets, musicians, sorcerers, drummers, and buffoons. We should all be so lucky.[5]

Viewed on a distribution map showing the entire continent, the trees completely ring the immense Congo basin, an area comprising about a half billion acres, although they are less frequently found in the basin itself. They're widely and erratically spaced, and individual trees are sometimes separated by miles. Across its eight species, the baobab family has many similarities, but *A. digitata*, named for its "digits," or leaves, reminiscent of the fingers of a human hand, has the broadest geographic distribution of the group. It's found in disjunct populations in western, southern, and eastern Africa, occurring naturally in about thirty countries on the continent. It also ranges from these continental locations to the Cape Verde archipelago off the African east coast. As with many other trees, though, individuals have taken root in other places, often centuries ago. It lives in tropical and subtropical locations around the world, including China, and India, where the trees' introductions seem to track with medieval Arab trade routes. The African baobab has also made the journey to Madagascar in more recent times. The specimens at Moramba Bay, on Madagascar's west coast, grow straight out of the water in places—strange, beautiful creatures rising from the sea like islands. Some have probably been standing in water for a thousand years.

But a long life is no guarantee of a viable future. The African baobabs, sharing territory with big elephants, are under attack. Almost every baobab tree in southern Africa is covered with healed scars from past elephant assaults. Thirsty pachyderms know that the trees are big jugs of water, and they attempt to penetrate the bark to get at the liquid. There's a lot of it; several species in the baobab genus can store up to a mind-bending thirty-two thousand gallons. Its water-storing ways are still being studied. Scientists aren't sure why the tree seems to store far more water than it needs; it's a confounding idea that the trees probably aren't storing the water for their own survival. As we improve our understanding of how symbiotic trees can be, it's possible that there is a sharing strategy that we haven't identified.

The ways that elephants extract water from baobabs is violent, involving spearing the tree, and chewing deep into its trunk to obtain moisture from its pulpy interior. The elephants also eat the bark. Gouging and eating into the baobab is often enough of an affront to the tree to kill it outright. The damage to a tree can be so severe that the tree takes on an hourglass shape and collapses under its own weight. Younger baobabs, tender and of an accessible height, are especially appealing to the elephants, who sometimes push the tree over while feeding. Trees in steeper terrain are less affected, because the sloping land restricts access by big animals, but elephants can range widely.[6] During droughts, elephants can become almost entirely dependent on the baobab. With a daily plant and fruit consumption surpassing three hundred pounds, an adult elephant needs a lot of fuel, and finds easy picking with the baobab: simple to spot, easy to reach, and hydrating and nutritious. These actions don't always kill the trees, some of which show evidence of healed scars. Still, the net effect is devastating to the overall health of *A. digitata.*[7]

At the same time, African elephants are endangered. Climate change means a hotter, drier continent, which means less water for elephants, who then turn to sources such as the baobabs for sustenance—while in wetter circumstances, watering holes would provide a more ready supply. *Loxodonta africana* is the main offender; it's one of just two species of elephants on the continent, the other, smaller one being *L. cyclotis*, which favors forests and is critically endangered. The two were long thought to comprise just one species, until genetic evidence in 2021 led to a revision by the IUCN. Both species have been at risk for poaching for their ivory tusks for centuries. They now number fewer than a half million individuals on the continent, and *L. africana* is ranked as Endangered by the IUCN.

In the case of the elephant and the baobab, it's been well documented that more elephants mean greater baobab mortality; conversely, when elephant populations have dipped, baobab numbers have increased. This complicated status for some species has overhauled conservation narratives. Competing needs have existed for a long time, but it's only through closer observation and scientific testing that we've come to understand how different species at risk can both diminish others while helping themselves and, at the same time, help others while being hurt. We need a new calculus to account for these simultaneous threats—some kind of metric quantifying the relative risk each poses to the other. One proposed solution in South Africa's Kruger National Park is to keep the elephants and baobabs separate from each other, dividing the park into six management regions. This split removes the trees from the elephants' water and food supply. But although the arrangement protects both tree and pachyderm, park rangers need new management solutions to get elephants more ready access to water.

Studying the tree's strange ways has provided clues about both how it stores water and how it responds to drought. But it's only in the past decade that scientists have examined the tree's biomechanics. It turns out that the tree always grows multiple stems hidden in one big enclosed column, unlike most trees, which grow a single external stem, the visible architecture of the tree. The baobab's multiple stems also often form around the false cavity. And here's the strangest part: many of these stems grow bark, which is internal, encased within the thick, lumpy, ultimate outer skin of the tree. It seems like those strange medical instances where people are born with five sets of teeth, or an extra pair of arms, or some other strange duplication that makes them stand apart from the great majority of their fellow humans. But with the baobab, these internal trees-within-a-tree aren't aberrations, for it's their regular way of developing.

Because of these internal structures, which keep growing, the architecture of aging baobabs becomes complex. The differential growth rate of these parts within the tree means that the age of individuals isn't well-known, and the topic is the subject of much contention among botanists. The trees do produce faint growth rings, but they're not reliable, since they're not always present in old trees and because the trees' large internal spaces mess with obtaining an accurate ring count. Instead, they require AMS (accelerator mass spectrometry) radiocarbon dating to reveal their ages, which until 2010 only worked on dead trees. Dendrochronologists used AMS in 2007 to determine the age of a huge collapsed baobab in Namibia, a tree with the wonderful name of Grootboom. The fallen monster was determined to be the oldest angiosperm (flowering) tree in the world, around 1,275 years old.

Although tree-ring dating is much more accurate for dating trees, living and dead, radiocarbon dating—one of the greatest discoveries of the twentieth century, with its ability to provide objective age estimates for materials that originated from living organisms—has improved over time, becoming more accurate as it gets recalibrated.[8] In 2010, researchers used radiocarbon analysis of living specimens by dating samples that they collected from inner cavities of old baobabs.[9] Dead trees can provide a great deal of other information, but the baobab's wood, which consists of concentric sheets of fiber, is yet another idiosyncrasy. When they die, smaller trees quickly collapse into a pile of fibers, rather than remaining intact, as with most other woods. In death, the African baobab looks like piles of dirty wool that have been left out in the weather. We still don't know the outer age limit of the baobab. Estimates within the scientific literature have ranged from two thousand to five thousand years, but without substantial documentation to support these assessments.[10]

Most trees consist of a trunk with a central core of heartwood, which is usually darker than the lighter sapwood that surrounds it. The baobab, however, is sapwood all the way in, and like a handful of other sapwood trees around the world, it has a way to self-heal injuries. Most of the wood in a baobab is composed of parenchyma tissue: material that remains alive for a long time, deep in the trunk. The tree creates calluses by way of repair, a response that protects against not only thirsty elephants and their damaging tusks but also repeated fires. This healing ability has been the tree's savior in the face of depredations not only by elephants but also by humans hacking footholds into the tree's trunk to climb it for its fruit. But the baobab is not indestructible, and trees die regularly. Given the frequent scarcity of water in its arid setting, its root systems are relatively shallow, often running aboveground as well as just below the surface of the soil. Even a very slight rainfall can reach the roots and provide moisture. These shallow roots are a danger to the baobabs' long-term survival, as the trees can fall over in a very strong wind, especially as they get older and less flexible. Climate change can produce stronger winds, especially in coastal areas. The baobabs are common in western and southeastern coastal Africa, and susceptible to this tipping threat.[11]

The tree's architectural complications are most obvious in some of the biggest baobabs, such as the immense Sunland tree, on a farm in South Africa. Most of the tree died in 2016 and 2017 as the result of fire damage, but it was two trees, fused together at the base, and thus, technically speaking, one tree with two stems. This baobab had an open interior measuring sixty-five square meters, the largest known for an African tree. That's seven hundred square feet, bigger than many apartments in Tokyo or New York. It's no wonder that people have been able to convert the tree's inner cavities into rooms. The Sunland tree once had a pub inside one of the two stems. But there is a measure of incoherence in measuring the circumference of a large baobab, given that some huge ones have collapsed chaotically over time, dying off in stages.[12]

Naturalists assumed for centuries that the trees' legendary water-holding capacity helped them to survive periods of extreme aridity. Although the tree's water supply is a key to its survival, scientists have only recently learned that the water is also central to the baobab's structural stability. While its soft wood isn't good for lumber, the tree's ability to grow to some ninety feet is surprising. If it loses a lot of water, its spongy interior starts to collapse. But the trees are downright parsimonious with their liquid. All members of the baobab family drop their old leaves and produce new leaves only at the end of the dry season, and even then only use a small quantity of water to produce those leaves.

Measuring the amount of water a tree can store, known as whole-tree water use, is challenging, although hydrobotanists have developed a variety of methods. The simplest and crudest way to see how much water a tree holds is to cut it down, slice off a known percentage of it, and then let it dry out to see how much less it weighs. This strategy will give you the percentage of an individual tree's approximate weight in water. But cutting down endangered trees to weigh them is not a great conservation strategy. Because they topple over from time to time, though, we know that a newly fallen baobab trunk weighs on the order of 850 kilograms per cubic meter, depending on the time of year. Once it's dried out, it might weigh only 200 kilograms per cubic meter. The tree can thus store 650 liters per cubic meter, which in turn tells us that more than three-quarters of the tree's weight comes from water. When you figure that the human body is up to 60 percent water, the baobab is pretty watery. But the similarities end there; the baobab does not let go of its water in anything like a gush. It's a slow, graceful release, patiently pulled up the trunk to nourish the leaves, fruit, and flowers in the upper canopies.[13]

Close studies of members of the *Adansonia* genus have revealed a number of clues about this water use. First, by studying sap flow data, researchers showed that the baobab used its stored water seasonally, rather than daily, to replenish the water supply to its upper canopy. Another way that baobabs stand out from other trees is that their diameters can fluctuate significantly, depending on how much water they hold at any given time. So trying to understand the tree's growth over time by measuring its diameter is ineffective, whereas for other tree species, it's a fairly reliable indicator.

Humans also use baobabs as static but strategic storage vessels for precious rainwater, which accumulates in its various orifices. People carve out deep wells in the trees' trunks, taking advantage of the natural cavities present in most baobabs. These collect water during the rainy season, which can then be used during dry spells. Not all baobabs have the same kinds of cavities or relative shapes. The trees vary in their particulars, shaped by their regions and genetic differences. The African baobab has been a tree on the move, constantly relocated by humans, and this process has affected gene flow. The morphometric diversity of differences in size and shape often indicates genetic variations, and we can see those variations in other aspects of the tree. The fruit can taste different depending on the region, and the flowers smell different. Fruit bats in southern Africa rarely pollinate the tree, although that mechanism is common to the west and north. Coastal trees and those further inland vary in water use, seed dispersal, fruiting frequencies, and pollination strategies.[14]

Despite these numerous differences across regions, one aspect remains constant: the teamwork between the tree's fruit and its water. One of the benefits of storing water in a gigantic, swollen trunk year-round is that it is always available to the nutrient-dense fruit that the trees produce. The process of fruiting begins with the baobab's flowers—a process that is one of the rare truisms of the natural world: all fruits come from flowers, without exception. And the flowers of the entire *Adansonia* genus are bizarre. Some species' flowers can open in thirty seconds. The flowers are born at the tips of the shoots of branches, usually with only a single flower present on each shoot. *A. digitata*'s flowers, which bloom between about November and January, are big and beautiful, on pendulous stalks. They're as wide as they are long, and emit a carrion-like smell that attracts bats, a common strategy in the plant world to ensure visitation for pollination. The flowers have been described as smelling like sour watermelon, urine, mice, and sweaty feet. This diversity of odors makes sense, as bats have a better sense of smell than of sight. Bat scientists (called chiropterologists) speculate that the scent is akin to the bats' own odor, and thus recognizable. As many as two hundred flowers have been observed opening on a single tree during a single night, although there are usually somewhere between a few and as many as fifty flowers on a tree, on average.[15] Not only do they open quickly, but they only open at dusk, like some mysterious creature driven by the coming of night.[16] On a single tree, the flowers will typically open within a half hour of each other, a slow-motion symphony of color and movement, especially visible when there's a full moon. This stutter-step timing of opening means that bats are prompted to move from tree to tree rather than lingering at a single tree, promoting cross-pollination and thus more robust genetic diversity.

Moths and several bush-baby species also pollinate *A. digitata*, while humans and big mammals (primarily elephants and monkeys) are the main dispersers of its seeds, since the fruit is large and not easily eaten by smaller creatures. There are plants that open and close their parts a lot faster than the baobab, such as the well-known

Venus flytrap, or hilahila grass (*Mimosa pudica*) from my childhood in Hawai'i, or the all-time champion of plant speed, the dogwood bunch-berry, which opens and fires out pollen in less than half a millisecond. But *digitata*'s much bigger flowers have many charms. It's the only species of baobab with flowers on long stalks, robust enough for bats to cling on to petals and stamens while eating pollen or nectar, and accessible enough in the dark so the little mammals don't get snagged in twigs or branches. The flowers of all the other baobab species are pollinated by birds and insects, rather than bats, because they grow on much shorter stalks, protruding either straight up or horizontally. But evolution isn't perfect; it's just good enough: fruit bats also love figs, such as those found on *Ficus bussei*, and in the course of carting them off, they can drop fig seeds into the forked branches of baobabs, con-demning the tree to death as the fig grows and chokes off the baobab.

Depending on the region, as many as three different species of bats feed on the nectar.[17] One species of African false vampire bat roosts in the hollows of baobab trees in groups of up to eighty indi-viduals and forages almost all night, listening for and gleaning prey on the ground—beetles, centipedes, scorpions, locusts, moths, and other insects—and at times breaking into song. (Yes, bats can sing, although they're in an altogether different sonic territory, being very high-pitched.)

And what's false about this bat, as its name says? It's because of the long misconception that they really did consume blood, as some bats indeed do. Taxonomy is wonderful: it describes not only what an organism is or does, but also what it was thought to be but isn't, and sometimes what it plainly is not. (The evening grosbeak? Fast asleep after sunset. Swedish ivy? Not from Sweden, and not even an ivy.) But taxonomists can also correct these matters, and the false vampire bat was recently renamed the heart-nosed bat. The bats also help to turn the entire baobab into a kind of singing tree, with birds singing during the day and the bats at night.[18] *C. cor* even has a soft song and a louder song, and it probably sings, as birds do, to defend its territory, and to foster social interactions by identifying individuals to one another. With all these actors, and all this activity, much of it taking place at night, it's no wonder that the tree has reverberations for the human settlements clustered near many of the trees. Peter Matthiessen, in his book *The Tree Where Man Was Born*, noted the tree's spiritual ties to the people: "For many tribes, the baobab, being infested with such nocturnal creatures as owls, bats, bushbabies, and ghosts, is a house of spirits."[19] Over time, African languages have accumulated many different names for the tree. My favorite is the French *arbre de mille ans*, with its implications not just of the age of the tree but of its aspirational presence in the landscape.[20]

The flowers pollinated by the bats take about five to six months to grow fruit, which consists of a pod about the size of a small coconut with a hard outer shell. Their otherworldliness extends to the fruits, which have been described as looking like dead rats hanging from the tree by their tails. When the fruits fall, they often break open, and termites eat the pulp, which liberates the seeds from their fleshy enclosures. Monkeys (and sometimes baboons) transport the seeds, offering a satisfactory explanation for the occasional presence of a baobab sitting high atop a hill or rocky outcrop.[21]

The velvet-covered, nutrient-dense fruit the tree produces in the dry season provides sustenance to villages throughout the tree's range. Sub-Saharan Africa is a place rife with famine; it has one of the highest levels of child malnutrition in the world. The fruit from the baobab has diversified and bolstered local diets, and local economies, for centuries. It's also a key ingredient in consumer products around the world, including smoothies, juices, ice cream, cereal bars, and much else. The fruit, which looks alarmingly like a set of human teeth grimacing at you when you slice it in half, is a high-fiber, nutritious food, and a tart, sweet, and chalky mouthful when eaten by itself. It's high in vitamins A and C, iron, calcium, amino and fatty acids, and antioxidants. It also shows up in noncomestible items such as toy drums, lampshades, and jewel cases.[22]

The fruit offers numerous advantages in a region plagued by food insecurity. Its pulp is highly adaptable for different uses. It can be safely stored in its natural dry form for months, and then dissolved in water or milk and used as a drink, as a sauce for food, or as a fermenting agent in brewing activities. Because it contains high levels of tartaric acid, the pulp is also frequently used as a substitute for cream of tartar for baking; the tree is commonly known as the cream of tartar tree. The stuff you use in your kitchen for baking is similar, because it's also derived from a fruit: a by-product of the fermentation process that turns grapes into wine.

The commercialization of baobab fruit has faced some of the same difficulties as African ebony: for years, corruption upended the value chain, so that by the time the product was finally sold, the harvesters themselves received a tiny fraction of the sales income. Enter the Micaia Foundation, a Mozambican NGO working to alleviate poverty and build sustainable livelihoods. Using a highly localized approach centered in the province of Manica, with about 1.3 million residents, the foundation has financial and logistical support that reaches more than one hundred thousand people in the province.[23] The enterprise has received high marks for alleviating food insecurity in Africa.[24] It also has addressed imbalances in gender roles in Mozambican society. Women tend to be the harvesters of the baobab fruit, but they have little control over the baobab trees and fruit in the route from harvesting to sale. Before Micaia's work, baobabs in the province were only sold to one group of traders, rife with bribery, and with a very low return on investment of labor. The women workers' livelihoods as harvesters have also been vulnerable to the rapid, uncontrolled deforestation of baobabs, which in turn has been a reflection of a lack of effective land governance and natural resource management. Micaia started its own operations, buying tons of the tree's pulp and seeds, and is now one of the leading producers of high-quality baobab powder in Africa, regularizing the harvesting, preparation, and sale of the fruit, in much the same way Taylor Guitars has done in Cameroon.

Part of Micaia's success comes from working within the traditional male community hierarchy to increase recognition of the baobab's value while also safeguarding resources for women. The foundation has also simplified the supply chain by removing intermediaries, and has given the women workers and harvesters a greater share of the profit, creating a lucrative and inclusive market for local baobab harvesters. We can thus draw a line from the tree's survival and potential expansion to that of women's rights and influence. In one survey, nearly half the women respondents reported that they had gained greater influence over household and community affairs—not a trivial feat in a male-dominated culture.[25]

The baobab's products also support indigenous housing, clothing, and medicine, as well as material for farming, hunting, and fishing. Locals use the tree's leaves, roots, tubers, and virtually all its other parts. The thick bark, with its long strips of fiber, is especially functional, and fabricated into rope. Baobabs are highly resilient, but are subjected to other abuses in the name of subsistence practices. To get at the fruit on the upper part of the tree, villagers often hammer wooden stakes into the side of the tree to climb the branchless lower trunks to reach the fruit. When the stakes rot away, the remaining holes serve as footholds over the years.

The substantial benefits the baobab can offer in the face of human suffering mean that there is more in the balance than just the tree's own right to survival. There are not enough trees to meet humans' needs, and many baobab stands are heavily overexploited. Communities plant baobabs in efforts to keep the trees' tomorrows secure. Baobab seeds have been placed in seed banks around the world, conserving their genetic material. But it's not just a question of protecting the tree. Assessment is the other critical element. Without knowing their rate of decline across a large geography, it's almost impossible to reach conclusions about its chances for survival. No conservation group, large or small, is willing to offer even the most general estimate of the number of surviving trees. Determining just how endangered a species is, and whether it should be considered endangered at all, can be complicated and confounding, with practical, legal, and policy ramifications. Extensive surveys of individual trees and their coordinates, the climates they inhabit, and the human populations near them, should now be mandatory. There are numerous tasks to be sorted out by geographers, botanists, statisticians: deciding who will aggregate existing data, square any inconsistencies, and undertake new studies. The future is now.

Some global conservation organizations are very effective; some are quite ineffective, and even counterproductive; some swing from effective to ineffective based on criteria like the current level of support, government interest, changes in policies within or outside of the organization, and the vagaries of humans' desires to support conservation. Some conservation entities, such as The Nature Conservancy, buy up large tracts of land to preserve. Others, such as Earth Justice, work the legal aspects of land, water, and species protections. Still others, including the World Wildlife Fund, have a broad brief: to conserve nature and reduce the most pressing threats to diversity. There are many more groups dedicated to specific kinds of plants and animals, or to specific conservation strategies. But the IUCN stands apart. It has made distinctive assessments of threats to thousands of species, and its active role is in not just conservation matters per se but in humans' involvement in these matters. Some scholarly work has been done on this sprawling, vital international organization, but nowhere near enough. As the pioneering environmentalist Max Nicholson noted in 1999 about the IUCN, "Its peculiarities, subtleties and complexities are sometimes mind-boggling."[26]

I'm a commissioner for the IUCN's Species Survival Commission, serving as a member of their Bird Red List Authority. I've had a chance to see up close the entanglements of conservation science, politics, law, and culture. No conservation efforts exist without resistance: a tension between decline and survival. Humans have caused every species extinction in the last two hundred years. Some of these losses have stemmed from malignant or unthinking neglect, greed, or economic motivations. We've eradicated species once considered pests and taken other bad actions—all the reasons you've read about in earlier chapters. The tensions inherent in the conflicts between humans and the planet's other residents mean that the numerous strategies necessary to save species are part of a long and often discouraging war, and the IUCN is the point of the spear in this battle.

After reading these details of the threats to the tree, it may surprise you to learn that the IUCN's ranking of *A. digitata* is Least Concern, its slackest category. One of the challenges for the IUCN's scientific staff is that they're forced to rely on existing research, much of which is necessarily regional and specialized, and which is often out of date and sometimes anecdotal. And once other taxa are involved, the obstacles to a clear understanding of threats multiply. Tracking data on the elephant as a threat to the baobabs is challenging, partly because the quality and precision of that data are inconsistent, and partly because numerous countries have had different experiences. An obscure account in 1960 by a park ranger in what was then Rhodesia who had inspected a game reserve in the enormous Hwange National Park found that of thirty-eight baobabs examined, only two had not been scarred by elephants over a span of two weeks; the ranger noted that this was the first time such behavior had ever been observed in the valley. A master's thesis from 2013 on the impact of elephants on baobabs in Mana Pools National Park in Zimbabwe provided useful but local data, as did, say, a 2013 paper on bark injury from elephants to the tree in Benin, or a study of the risk to the tree from elephants in Limpopo National Park in Mozambique.

If extrapolating conditions in one region to make continent-wide generalizations is hard, getting at the truths of individual trees for range-wide assessments is impossible. Finding trees in a comprehensive way across its range would be like searching from a helicopter for a lost swimmer in the open ocean, but with only a rough idea as to her location. This wide distribution has meant that studies have almost always tended to have a regional focus: Namibia, Kenya, Mali, Sudan, Ethiopia, South Africa, and elsewhere. The tree is favored by its extensive genetic diversity, but understanding those distinctions as aids or obstacles to its survival is an ongoing task. Think of the different populations of the African baobab as analogous to accents and dialects, and the idea of its messy variation becomes clearer. There are some two thousand distinct languages on the African continent, and about eight thousand more dialects. There are also lots of middling variations within those accents, with hyperlocalized differences in pronunciation and intonation. Distinctions blur, and people's individual characteristics and different upbringings make precision in identifying various inflections difficult.

Full Red List assessments are slow and expensive. Conservation concerns for entire species often span very large geographies, so they often cut across countries. Assessments by the IUCN often involve making one set of data from one region consistent with data from other locations, harmonizing language differences, and regularizing the ways we measure and count species. Cultural differences can also affect data on endangerment. Even a small leak in our estimations of true species endangerment can cause a cascade of errors, and an enormous amount is riding on these decisions. A misclassification of a species' threat can mean that vital resources are deprioritized and shunted elsewhere. It feels like an impossibly fraught undertaking.[27]

The IUCN isn't in a position to provide different threat rankings for a species depending on its locations. It's necessarily a generalized ranking, for research resources are finite, if not impoverished, depending on the species and the part of the world. But science is done in particulars, resulting in case study after case study, from which we can extrapolate. Scientific research isn't a blanket that covers a topic; it's more like a series of wells drilled into a broad landscape, a search for evidence, clues, data.

Trees take their own time. They often grow slowly, and take even longer to understand. This pace is only a tragedy when trees start to disappear and we don't know why, and thus don't know what to do. We've learned so much about the baobab, and we know so little. With relatively little data quantifying the trees' pollination, and the ecosystem strategies of the pollinators, it's hard to tell how successful those pollination efforts are. We also don't know how long the tree takes to regenerate naturally. Not only are younger baobab trees similar to other species, but even up close, tiny seedlings are quite difficult to tell from other generic-looking seedlings nearby; the young plants lack the palmately digitate leaves and the thick trunks.[28]

The IUCN has a hard route forward to ranking the baobab's level of threat not just because of regional variation, but also because of what the impacts of that ranking can be. The nine categories range from most woeful to most hopeful: Extinct, Extinct in the Wild, Critically Endangered, Endangered, Vulnerable, Near Threatened, Least Concern, Data Deficient, and Not Evaluated. The trees' placement into a particular category can have radiating effects on exports, local laws, the use of the tree's by-products, funding to further scrutinize the tree, and more. The Red List is well-known, having appeared in innumerable popular conservation pieces in magazines around the world, but its own history and evolution as one of the world's key conservation policy and procedure systems, and other aspects of its work, are much less recognized. The IUCN established the Red List in the 1960s, and the early versions relied on common sense and the experience of experts, not on any particular protocols. Simple assessments by authorities proved insufficient, and the IUCN introduced new criteria in the early 1990s. Today, going from raw data to Red List means involving global partners, identifying expert consultants, undertaking workshops and consistency checks, and undergoing a long and involved set of protocols. The process can take years, and during that time, the on-the-ground conservation status might change. So the reasons the baobab hasn't had a change in status yet are understandable. But it's still overdue.

Species survival is far from the only key that fits the conservation lock. Conservation of ecosystems, which are support systems for not just one species but many, became part of the IUCN's efforts with the formation of the IUCN Red List of Ecosystems (RLE) in 2013, which provides a global framework for documenting the status of ecosystems around the world. Within five years, the RLE's protocols have been used to assess 2,821 ecosystems, at a variety of geographic scales, in a hundred countries—protocols all geared toward assessing the risk of ecosystem collapse. You might have a healthy tree, or a healthy forest, or even an abundant species, but if its home is in decline, those trees are at risk. Saving ecosystems is often the most effective tool for saving species, for in any one ecosystem, a dense number of species exists—ranging from the common to those hanging on by their pretarsi.[29]

Despite the threats it confronts, the African baobab has assets. The tree is easy to transplant and to grow. Regeneration of the species might hinge on a conservation strategy that involves planting seedlings in many locations across the vastness of the sub-Saharan region. For now, it survives. It has many advantages for potential survival along the long, dark runway of the future: far-flung, genetically diverse, numerous, lousy for lumber. The baobab has many disadvantages, too: thirsty elephants, shallow root systems, intense consumer pressures for its fruit, and the perils of a warming planet. As with every tree in this book, the baobab is tethered to humans for its survival. But the tree survives, out of a deep, resonant past. As Peter Matthiessen wrote, "The present is wild blowing light, the sun, a bird, a baobab in heraldic isolation, like the tree where man was born."[30]

CHAPTER 11

Waterlogged: The Bald Cypress and the Wonders of Wetlands

"To love a swamp . . . is to love what is muted and marginal, what exists in the shadows, what shoulders its way out of mud and scurries along the damp edges of what is most commonly praised. Swamps and bogs are places of transition and wild growth . . . where the imagination can mutate and mate."

—Barbara Hurd, *Stirring the Mud*

Big Cypress National Preserve in South Florida is a land without any anchors to the present. Wading slowly through dark water that reaches up to your hips, your eyes land only on flora and fauna, with no sign of your fellow humans, and as you walk through the swamp, you could easily be a lonely traveler in any era. Birds call in the distance, insects hover, and dappled sunlight dances. Some three-quarters of a million acres constitute the park, and you'd walk for a very long time before you came to anything resembling civilization. You would, however, be in excellent company for almost all of your journey: the big bald cypress trees standing like sentries, rising straight out of the water. This is a scene still possible in other parts of the Southeast, in the enormous Great Dismal Swamp National Wildlife Refuge in Virginia and North Carolina; the Four Hole Swamp in South Carolina; the Atchafalaya

Basin in Louisiana; and in numerous smaller watery pockets and backwaters across the American South.

Trees need water, this much is certain. But a few have adapted to exceptionally wet conditions, and the bald cypress can live, and thrive, with significant parts of its trunk and root systems underwater. A deciduous conifer, the tree is so named because it loses its tan, cinnamon, and fiery orange leaves early in the fall compared to its more sturdily coiffed evergreen neighbors—the loblolly, southern live oak, and longleaf pine. It is a resident of wetlands, the most valuable and important ecosystems on the planet. It's frequently written, and said, as "baldcypress," one quick three-syllable word. Scientifically known as *Taxodium distichum*, the tree once covered some forty-two million acres in the southeastern United States in prehistoric times, and is now down to about three million acres, tracking across the Atlantic coastal plain, from southern New York down to East Texas, running in higher concentrations along the Mississippi River due to its love affair with water, and down south to the tip of Florida. There's also a nearly genetically identical version found in Mexico: the Montezuma cypress, *T. mucronatum*, that figures in the survival story of the bald cypress.[1]

The bald cypress has several qualities that are to the world's great good fortune. It's a tough plant, well adapted to standing water or flooding, with a deep root system and strong resistance to high winds. It has been in its current habitat for a very long time, but has adapted to other drier habitats as well. Even as its environment changes at the hands of humans and inclement weather, its longevity and flexibility are in its favor. The tree also provides a crucial buffer against storm damage on the Gulf Coast. But although bald cypresses are moderately salt-tolerant, the potential intrusion from salinity due to rising sea levels is one of its most substantial threats because of climate change–driven storms and rising tides. Numerous studies are underway seeking means to increase the tree's salinity resistance.

The cypress's stability and excellent integration in its botanical neighborhoods contribute to its continued well-being and presence on the planet. It's a tree that seems to have a positive future—albeit with some important caveats.

We know the lessons we can learn from the fossil record, and from dendrochronology, but there are other ways trees' informational freight can be rescued from antiquity. Divers recently found a bald cypress forest more than seventy thousand years old sixty feet underwater several miles off the coast of Alabama, in the Gulf of Mexico. Although the trees were dead, they were still standing in place, arranged as a forest, with some trees upright, and others lying flat where they had fallen before they were buried in sediment. The forest had probably been uncovered by Hurricane Katrina in 2005 and became an artificial reef, attracting a myriad of species and swarming with life. The logs were huge. Some of the stumps were more than six feet in diameter, and probably thousands of years old before they died. Samples from these giants—dating to the late Pleistocene but still made of wood, not petrified into stone—were brought to the surface and cut, whereupon they released sap, and the odor of fresh cypress. The trees contain a cargo of organic content from many millennia ago, including lignin, cellulose, pentosan, benzene, ether, and other components. These samples will prove instructive as to the effects of climate and environment on wood from that era, as well as to the evolution of the tree itself, over those seventy millennia. As a bonus, they also include growth rings useful for all the facets of dendrochronological study.[2]

Decades ago the bald cypress was better known by different, water-soaked common names: the marsh cypress, and the tidewater cypress. It has adapted to have unusually long root systems, which help anchor the tree so that it is supported in muddy, saturated soil. It also has a liquid way to spread its seeds, through a process called hydrochory, or dispersal by water, rather than the more usual strategies of being eaten by animals and then pooped around, or borne on the wind. The tree's wood also resists bugs and rot, an adaptation that has allowed it to thrive in damp places. Cypressene oil, found in old-growth cypress heartwood, is a natural preservative that provides the wood's characteristic insect resistance, although the oil's creation and precise role are not well understood. Because it takes decades for cypressene oil—a yellowish-green, viscous, and almost odorless substance—to build up in the wood, old-growth trees are more resistant to rot than younger ones.

Climate change has shifted future sea level rise from a possibility to a scientific certainty, and salt water will test the ability of the bald cypress and other trees in low-lying areas to survive. There is much hopeful work being done along this front. Hydrologists have noticed that some stands of the tree survive fairly well in areas that have been encroached on by the sea, while others do poorly. These fluctuations in salinity tolerance mean that there is some natural variation within the species to survive salty conditions. If botanists can manipulate the tree, through either selective breeding or genetic manipulation, a whole new defense against rising sea levels could be possible. Excess salinity is an old problem for plants, and while botanists understand many of the biochemical interactions at play, others remain elusive. Fostering salinity resistance in the bald cypress could also help efforts to protect other coastal trees susceptible to sea level rise.

It's already in the tree's nature to serve as a sentinel along the coasts, defending against storm surges, filtering water, absorbing contaminants, and harboring a broad spectrum of life. As rising ocean waters intrude into bald cypress habitat, multiple approaches have been proposed as solutions to the salt problem. One recent and promising approach has been the use of salt-tolerant endophytes—fungi and bacteria—to inoculate trees and improve their saline resilience. Ecologists hope that these inoculations will allow the endophytes to take up long-term residence in root systems. Another potential tool is the use of salicylic acid in water, which the tree absorbs to gain significant benefits in the right concentrations: improvement of shoot and root lengths, increases in the quantity of chlorophyll, and other subtle signs of beneficial growth. Research continues to tease out the tree's mechanisms better, such as the study of aquaporins—proteins, found in all living organisms, that transport water across cell membranes. Many aspects of the influence of aquaporin activity on plant water movement remain unclear, but new studies have provided mechanistic and functional insights into plant hydraulics.[3]

Writers have spoken of the bald cypress's ability to remain aloft in wet conditions, and Rutherford H. Platt, an American nature writer, put it as well as anyone has, a half century ago, as a rhetorical question: "With roots groping in unstable, virtually bottomless mud, how can a tree erect a trunk a hundred or more feet in the air?" Bald cypress wood is so heavy that a freshly cut log sinks in water. It seems that the slightest sway of its unwieldy trunk would easily rip its roots from the mud and topple it. But *T. distichum* has pulled off an outstanding feat of engineering. The base of the trunk flares out at the water's surface. Where drought or drainage has lowered the water level of a cypress swamp, the bulbous base is visible, and continues to widen for four or five feet below the surface. The bald cypress is shaped like a giant bottle with a long neck, which helps to keep it in a vertical position, which Platt described as making the tree "a toy clown, weighted so that it cannot be tipped over."[4] The key question, though, Platt notes, is how could the tree possibly get oxygen to its roots? The trees' "knees" were long thought to be the answer: stilt-like projections that rise a foot or more above the waterline, providing stability. Biologists previously thought that these knees served as an aide-de-camp to the roots, carrying oxygen down and under the water, a kind of root snorkel. Recent studies, however, have shown that there is no oxygen or carbon dioxide exchange between the roots and the knees, and the means by which the roots survive is still a mystery, despite 180 years of sporadic botanical attention.[5] The tree has kept the exact nature of its relationship to water to itself.

Survival in the natural world is a pitched battle (sorry; tree puns abound): organisms respond to changing conditions, and to threats

from other organisms, which in turn evolve to better take advantage
of their surroundings. The combination of the bald cypress's naturally evolved defenses against water and the possibility of breeding
intervention could be a harbinger of more robust times to come. The
time to work on a tree's survival is when it is at its most abundant, not
when it is in decline, and there is much more to learn from abundance
than from loss.

But don't rest easy. It's a long, painful, and tedious list, abundance
sliding into decline. Witness the Atlantic halibut, now classified as
Endangered by the IUCN and but a fin flick of its historic population from overfishing. In 1879, Gloucester Harbor in New England
landed and sold more than eleven million pounds of halibut, most of
it brought from deep waters by a fleet of some fifty vessels. Multiply
this localized haul by the numerous other fishing ports on the Atlantic
coast and the numbers grow into the hundreds of millions of pounds
of halibut per year. "It is nothing uncommon for a trip of 75,000
pounds of halibut to be taken from a vessel, weighed, packed, and
loaded onto the [rail] cars within a few hours in one forenoon, and by
the next morning to be marketed in New York and Philadelphia," an
1884 government report on the fishing industry noted.[6]

The bald cypress's disappearance would diminish the world, no
longer serving as an amphibian nursery for toads, frogs, alligators,
and other species, nor as a valuable food source in the form of seeds
for birds and small mammals. The tree helps waterfowl, because its
shallow swamps are rich in shoreline vegetation, crustaceans, and
insects, all of which feed geese and ducks. Slide the lens in closer and
you'll see that there is a world within and among the bald cypress.
None are sterile poles in the ground; all are elongated miracles of
growth, photosynthesis, respiration, oxygenation, absorption, and
interaction. Its seeds nurture the sandhill crane and the great blue
heron, and birds feed on the Spanish moss that often drapes the tree.
Small insects eat its foliage; the fall webworm, the Monterey cypress
scale, bark beetles: all have worked the tree into their diets, and all
rely on it for food. Both individually and collectively, the bald cypress

carries ecological freight; remove it from the landscape and its bio-diversifications would disappear—another dent in the planet.

A bird has also been enmeshed with the bald cypress's history: the ivory-billed woodpecker. Because of its size, the huge woodpecker was known as the "Lord God Bird," for people's response upon seeing it for the first time. It's an extinct bird story, played out in the tangles of the deepest swamps and stands of cypress. One writer called it the "ghost bird," because "the quarry is a kind of ghost bird, a creature that does and does not exist."[7] Its survival has been hotly debated and continues to be picked at, up to the present day. Life histories of the bird over the past two centuries tell us that its primary habitat, especially in Florida, was bald cypress, because the trees so thoroughly dominated the same landscape.

While the ivorybill's story is one of life and possible death, the bald cypress, through its death, also contributed to the survival of the woodpecker. Ivorybills needed grubs and other insects gleaned from the trunks of dead trees. It is these larvae that the bird found most palatable. Because its beak was the largest and strongest of any bird, at least in the far-flung region of the bald cypress, it took exclusive advantage of its ability to lever up the remaining bark on a log and get to the tasty larvae that lived between the bark and the sapwood, in the soft outer layers of the tree. These beastlets include a number of beetles, among them jewel beetles, along with one of the most voracious types of beetles anywhere: the scolytids, known as bark beetles for their habit of lodging themselves just below the bark. Well adapted to warm and humid climates, these scolytids have caused untold mischief by damaging forest systems, crops, urban landscapes, and nurseries. But for the ivorybill, their larvae were delicious. The trees provided shelter as well as food; with their large nesting cavities, they were ideal habitat. If the bird does somehow still improbably exist, it's likely that it survives in the crucible of bald cypress swamps. But if the tree had not survived in the areas where the ivorybill population was in decline, there is no doubt the bird would have blinked out long ago.

Beyond the iconic woodpecker, and those beetles, a large menagerie has evolved to make specific use of the bald cypress. The bald-cypress coneworm moth (*Dioryctria pygmaeella*) is a snout moth, so named because of the nose that extends from above its mouth. *D. pygmaeella* is a serious pest that eats the cypress's cones, which contain the tree's reproductive parts. The tree is also prone to predators, such as the swamp rabbit (*Sylvilagus aquaticus*), a curious creature that feeds on the bald cypress's roots and then poops the material out; the poop is then eaten by other rabbits and digested and divested a second time. And if the swamp rabbit sounds familiar, maybe you recall the "killer rabbit" attack involving then president Jimmy Carter, who was out one day alone in a boat and apparently charged by a swamp rabbit.

Trees can also speak to the skies, through tools that study them from high above, with satellites and other devices closer to Earth's embrace. These tools from on high sense the mechanics of wetland environments. David Thompson, an instrument scientist at NASA's Jet Propulsion Laboratory (JPL) in Southern California, told me to think of trees as optical machines. "They survive by presenting photosynthetic area to the sky," he observed, noting that their diverse evolutionary tactics for doing so, and the associated variability in chemistry and structure, lead to equally diverse optical "fingerprints" visible from air or orbit. Mathematically, their color diversity is wavelengths beyond what our eyes see, and exponentially more diverse than anything we would recognize or even have the neural architecture to perceive. Spectroscopy can measure that diversity, and lets us use math to quantify where our intuition fails.[8]

Kerry Cawse-Nicholson, with the Carbon Cycle and Ecosystems Group at JPL, provided me with an instructive list of additional ways that remote sensing can be used to study the larger environment that trees live in: sensors' abilities to measure moisture in the ground, or in the surface of the soil; how the landscape temperature varies throughout the day, across seasons, and over long time periods; how the atmosphere and clouds are behaving over that ecosystem; and how much CO_2 the trees are absorbing or emitting.[9]

Wetlands are the focus of conservation efforts around the world. They serve as water supply reservoirs; they trap and accrete sediment in river delta systems; they buffer against weather and storms; and they may slow down inrushing water long enough for sediment to settle. Cypress swamps can lay down up to a meter of organic matter, which helps as a mat to hold water. If you've heard of slow violence—the role of environmental degradation in creating a slow-motion disaster—swamps are slow peace: the calming and salubrious effects of wetlands.

The bald cypress is not just a North American phenomenon; other countries have a stake in the species' success. China has the planet's fourth-largest total of wetlands areas, and the country's scientists are fighting similar battles against wetlands loss and degradation. The tree's stability and its downright enthusiasm for swampy territory make it an ideal candidate for new plantings there, especially because China's wetlands climate is similar to that of the American South. Chinese botanists have begun hybridizing trees such as the bald cypress with other allied species to take advantage of their adaptability to wetlands. This hybridization involves breeding the bald cypress with the Montezuma cypress from Mexico: two geographic variations of what is essentially the same tree. These attempts aim for the best qualities of both: the Montezuma cypress's adaptability to the kinds of alkaline soils commonly found in Chinese wetlands, and the bald cypress's physical stability in waterlogged environments.

Cawse-Nicholson also observed that wetlands are often more difficult to study than other ecosystems simply because they sit at the blurry border of water and land. Historically, the scientific communities studying water and land have worked separately from each other. The algorithms designed for remote study of land aren't optimal for wetlands, but neither are the algorithms designed for water. There is also a relative lack of field data in wetlands, because getting across dry land is faster and easier than working your way across shallow waters. The technologies that provide better spatial resolution, mapping frequency, and data availability all work best with large acreages of land, which provide more study areas, along with greater variety and nuance.

The decline of the bald cypress during the nineteenth century, and into the twentieth, has meant that there are fewer regions for study. The first statistics for production of bald cypress lumber don't appear until 1869, when about 29 million board feet were produced. Accounts in the early twentieth century noted that the amount of standing cypress—"merchantable" trees, in the argot of the era—equaled 33 billion board feet. Lumber produced from the bald cypress peaked in 1913 at 1.1 billion board feet, then declined steadily. The most recent lumber statistics available for the bald cypress were taken in 1954, when the species continued to be logged substantially. That year, it accounted for just 240 million processed board feet. However, that's still a ton of wood, making for about nineteen thousand homes of two thousand square feet each.

Lumber commerce still swirls around the bald cypress. But much of the industrial interest in the wood now relates to its underwater life. There is sinker cypress, which comes from old-growth cypress logs cut early in the nineteenth century, then submerged in the southern swamps, bayous, and rivers in the South; and in particular, pecky sinker cypress (a particular grade of sunken wood that's been inundated by a fungus while still alive—*Lauriliella taxodii*, which creates tubular pockets in the tree, giving it an artisanal look). It's probably not ideal for a dining room table, as you'd be constantly suctioning out bits of your kids' waffles and trying to blot up spills into the characteristic tubes. But although these pockmarks provide a distinct aesthetic much favored by architects and craftspeople, the fungus damages the living tree, typically starting in the crown and working its way down-trunk. It's a battle scene written in wood.

The location and restoration of sinker cypress is big business for many small industries throughout the southeastern United States. Old bald cypresses with tight grain have many uses, and underwater logging efforts find and reclaim these rare, old-growth woods. Every tree retrieved from a dark river is a tree that doesn't have to be cut down to meet demand. As decades rolled by, loggers downed many of these large, waterlogged trees but never harvested them; some were cut and then tied to rafts to float downstream to mills but broke loose and sank; and still others probably succumbed to old age along riverbanks. Divers attach big eye bolts to the logs and pull them up one by one. When the old wood is sold, it goes for as much as ten times the cost of new wood. One of the holy grails for waterlogged wood harvesting is its potential use in high-end violins and other musical instruments. Stradivarius soaked wood for his eponymous violins in water, removing the resins and gums. Finding just the right sunken wood, which can be centuries old in some cases, for use in musical instruments is an erratic enterprise; fewer than one in a thousand logs of different kinds of woods might meet the quality requirements.

People make endlessly clever use of wood, but no tree is everything to everybody. The British government bought large quantities of bald cypress during World War I for aviation purposes, the wooden airplane having just taken off. But government administrators discovered that the wood proved unsuitable and led to what one expert described as "deplorable results." In general, though, the wood has had remarkable durability. It's moderately soft as well as long-lasting, which has made it popular for centuries, proving to be one of the great resources of the southern United States, valued for railway ties, posts, shingles, and lumber for general construction purposes. Its relative immunity to insects and parasites, however, was probably its greatest commercial benefit, and growing cities and towns recruited the wood for use in big water tanks, barrels, and other structures subjected to water, weather, or high humidity. It was good for making liquor in casks too, because it didn't include any objectionable flavors that could be transferred to the liquor being stored. Shipwrights also used the wood for boat hulls and boat decking because of bald cypress lumber's length and relative density, and Native Americans crafted thirty-person canoes from its trunks.

The tree also shows up frequently as Japanese bonsai. Miniaturization changes tree nomenclature. Bonsai people talk about the bald cypress's sloping roots as fluted, not buttressed. This nomenclatural pivot makes sense, as the former term implies a delicacy that you wouldn't use for the full-sized version found in swamps in the American South. The pint-sized tree's ability to grow successfully in the hot, dry Mediterranean climate of places such as inland Southern California means that the bald cypress's miniature form allows for manipulations not possible with its larger congener. In the process of developing roots, they're weaned from their watery environment and turned toward a drier lifestyle. Bonsai enthusiasts collect them in the winter, and if you're on the hunt, your quest might involve walking through shin-deep water in Louisiana, amid surrounding trees that are twenty-five or thirty feet tall. When you find a small one with good fluting, you reach down and cut it off at its widest spot below the water. The top is also severed, leaving the bonsai master with what is effectively a log. The tree then grows at both ends, rooting and budding, and turns into a miniature green promise. It's an amanuensis for the big tree, representing its bigger, older ancestors and inscribing its botany into a smaller form. Bonsai, like their larger versions, can live for thousands of years.

The Mexican variety of the tree, the Montezuma cypress being cross-bred in China, like its sibling in the southeastern United States, is also mostly riparian. The Nahuatl name for the tree, āhuēhuētl, means "upright drum in water," and also "old man of the water." To a much greater degree than the United States version, this tree saturates cultural life in the country. It's been the national tree of Mexico since the outbreak of the Mexican Revolution in 1910, and numerous native groups hold it sacred. The Montezuma cypress features in both Zapotec and Aztec prehistory; the combined shade of an āhuēhuētl and a pōchōtl (*Ceiba pentandra*) represented a ruler's authority. As they did with its counterpart in the United States, builders made steady use of the Montezuma cypress, but in Mexico, people found numerous additional uses: over the centuries, its resin treated gout, ulcers, wounds, and toothaches, and the pitch from the wood was used a palliative for bronchitis.

Trees respond to countless stimuli, many of which we have yet to categorize or understand. Thus, the evolutionarily shaped Mexico tree is amazingly different, despite being nearly genetically identical to its northern brethren: rather than standing on knobby knees, the Montezuma cypress gets stout. Really stout. Especially in the highlands of Mexico, where one specimen in Oaxaca holds the record for the widest tree known, with a diameter of 38 feet. That means the tree is 119 feet around, larger than the largest coast redwoods and of greater circumference than the gigantic water-storing baobab.

And while the Montezuma tree gets rotund, the bald cypress gets old. Among its numbers is one of the ten oldest trees in the world, found in Three Sisters Cove on the Black River in North Carolina, which runs through an ancient forested wetland. This particular bald cypress clocks in at 2,629 years old, making it the oldest living tree in eastern North America. That means the tree was first sprouted in 605 BCE. The cove in which it grows contains trees of similar ages, pushing the paleoclimate record in the southeastern United States back another nine hundred years.

That's part of the unique beauty of dendrochronology: it can pinpoint a tree's growth to a precise year, or even a specific *time* of year. For dendrochronological analysis, it helps that the water in these particular wetlands is clean, free of pollutants and toxic elements. Ancient bald cypress and bottomland hardwoods survive today only because they were too low-lying and frequently flooded, unsuited for harvesting. The scientists who studied these old trees used both dendrochronology and radiocarbon dating to pin down the date, documenting the extreme longevity of the trees at Black River.

Although these dating tools provide intimate details about age and environment, it's also possible to size up the bald cypress visually, as well as some other trees, to estimate their ages. It's not always reliable, but it lets you move through many trees to reach general conclusions. Bulk or height alone is not necessarily a determinant. But a tree whisperer who knows her species' idiosyncrasies can identify age through more subtle clues: the ways that the trees are twisted; burls, or deformities along the trunk or a branch; heavy limbs; and hollow voids, usually at the base of the tree. As they grow old, they accumulate lumpy, wrinkly evidence of their life experiences: hardships endured; growth and survival; and the reshaping of their bodies.

While there's talk in all quarters about carbon dioxide and its role in the planet's decline, most of this conversation has been about green carbon: its sequestration or release on land. But coastal regions and their plants are mighty citizens in the carbon conversation, storing what is called blue carbon, a term first coined in 2009—carbon that's locked in coastal and shallow marine ecosystems. Tidal swamp forests that contain bald cypresses engage in both emissions and containment of carbon dioxide. This carbon is stored in both plants and sediments, and coastal habitats account for about half of the total carbon sequestered in ocean sediments. The Blue Carbon Initiative, founded in 2015, is an important part of the scientific efforts to manage the challenges of carbon in watery environments. The initiative is a nascent version of the IUCN: a global program that's focused on mitigating climate change through conservation—in the initiative's case, through the restoration of coastal and marine ecosystems.[10]

Wetlands restoration involves various techniques, including planting native vegetation, removing introduced species, and replacing them with plants having longer evolutionary tenure in the region. Putting water in motion through tidal action is another strategy, because it reduces sediments, helps to promote plants that crowd out invasive species, and diminishes the buildup of mosquitoes. The exchange of salt and fresh water also helps to reduce emissions of methane—a greenhouse gas we don't talk about enough. Methane is produced when organic matter decomposes in the absence of oxygen, a process called anaerobic decomposition. Wetlands are particularly good at producing methane because they are often anaerobic environments. Methane doesn't reach the headlines as much as carbon dioxide because it accounts for a considerably smaller percentage of all greenhouse gas emissions. But it's a huge driver of global warming, and at least a quarter of today's warming, on average, is due to methane produced by humans (less in the United States, and more in other countries). Methane has more than eighty times the warming power of carbon dioxide over the first twenty years after it reaches the atmosphere. Its effects then diminish, and more abundant carbon dioxide has a longer-lasting effect. So those CO_2 emissions from your father's Oldsmobile are still up there in the atmosphere, warming the planet. In fact, those CO_2 emissions from the coal powering your great-grandfather's steam locomotive are probably also still in the atmosphere in some appreciable quantity. But methane is what's supercharging climate change today, and for coming decades.

At the same time, coastal blue carbon ecosystems are some of the most threatened on Earth, with an estimated 340,000 to 980,000 hectares disappearing annually. It's a lousy trend. Wetlands aren't just difficult to study. They're difficult to work in too, and hard to extract resources from, and generally a nuisance for the smooth turning of the insistent wheels of progress. So they're often drained, dredged, filled, leveled, and otherwise modified for other uses best suited for flat, dry land. In the course of these wetland modifications, removal of the plants and sediment that sequester the carbon dumps greenhouse gases into the atmosphere, doubling the problem: by removing the future benefits of wetlands to reduce carbon outgassing (and removing wetlands' roles in recreation, coastal protection, and more), these modifications simultaneously push long-sequestered carbon and methane back into the atmosphere.

We have a hard time controlling our noxious emissions into the sky, and although attempts to manage these outputs are politically fraught, the scientists working on solving the problems of greenhouse gases are taking an approach that skirts the issue of output and focuses on conversions. The most effective approach is large-scale wetlands restoration: bringing back benefits once lost. This work is difficult, and sometimes economically, legally, or logistically unfeasible. But smaller-scale efforts have been effective, and they add up. In Louisiana—hardly a wealthy or progressive state, ranking forty-seventh in the United States in infrastructure, forty-second in fiscal stability, and forty-ninth in natural environment promotion—a number of partnerships have restored tidal swamps of the kinds that grow bald cypresses. A 2013 project in the Louisiana swamp, funded by a private restoration group, restored tidal scrub-shrub habitat, removed invasive reed canary grass, revegetated the area with twenty-eight thousand native trees and shrubs, and removed a levee to allow tidal waters to flow twice a day into the swamp, restoring natural processes.

People often talk about the federal government as a bureaucratic obstacle to progress, but for environmental projects, it can be the opposite, providing an infusion of money and engineering resources, a timeline, and labor, all of which are often in short supply, especially in poor communities. In 2022, the National Oceanic and Atmospheric Administration (NOAA) began a massive project in Louisiana's Barataria Basin to produce a twelve-hundred-acre marsh that will create habitat to support diverse populations of fish and wildlife, reduce erosion, and lessen storm impact. In doing so, NOAA will dredge two Superdome stadiums' worth of sediment from the nearby Mississippi, and pump it thirteen miles to fill the target areas. Swamp by swamp, these are the kinds of projects that, scaled up, begin to loosen the rusted screw of climate change so it can start to turn in the right direction.[11]

Here's a twist on the salty-wetlands problem: although higher salinity puts the bald cypress at risk, the increased salt provides a strong cooling effect on climate. The greater the presence of tides in wetlands, the more effective the reduction in emissions from both methane and CO_2. Currently, coastal wetlands are fragmented in their access to seawater, consisting of a patchwork of desalinizing efforts undertaken in the past for many reasons, including aquaculture, rice production, and waterfowl management. Opening more and more of these wetlands to the sea would increase salinity. But this approach probably isn't great for the bald cypress. So perhaps this means that while increased salinity for the tree becomes ever more inevitable, we double down on our efforts to find solutions for the bald cypress to embrace the salt.[12]

We are awake now to the complexities of natural systems we barely understood a century ago, and to the perils now facing them. And always, through all the byways and backwaters, human emotions provide a conservation through line. As we talk about satellites, genetics, and optical machines, let's not forget that the homes of bald cypresses are beautiful places that call to us, teeming with riotous life. Science and desire arrive at a similar conclusion: these trees, and their homes, deserve to be saved. Henry David Thoreau, an aficionado of dark and wild places, understood their inviolable nature when he wrote, "I enter a swamp as a sacred place—a *sanctum sanctorum*. There is the strength, the marrow, of Nature."[13]

CHAPTER 12

Tall Stories: The Mighty Ceiba Tree

"What did the tree learn from the earth to be
able to talk with the sky?"

—Pablo Neruda, *The Book of Questions*

I t's September 11, twenty years after the Twin Towers fell in New York City, and I'm about as far from civilization as I can get, working my way northward in a small motorboat on the Madre de Dios River in Amazonian Peru. Despite the somber date, I'm a world away emotionally as well as physically. At the moment, I'm all about resurrecting my own towers, in the form of big tropical trees. We're about to enter the so-called gateway to the Manú Biosphere Reserve, known as Manú National Park. It's taken a heavy push to get here, endless obligations back home reorganized, postponed, rearranged. I'm so giddy that I start free-associating in my notebook. Gateway drug. Gateway to the wildest places. Gateway to heaven. Scratch that last one. There is no heaven, only life here on Earth. But that doesn't mean that there isn't room for heaven on Earth. It's late in the afternoon, and the sun is low in the sky, a warm, round mango to the west, with the Pantiacolla mountain range in the distance.

It's been a day. For almost all of the two weeks of our trip, we're up at four fifteen in the morning; breakfast in the dark at four thirty; and then into the boat by five. Almost every morning on the river brings a fiery sunrise, lighting up scattered clouds in fragments and fits and starts until it spills onto the scene, sliding across the horizon and staining the sky in impossibly beautiful hues. We are six bird nerds in a boat. The sun rarely bites; we're in the shade of the canopy, with breeze from our forward motion. We glass the trees with our binoculars, looking for avian life. Preston invited all of us. Preston is getting married soon, and for his bachelor party, he wanted to mount an expedition to Peru to look for nests of the harpy eagle (*Harpia harpyja*), one of the largest and fiercest birds in the world. He was the subject of a *National Geographic* documentary the previous year, about a project he initiated more than a decade earlier: the Sibinacocha Watershed Project, more than sixteen thousand feet up in the Peruvian Andes. I met Preston nearly forty years ago. He's a decade my junior, serrated around the edges when we banged into each other, and now a sophisticated marvel of an environmentalist, photographer, climber, and adventure enthusiast. Preston has made some ten trips to his Sibinacocha archaeological site in the Andes, where his work has led to the discovery of new species of flora and fauna.

We're not that far south of the equator, but it's not as hot as the stereotypes about the tropics dictate. Vegetation rises up from the riverbanks, and it's a broad, green, sunny day. The motor is pushing us up the river, sometimes over rough passages that splash water up into the boat, sometimes smooth and calm. The entire time, the green-brown snake of the Madre de Dios River flows by us. Kingfishers, fasciated herons, swifts, swallows, parrots, and other birds appear as we motor. Along with our harpy eagle obsessions, I'm looking for *Ceiba pentandra*, the majestic tree, which towers over the canopy in the Amazon; it's the tallest life-form on the continent. Sacred to various endemic peoples, the ceiba (as it's commonly known) is armed with thick green conical spines and huge umbrella-shaped tops, and like all trees, it is the nexus for a wider, complex ecological community.

Miguel, our own little community's full-time guide for two weeks, has a remarkable ear, like all really good field naturalists who study birds seem to have. It's often the first way to narrow in on a bird, because they're frequently heard long before they're ever seen, and sometimes they're never seen, only heard. Today, we also have an additional local guide whose specific job is to get us to a harpy eagle nest. He goes by Isaiah, presumably after the prophet by that name in the Old Testament, an authority figure in ancient Jerusalem, and best known as the Hebrew prophet who predicted the coming of Jesus some seven centuries before the start of the Christian era. Our Isaiah is a prophet, too: he's confident of our route to the site this morning, which he claims has not yet been visited by white outsiders like ourselves.

We get to the eagle's nesting site by midmorning, and there is the chick. It's odd to call a bird that's three feet tall a "chick," but it's ornithologically accurate. The nest is correspondingly gigantic, and constructed in an enormous tree, about 150 feet tall, but not a ceiba, which disappoints. But nature doesn't work with our narratives; it labors on its own schedule and plan. Statistically, though, the ceiba is the tree in which adult harpies most often choose to build their nests. The center of the tree is typically broad and flat, large as a good-sized one-bedroom apartment, and the perfect platform for the nests of one of the largest birds of prey in the world. This chick is a female. She's scowly, with big tufts of gray feathers and dark, piercing eyes. She's also precious, in that the harpy eagle has the longest known reproductive cycle of any of the planet's eleven thousand bird species, with just one fledgling produced every thirty to thirty-six months.

Sometimes, a chick will become overweight, and as an evolutionary strategy, the mother will stop feeding the chick for days at a time to get its weight down so that it will be able to fly when it leaves the nest. We wait for hours for the mother to come back to the tree, but she never does. We worry, we wonder, we wait, spending a half day on a muddy hillside with the unblinking eyes of our spotting scopes and binoculars and cameras trained up into the canopy. Seeing the baby bird is wonderful, despite the absence of a parent, and we get hundreds of photographs, along with audio and video footage. The nesting sites for the bird are not well recorded, and we're glad to be able to add data to the known set of existing locations, for another harpy will often use the same site later. Miguel concurs with Isaiah, telling us that we're probably the first white people to visit this particular tree deep in the forest.

As dusk falls and we leave the tree, the locals along with us turn and say, "Takichi watopo," which is an indigenous Amazonian thank-you to the bird for letting us pass. We return to the boat, which fittingly, although only coincidentally, is named *Aguila Arpia*—the harpy eagle. On our way back we see several hoatzin, bizarre, prehistoric-looking birds that seem scared of their own shadows. Then a red-capped cardinal, a social flycatcher, a blue-headed parrot.

We've been on the water, and sometimes on solid if muddy ground, and occasionally on rocky flats midstream for days, looking for birds and other taxa, six very different men. It helps that the whole team has been indoctrinated into my quest to see *C. pentandra* in its natural setting. Everyone keeps pointing them out along the river. Despite how huge they grow, it's often not obvious, at least to me, which trees are the ceibas. Their density is relatively low, so they're often several miles apart—and of course, young ceiba trees aren't huge like old ones; they're harder to spot in the midst of countless ribbons of green.

White-winged swallows dart around the boat, which moves most days at a leisurely twenty miles an hour, powered by an old Yamaha outboard motor. Waterbirds abound: egrets and herons of various kinds, and lots of fliers higher up in the air, but especially birds of prey—king vultures, bat falcons, and hawks of different sizes, all reminders that it's nature red in tooth and claw in the jungle. The clichés are true: it's a dangerous place. As long as you're mindful, though, you'll be okay, barring some spectacular bad luck. Human health and well-being is like that of trees: one day you're alive and thriving; the next you've fallen down, through accident or incident. Nothing is ever certain.

Some of us in the boat don't know each other, joined together only by our friend Preston. But we all end up getting along famously for the whole journey. There's my roommate, Stephen, a tech company CEO from Colorado. He's built like a house and is the sweetest, funniest guy, chattering constantly to himself. He's also brought along a satellite phone, which lets me get a few reassuring messages to my family back home. And then there's Jon, an ultramarathoner who's one of the fittest, most athletic people I've ever met, a gentle soul who's quick with a funny, sarcastic crack. And Robert, at thirty-eight, the youngest in our group, living an itinerant life on the West Coast as an assistant director of photography working in film and television around the world, which suits his nomadic lifestyle.

I'm a bit taken aback to meet Robert for the first time, as he could pass as a movie double for my late brother, Gene. They have the same soft, quizzical blue eyes, the same tall, thin frame, the same long, blond hair tied back. He is gentle like Gene, but steely like Gene was not. Robert has extensive natural history experience; he's already spent five years working with big cats in Bolivia at a rehabilitation facility. I keep wanting to pester him to see the scars from the bites he mentions in passing, but that seems weird, so I don't. He's also led wildlife safaris in Namibia, which is where he got his first field guide and became interested in birds. His great obsession, at least on this trip, is with Peruvian birds. He knows almost as much as our guide Miguel (although I overheard him one night, out with Jon to look for owls, muttering, "Without Miguel along, I'm just a B-list birder"). He's also the only member of our group besides Miguel and our cook who's fluent in Spanish.

Robert also knows a lot about the ceiba, probably from his years in Bolivia. I sit next to him for many of the hours we spend in our boat going up the river. He points out some of the trees as I try to build a visual vocabulary for the ceiba in a jungle setting. Robert's scars are on the outside, but Gene's were on the inside, and he wanted to bring life to an end, and finally did. Robert, in sharp contrast, wants to spin it up. "Nobody ever regrets a sunrise," he notes one morning on the boat, to no one in particular. I find it deeply satisfying to hang out with him. Life comes to a halt at the same time that it moves forward, for every species on the planet.

The river—green, brown, or oil-dark, changing every day depending on the weather and the load of sediment it carries, but always moving slowly and steadily—is a deep tonic for all of us, I can tell. It's an antidote to all the complexities and challenges of daily life back home. The timelessness of the location also changes the calculus of my place on the planet. The two rivers we traverse during the trip (the Manú River and the Madre de Dios River) have been floated by humans for at least ten millennia. It feels like an honor to be a particle of shared life, one in an uncountable expanse of travelers who've come along these astounding waterways.

The sixth member of our tribe is Kyle: warm, kind, gentle, funny, smart, and an unreconstructed hippie, and Preston's oldest friend; they've known each other since seventh grade and have traveled the world together for months at a stretch. We're all bird specialists after a fashion, but Kyle is a masterful generalist. He's not all that interested in birds but is watchful. He's our eyes, our ears, and, in some ineffable way, an embodiment of the forest entire. He stops on the trail to photograph fungi, plants, small creatures. He has a global view of the forest: its moods and its themes, its comings and goings.

We're pretty much drunk on birds twenty-four hours a day, and it's a thrill that we're in the middle of one of the most biodiverse aggregates of avian life on the planet. We end our evenings sitting around a table or campsite in the dark with our headlamps, reviewing the day's sightings in our field guides; we review calls and songs on our phones; we laugh and drink Scotch and wine; we argue over identifications. Because of the global pandemic at hand, we end up at encampments at various rustic lodges where we are the only people;

and in a few cases, we're the first people there in many months. Lots of buildings and trails are in disrepair, rusty or overgrown or clearly unused for a long time. But our spirits are high. We do love not seeing other people, as it turns out. And Miguel, if possible, has even more birdy enthusiasm than we do; he insists we go out every evening after dinner to look for owls and nightjars by lamp and headlight. And every morning he wraps up breakfast with the same phrase in his broken English: "Time to make birding!" It makes us all smile, and I come to love the active nature of the phrase: "making" birding, which says that we're working at it, bringing it to life.

I'm worried about having a chance to get up close to a ceiba, given everyone's preoccupations with birds, and fret to Miguel. Little do I know what he has in mind. One day, we hike through the forest, as we do most days, heading to specific ecosystems to spot new bird species. We stop for lunch, where Miguel and the cook have set up small camp tables and chairs for us. Someone calls my name, I turn around to take in the scene, and there, not thirty feet behind me, is the most gigantic tree I have ever seen in my life—a monumentally huge ceiba, with its enormous buttress roots radiating out in all directions. I'm quiet for a second, and then do what I do when I'm excited: let loose a stream of epithets. Photographs just can't do justice to the size of the tree, although I take many dozens of pictures. Its trunk is immense, and dwarfs all the other surrounding vegetation below the canopy. It's not as tall as a coast redwood, but nothing crowds it or obscures the view to the top, sighting up its smooth, unbroken column. Strangler figs make token gestures of wrapping themselves around parts of the trunk, but they're like filaments alongside the tree's impossible bulk. The upper canopy of the ceiba flays out like a giant mushroom—a quiet, green nuclear explosion in the forest. The harpy eagle is one of the heaviest birds in the world, and you can immediately see why the upper canopy of the tree is so well suited for it and its progeny. I touch the rough bark, circumnavigate the tree, commune with it, climb up a bit into its branches, trying to bring its world more fully into my own—and to create a tall story all my own.

Inevitably, there's also pain in the forest, and in the stories at hand. Humans can't stop themselves from doing wrong by nonhuman life. Miguel and another guide tell the story of how this tree housed a harpy eagle nest back around 2006, until someone shot the adult bird. Its chick eventually fell from the tree, and survived; park rangers rescued it and took it to a rehabilitation facility somewhere, its ultimate fate unknown. I wonder whether any of the current bird residents, or any other intermediate ones, could sense the trauma that had taken place earlier. Was there old eagle blood on the scene? Was it distressing to be there? But home is home, and necessity is the mother of habitation.

Meanwhile, Miguel belies various stereotypes about a rural Peruvian from Cusco with no college education. During the pandemic, he has made a point of learning the Greek and Latin etymologies for many Peruvian bird names, derived from their scientific epithets. He can thus discuss, with some authority, the ancient linguistic derivations of the Latinate names, and plans to publish a book about these etymologies.

Miguel was born and raised in Quillabamba, located in the high jungle in southern Peru. His father was a farmer, raising coffee and coca and rice. Seed-eating birds came to the rice paddies, and when he was thirteen, his father told him to take a small pair of plastic binoculars to the rice paddies, and asked him to check the farm to see what small birds were eating the rice. He tried to run them off with his slingshot, but once, a shining pair of black-and-white birds caught his eye, different from the others. He determined to kill just the usual birds, and leave the black-and-white ones to live. Several days later, he saw them mating and understood that one was male and one was female. Around the same time, a French ornithologist doing research in the area stopped by his remote village and asked whether he could have permission to go onto the family property to look for birds. They invited the ornithologist to stay at their house, and in the morning, he was up early watching birds. That caught Miguel's attention;

when he got closer, he saw the man's field guide. In the book he recognized some common birds he had seen and pointed those out to the ornithologist, who spoke good Spanish. So the two took off into the jungle; the Frenchman loaned Miguel some better binoculars, and Miguel helped the ornithologist. They "made birding" for fifteen days. Miguel then worked his way to Cusco to attend high school, filled up with birds and desire.

One day we take a swim in a dark, nameless pond deep in the forest, up by a small waterfall. It's dark with tannins from decaying vegetation. Nothing tries to eat us. Huge ancient mahogany trees overlook the pond. We are happy to shed our stinky clothes and rinse our bodies and soothe our itchy skin in the cold water. We're a field guide for bug bites; you could map the region's insect biodiversity simply by how many different flying pests make a blood meal out of us. September 12 comes and goes. It's the twenty-second anniversary of my first date with my now wife. Ridiculously tiny time frames are still significant and are embedded in the historical record: small events tucked into a huge narrative that spans generations, and eons. Time has many registers. Daily lives matter, because what else is an eon but a vast collection of days? On another outing, we climb an old but rock-solid observation tower, going up about two hundred feet, the top rising above the canopy. It's the perfect place to see monkeys, birds, and the setting sun. There's not a ceiba in sight. The tree seems uncommon to me, even deep in the jungle. There's a long, tiresome argument about how tall the tower is. Who cares? One golden afternoon finds us at a small lodge with hot mineral springs, where we can slip in and soak our tired bodies.

It was truly idyllic, but that's not to say that it's not damned dangerous in the jungle. There are poisonous or painful snakes, frogs, plants, fungi, fish. It's a rule of the trail not to lean or hold on to a tree or branch, lest an insect or reptile crawl up your arm or down your leg. Preston's initial email noted, in capital letters, "SAFETY NOT GUARANTEED!" A diver died on one of the trips to his Sibinacocha site. Miguel recounts a story about being bitten by several bullet ants once, paralyzing his arm for several hours. It's supposed to be the most painful of all insect bites. We get through the trip with nothing more than a few blisters and some garden-variety insect bites—if your garden is in the deep tropics, that is.

And it's a crowded garden. Forests in South America contain a bewildering variety of trees, topping more than thirty-one thousand different species. There are stands of plants so dense that nothing bigger than a rodent can pass. The selva is hot, humid, and close, trembling with life. Even the leaf and branch litter at the base of trees is sometimes impassable. The plants and animals are all a patchwork quilt of nature, working both with and against each other. A huge assortment of birds sound all day long and into the night. Insects are everywhere. Creatures flit, fly, crawl, slither, swing, and crash through the trees, from ground level to the canopy. Sometimes it's also quiet. But moving or still, the entire forest practically vibrates with entangled life. Strangler figs, usually starting life as a sticky seed somewhere up in a tree canopy, then heading down to root in the ground, are everywhere, trying to bring down trees. Known in Spanish as *matapalos*, or tree killers, they're like pythons, wrapping themselves around bigger trees and choking the life and nutrients out of them until they're a tree unto themselves, the husk of their prey running up through their middles.

The entire Amazon basin in South America is one of the watery wonders of the world. The Amazon River discharges, on average, more than seven million cubic feet of water per *second* into the sea, accounting for a fifth of all water flowing into oceans worldwide. On a typical day, close to 390 billion trees pump water up from the ground and surrounding air. The volume and significance of water in the Amazon mean that droughts are exceptionally impactful for trees. The Madre de Dios region lay in the epicenter of severe droughts in 2005 and 2010, both extreme climatic events that affected livelihoods across the region. Many rural Amazonian communities rely on the region's seasonal water cycles, making them vulnerable to climatic variability. Extreme drought makes fire less predictable, too. Conflagrations of various sizes serve as a tool throughout the Madre de Dios region, used to remove unwanted vegetation and insect pests, and to ultimately fertilize land with ashes—a practice seen as both necessary and culturally appropriate for farmers, who cannot typically afford commercial fertilizers or the requisite machinery. But drier lands increase the risk of runaway blazes that can occur when farmers kick off their seasonal burning during the driest moment of the dry season. Burning has gone from a benefit for traditional farming practices to being a menace under climate change's drought effects, for an out-of-control fire can destroy capital and resources, hopping into nearby pastures and adjacent forested areas.[1]

What's a tree to do to survive? Let's look at its specific gifts. The ceiba, known as *huimba* or *lupuna* to Peruvians, is considered by many natives to be the mother of the forest, with its sometimes swollen, gravid shape and its outsized presence. The largest known example tops out at 252 feet, taller than most mature coast redwoods. The tree's great height above the canopy also means that its oily, edible seeds can be blown quite far across the forest landscape. Once mature, the tree readily bears fruits, producing as many as four thousand at a time, each containing as many as two hundred seeds. With maturity comes other advantages: taller trees in the Amazon basin are less susceptible to drought than shorter trees. It's also a fantastically fast grower, sometimes gaining as much as thirteen feet of height per year.[2]

While the tree's height and the fecund distribution of its seeds give it natural advantages in the tropical forest setting, it's also extraordinarily stable, and not prone to getting knocked down, blown over, or tipped onto its side. As it grows, the ceiba's buttress roots increasingly prop up the tree. Differently shaped than those found on the bald cypress, these roots distribute mechanical stresses very effectively, and tend to be more developed in wetter areas. In one experiment in Borneo, trees that had their buttresses removed quickly fell.

The IUCN gives the ceiba a ranking of Least Concern. Unlike trees such as the baobab, however, its timber is of great interest and use. As the IUCN noted in a 2017 assessment, its population trend is not clear. It might be in decline in some areas and stable in others. It is, however, native only to Central and South America, where it was born, evolutionarily speaking, and grew up, both figuratively and literally. But the biological record provides abundant warnings about the plunge species can take from abundant to nonexistent. The Rocky Mountain locust, so prevalent in the late nineteenth century that observers of one famous sighting in 1875 estimated that its extent reached 198,000 square miles—27.5 million tons of biomass comprising 12.5 trillion insects. The locust was so pervasive that it would eat the clothes of people working in the fields. Oil from the crushed bodies of the insects could stop a train from going uphill, so slippery were the rails. But by 1902, it was extinct, disappearing so rapidly, for reasons still not fully understood, that just a handful of specimens survive. No one even thought to memorialize the bug in museum collections, since no one conceived of its possible extinction.

The ceiba won't eat your clothing, but it does cover vast territory. Besides its wood, the tree's primary economic feature has been its fluffy seed fiber, known as kapok (although at least two other trees bear that same common name). It appears as stuffing for teddy bears, pillows, upholstery, and other soft domestic products. It was also used in life jackets in World War II, but they wouldn't stay buoyant if the outer plastic coverings were punctured or cracked, becoming more millstone than survival tool as the kapok quickly became waterlogged.

No tree is an island. To better understand the harpy eagle is to better understand the tree, because they're respective fauna and flora giants of the ecosystem: the big kids at the prom, made for each other. An apex predator, the harpy is gigantic. Its tarsi—lower legs—are about as thick around as your wrist. It's the feet that do the killing with hawks and eagles, not the bill, which is primarily used to tear up dead prey. People who see the harpy in photographs with something next to it for scale, such as a human, often refuse to believe it's a real bird, because it looks for all the world like a person wearing a bird costume. Its wingspan, another often cited marker of big birds, is not especially notable, but that's because it has evolved to live in fairly crowded tropical forests, rather than in open woodlands. Its stubbier wings give the bird the ability to navigate rapidly in close quarters. Like the tree, it's native only to the Americas. Nesting and living in the tallest tree in the Amazon's forest canopy provides great advantages to the bird as a nesting site, lookout, and launching point. Objects of the harpy's culinary affections include sloths, monkeys, porcupines, anteaters, and even kinkajous, coatis, and tayras. It's been known to eat at least sixty-nine different species of animals, the kind of generalist behavior that helps species remain viable in the face of disturbances. The harpy's culinary interests can drive population densities of these animals, and thus the radiating effects of their influence on seed distribution and other activities.

Some thousands of eagles survive, but no more accurate census assessments than that exist because of the difficulty in accessing remote nesting sites across an enormous sprawl of many millions of acres and numerous countries in South America. But as their habitat disappears, so too certainly does the bird. Over millennia of evolution, birds tend to imprint on specific trees for nesting. The red-cockaded woodpecker is irrevocably wed to the longleaf pine, and Clark's nutcracker to the bristlecone. Plants and animals strive to adapt to their neighbors. It's how they survive. Humans are at a great disadvantage here: Our big brains keep us stubborn, resistant to natural pressures. Our habits keep us stuck. Our egos keep us removed from the natural world and make us a danger to the natural world.

It's not just white people who threaten the big eagle. There is also ubiquitous enthusiasm among Amerindians for the harpy's claws and feathers, which often show up in arrow fletchings and headdresses. The birds are also sometimes captured live by natives and kept for the feathers they produce.[3] Big raptors such as the harpy eagle also depend on big trees that are natural targets for lumber harvesting. Nestlings also are often lost when big trees are cut down—killing young birds at the same time as removing habitat for the adults. And although the ceiba tree continues to do well in the face of climate change, pollution, and other threats, the continuing wide-scale habitat destruction on the continent puts the tree at risk, which puts all of its affiliate species at risk, including the harpy. "Bird is the word," as the Trashmen sang in 1963, but destroy its habitat and life spirals down. We all need a workable place in which to survive.

But still other warning bells are ringing. As we went downriver, passing near the city of Puerto Maldonado, we saw many dozens of sticks pointing up out of the ground in the shallow waters along the banks, surrounded by tailings—piles of earth, evidence of gold mining, the common coinage of pioneers everywhere. But it's fool's gold, and a fool's errand: a study published after my return from Peru shows a stark and alarming development related to these small-scale mining sites. Mercury is used to separate gold from surrounding sediment, which is then burned off to reveal the precious metal. This burning also releases the mercury into the atmosphere in different forms, including methylmercury, which is poisonous, formed when bacteria react with mercury in the water, or in soil or plants. The terms that describe it and its effects on humans and other animals are all nasty: Neurotoxin. Cognitive decline. Neurodegenerative.

Worst of all, it bioaccumulates, getting more and more concentrated as it moves up the food chain. The dust from the burned-off sediment drifts through the air, landing on trees such as the ceiba, which sits highest in the canopy, and eventually into the bodies of songbirds and other animals that live in the forests, from the ground up to the treetops. The study showed that mercury has been transferred up the food web to the birds, which had levels of mercury between two and twelve times as high as those in areas farther from the mining activities. The three bird species studied—the white-flanked antwren, the black-spotted bare-eye, and the band-tailed manakin, all of which I saw on the trip—had elevated levels of mercury. "The patterns were so much more stark and so much more devastating than we expected to find," Jacqueline Gerson, the biogeochemist who was the lead author of the study, told the *New York Times*.[4]

So that's another confounding tangle. When you're working to protect land from threats on the ground, including clear-cutters, poachers, trappers, loggers, and others intent on monetizing the forest, and keeping an eye on the effects of a changing climate, it's easy to miss a threat from above, such as pollutants floating in from on high. There are more than a thousand species of birds in the Manú National Park alone, well more than in the entire United States. Many of these Peruvian birds are at risk from the mercury. And it's not good for any of the trees, so dense in places that they're like a geological formation. The various threats to so many different trees also risk biodiversity. One famous 1988 study of Amazonian trees noted that two of the relatively small plots surveyed for tree diversity numbered more than three hundred species, far exceeding tree density in any other known site of the same size in the world.[5]

There has also been a move to use *C. pentandra* as a source for biofuel, because it has shown promise in this area. This is a terrible idea. As the world works to convert to renewable resources such as wind, waves, and solar energy, pressing the seed oils from an abundant tree into service to provide fuel on a global scale risks the kinds of resource thrashing and diminishing that have marked many other such endeavors. The problems are numerous. As soon as you turn something into a commodity, especially a large-scale one, commercial aspirations grow like a tumor. To make such production work, you would need to dedicate specific regions to bioenergy production—to growing trees in farms. This monoculture approach lowers the biodiversity of a region, because you can't have all the messy accoutrements that come along with trees in their unregulated ecosystems when you're trying to maximize oil production and profits.

Most biofuels do reduce emissions by about 30 percent compared to fossil fuels, and governments around the world have touted them as miracles for mitigating climate change. When you factor in all the resources involved in their creation and extraction, though, nearly half of all biofuels have *greater* overall environmental costs than do fossil fuels. It depends on the biofuel. This is an important distinction, because some biofuels are a good idea. Algae has a minimal impact on freshwater resources, has a high ignition point, and can be produced using saline water and wastewater. Using waste vegetable oil to power buses in Spain? A worthwhile undertaking, because it uses something that had already been produced for human consumption. But I can't imagine what the harvesting efforts of kapok seeds, from which the biofuel oils would be taken in vast quantities, would do to the health of the forest. And if the kapok is farmed, it seems problematic to have to cultivate new areas to hold these tree farms, because you have to clear ever more land to meet the demand you're trying to create.

Our tribe prepares to disband. We leave the river and board a pair of four-wheel-drives to get back to the big road to the airport, to the next airport, to the next ones after that, and then home. But our adventure isn't done and almost turns into a serious misadventure. The driver on the forty-five-minute leg to meet up with our next vehicle is young, macho, and very dangerous, taking risky chance after risky chance on the unpaved divided highway, and driving very fast. Stephen and I yell at him to slow down; he turns and grins.

We pass a big blue truck, with a slogan hand-painted on its back: VIVE TU VIDA, NO LA MIA. Live your life, not mine. I consider this and feel better. We've had an absolutely amazing time, and I'm still standing, as are many thousands of ceiba trees. I feel a bit of Stoic joy coming over me: imagine how much worse circumstances could be.

We are biomes; we cluster, we exchange carbon dioxide and oxygen and desire, and we need each other.

Being iconic is important to a species' survival. It's a rocky, cold fact that we don't love everything equally. But if we are to help species survive, we need to care about more of them, one way or another; we need to elevate their status to get others' attention. We love charisma, if that's not too much of a tautology. Publicity about endangered charismatic species helps to elevate awareness, raise money, and encourage political will. To my eye, the ceiba is the most spectacular of all of the trees in Latin America. Its towering, branching size can dominate a landscape. Its exotic thorns, its sprawling buttress roots, its cavernous spaces high in the forest tree line, and its enormous, cathedral-like presence all provide evidence of its magnificence, and its desirability.

Having a chance to see the mighty ceiba up close has been part of an extraordinary adventure. Our little team has offered up a microcosm of wonderful messages, to be bent toward trees and their futures. Take direction from experts, but see for yourself. Understand the living world in as broad a context as possible. There's usually a river nearby, providing a route to and from the forest, for most of us can't live among the trees forever; we need to return to our homes and our haunts to do work that can sharpen the planet's survival strategies. Be watchful and anticipate danger from all quarters, but don't dwell on it. Be joyous in your appreciation of the natural world.

In Praise of Recording, Reporting, and Remembering

Then a voice like a howling wind deep in the leaves said:
I'll tell you a story
about a seed.

—Mary Oliver, "Banyan," *Poetry* magazine, 1985

In 1958, on the summit of Mauna Kea, on the Big Island of Hawai'i, the environmental chemist Charles David Keeling began recording the accumulation of carbon dioxide in the atmosphere. The curve, when graphed, traveled up and to the right in a stair-stepped, unambiguous path, providing the first significant evidence to the world of the increase in carbon dioxide in our atmosphere. He had discovered Earth's breathing cycle. Keeling chose Mauna Kea because of its remoteness from continents, and because it had no nearby vegetation or dust to contaminate the readings. He persisted in his recordkeeping. When he ran out of funding in the mid-1960s, he moved the recording operation to the other big mountain on the island, Mauna Loa. The recordings of the Keeling Curve continue up through today. Because of Keeling's work, NOAA began to pay attention to carbon dioxide emissions, and to monitor them around the planet. Many other isolated sites have now been monitoring the greenhouse gas for years, confirming Keeling's findings, and going from a matter of theory to a matter of fact.

We record so that we can remember, plan, act, and memorialize. Without evidence, we forget our successes, our failures, and our germinating ideas. Science is a collective form of remembering but not a static one, for gathering knowledge moves science forward. The dozens of people detailed in this book have come to know trees and their pasts, presents, and futures in very large part through recordkeeping. Oral traditions are resonant with elegance, and can provide essential records from long ago, but the written record is different. Perhaps you've played the "whisper around a campfire" game, where you're given a short phrase to breathe quietly into the ear of your neighbor, who passes it to their neighbor, until it arrives at the last person in the circle. The final product is frequently unintelligible. But four-cornered documents, and now their electronic counterparts, give us stable footing. They allow for nuance at the same time that they support precision, reflection, and doubling back on an idea.

The science fiction writer Octavia Butler's ideas about keeping track appear in her book *Parable of the Sower*, where her character Lauren Oya Olamina maintains a journal, using it to develop a new set of ideas about the Earth's fragility and to inscribe new ways to think about the planet and its spiritual dress. Butler knew the importance of recordkeeping at a deep, instinctual level. Her seven thousand letters, journals, and diaries are at the Huntington Library, some of them kept in what she called commonplace books—a lovely, old-fashioned nomenclatural nod to earlier centuries of recordkeeping. She jotted down grocery lists, phone numbers, story sketches, quotidian tasks, and big ideas for her books. Her rough writings were her route to her published texts. She understood the ways that recordkeeping, above all else, was a connection: between her, her writing, and the universe. "Seed to tree, tree to forest; rain to river, river to sea; grubs to bees, bees to swarm. From one, many; from many, one; forever uniting, growing, dissolving," she wrote in *Parable of the Sower*.

Records connect us but also keep us accountable. There are different kinds of recordings, and all sorts of recorders. Memory is a slippery rascal, and evidence can be hard to come by. There's a reason that courts have stenographers, and students get grades, and undercover agents wear wires. Be a documenter. Outline and write and draft and draw and assemble. Keep track of the world. The planet's stories are all told in parts. Leave a record for the future, as our progenitors have done for us. Recordkeeping has gotten us where we are today.

The work of trees' outdoor partners—field naturalists, samplers, climbers, and counters—is matched by other partnerships that involve numerous and often overlooked literary labors: poring through a huge body of textual material, engaging in scholarship, and ultimately in publication. Without the written record, there would be no news of changes in science, no new discoveries, no claims. Praise be to writers who peer-review papers, craft journal articles, publish monographs, and populate the pages of the popular press. At the risk of waxing oxymoronic, let's call them indoor tree people. Scientists and others have written more than sixty thousand scholarly articles and many dozens of books about these twelve trees in just the last four years, with no slowing in sight. Understanding and interpreting trees, and their comparative international lives, takes a scholarly village, working across different cultures and in different languages, but all in the argot of science. Very often, the indoor work is also done by the outdoor people, creating a trajectory from field to footnote.

Fieldwork is a messy, essential, and often exhilarating discipline in the natural sciences, and writing pushes that work into the public sphere.

But there's another allied aspect of natural history work that warrants shoulders, arms, and hands to the wheel: the work done in libraries and in natural history museums' study collections to validate, inform, support, or disprove fieldwork. Collections work is the close cousin of recording and reporting. You can volunteer in these indoor places as well, joining a group of people whom nineteenth-century observers called, not unaffectionately, "closet naturalists." Many of these tasks involve amassing, organizing, and describing, and then doing comparative work: preserving specimens, and then looking at examples laid out across a table to reveal differences and similarities. To understand a species in physical form is to know what its biological allies are. Collections managers are the unsung heroes of the biological sciences, for they keep the archives of the possible. And discoveries still await not just in the field but in museum collections, where specimens—sometimes ones decades old—can be revisited to reveal new truths, ready to take their places in the skein of our understandings of evolution and survival.

And finally: recording and research don't just inform science. Learning the nuances of broader notions such as identity and camaraderie gives us context. It's a satisfaction to keep learning new tricks and to visit new tableaux. Make investigations. Seek to understand more deeply. Travel to the margins and stake your claim. *Carpamus diem*— let's seize the day together. In every context, relationships matter. A lot of the collective work we need to do for trees begins by acting with kinship. The best and most useful tree jobs are partnerships. If we can't foster good relations with one another, we can't build the strongest possible network to save trees. Cooperate, don't battle. Leave competition to the natural world, for in that evolutionary action, undertaken without value judgments, ill will, or any other human frailties, lies a good part of trees' salvation. They're born to succeed.

ACKNOWLEDGMENTS

Working at the Huntington Library, Art Museum, and Botanical Gardens in Southern California, where I've had a long and engrossing career, has meant access to some of the planet's best botanists, many of whom read portions of the text, talked with me about relevant matters, corrected errors and misconceptions, and much more. Thanks to Jim Folsom, the previous Director of the Gardens; Nicole Cavender, current Director; Sean Lahmeyer, Plant Collections and Conservation Manager; Brian Dorsey, Senior Systematic and Conservation Botanist; Raquel Folgado, Cryopreservation Botanist; Kathy Musial, Curator of Living Collections; Ted Matson, Curator of the Bonsai Collections; and in the Library, Steve Tabor, Curator of Rare Books. My thanks also to my terrific boss Sandra Brooke Gordon, the Director of the Library, for her enthusiasm, daily bonhomie, and extraordinary support—and not just for me but for all fourteen library curators.

Being at the Huntington also means I'm surrounded by a cohort of exceptional researchers, scholars, and collections. Ed Larson made a number of useful suggestions; Alan Marcus read the entire manuscript. Many others passing through my daily orbit made suggestions, asked useful questions, and talked about the topic with me over many lunches and gallons of coffee. Kristen Brownell undertook early research on the book on my behalf and made a suggestion one day that proved to be the kernel of the project.

To those who appear in these pages as subjects, or who helped behind the scenes, in depth or in passing, my thanks: Jerry Beranek, pioneer climber of the ancient coast redwoods; Dave Bottjer, paleontologist at the University of Southern California; palynologist Stephen Blackmore, His Majesty's Botanist in Scotland; Joe Burnett, the California Condor Recovery Program Manager at the Ventana Society; Faya Causey, who was at the Getty Research Institute; Vincent Deblauwe of the Congo Basin Institute in Cameroon; Vidal de Teresa of Madinter; Miguel Garcia of Perú Amazing Jungle; Susan Miller of the US Fish & Wildlife Service; Scott Paul, Taylor Guitars' Director of Natural Resource Sustainability, who graciously shared his deep knowledge of forest conservation across the length of the project; the late and greatly missed Jay Pasachoff of Williams College; Terri Edillon of the NSF Office of Polar Programs; Jaime Espejo of the National Botanic Garden of Viña del Mar in Chile; Kerry Cawse-Nicholson and David Thompson, climate scientists at NASA's Jet Propulsion Laboratory in Pasadena; olive-tasting authority Orietta Gianjorio; olive producer Arden Kremer; Björn Aldén and Åsa Krüger of the Gothenburg Botanical Garden in Sweden; climate change journalist Eugene Linden; Mike Maunder of the Cambridge Conservation Initiative; physician Mario Molina; Tom Senty, culinary manager for McMurdo Station in the Antarctic; Jesse Wimberley of the North Carolina Sandhills Prescribed Burn Association; and my bestie Bill Wheaton, a geospatial data expert who provided a few key bits for the book. Special thanks to the scientific staff at the remarkable Laboratory of Tree-Ring Research in Tucson, Arizona, where director David Frank spent a generous dollop of time with me during my two-day visit, as well as to the research scientists Matt Salzer, Connie Woodhouse, and Malcolm Hughes; and to the LTRR scientist Valerie Trouet, whose work and writing was essentially useful. My gratitude also to Rob Bartels, who read and commented on the entire manuscript; my Peru boys, who occupy a substantial part of the final chapter of the book; Eric Nyquist, the fiercely talented and highly collaborative artist who did the artwork; my agent, Wendy Strothman, who offered exactly the right tincture of editorial rigor and encouragement in helping me shape the book in its formative stages; Carolyn Kelly at Avid Reader Press; and Ben Loehnen, my editor at Avid Reader. Ben knew what the book needed even when (and especially when) I did not, and he has changed me forever as a writer, helping me craft a better story at every turn.

Finally, thanks to my wife, Pam, the inner chamber of my heart, and still the smartest, funniest, and most dedicated person I've ever known; and to our freaky, astonishing kids, Paxton and Kelso, who are probably really tired of hearing about trees.

NOTES

PREFACE

1. This quote is scrawled in Muir's copy of *The Prose Works of Ralph Waldo Emerson* (Boston: Fields, Osgood & Co., 1870), held by the Beinecke Rare Book and Manuscript Library, call number Za Em34 C869. It's written in pencil by Muir on the back flyleaf of the book.
2. Dorothy Wickenden, "Wendell Berry's Advice for a Cataclysmic Age," *New Yorker*, February 28, 2022.
3. Roberto Cazzolla Gatti et al., "The Number of Tree Species on Earth," *Proceedings of the National Academy of Sciences* 119, no. 6 (2022): e2115329119.

CHAPTER 1 · A BOOK OLDER THAN GOD: THE GREAT BASIN BRISTLECONE PINE

1. Stephen Tabor, personal communication with the author, October and November 2020.
2. Ronald M. Lanner, "Living a Long Life," chap. 3 in *The Bristlecone Pine Book* (Missoula, MT: Mountain Press Publishing, 2007). I've tried to channel Lanner's marvelous details in my own terms.
3. Matthew W. Salzer, Malcolm K. Hughes, Andrew G. Bunn, and Kurt F. Kipfmueller, "Recent Unprecedented Tree-Ring Growth in Bristlecone Pine at the Highest Elevations and Possible Causes," *Proceedings of the National Academy of Sciences* 106, no. 48 (2009): 20348–53.

4. Thanks to Ronald Lanner for the skyscraper analogy in his *Bristlecone Pine Book*, 23.

5. Ronald M. Lanner, "Dependence of Great Basin Bristlecone Pine on Clark's Nutcracker for Regeneration at High Elevations," *Arctic and Alpine Research* 20, no. 3 (1988): 358–62. "Stem clumping of pines in the subalpine zone is known to result from the activities of nutcrackers, and not known to result from the activities of other species."

6. An excellent and essential book on bird intelligence is Jennifer Ackerman's *The Genius of Birds* (New York: Penguin, 2016).

7. Robert M. Lanner, *Made for Each Other: A Symbiosis of Birds and Pines* (New York: Oxford University Press, 1996).

8. R. Croston et al., "Individual Variation in Spatial Memory Performance in Wild Mountain Chickadees from Different Elevations," *Animal Behaviour* 111 (2016): 225–34.

9. An LTRR scientist has recently written a lively and authoritative book on tree rings: Valerie Trouet, *Tree Story: The History of the World Written in Rings* (Baltimore: Johns Hopkins University Press, 2020); her book provided or reinforced a few key details in this chapter.

10. Andrew Ellicott Douglass, "The Secret of the Southwest Solved by Talkative Tree Rings," *National Geographic* 56, no. 6 (1929): 737–70.

11. Douglass, 763.

12. David Frank, interview, May 5, 2022.

CHAPTER 2 · AWESOME MATTERS: THE COAST REDWOOD

1. Natalie Breidenbach, Oliver Gailing, and Konstantin V. Krutovsky, "Genetic Structure of Coast Redwood (*Sequoia sempervirens* [D. Don] Endl.) Populations in and outside of the Natural Distribution Range Based on Nuclear and Chloroplast Microsatellite Markers," *PLOS ONE* 15, no. 12 (2020): e0243556.

2. A key reference is Reed F. Noss, ed., *The Redwood Forest: History, Ecology, and Conservation of the Coast Redwoods* (Washington, DC: Island Press, 1999).

3. Statue of Liberty weight from the National Park Service: https://www.nps.gov/stli/learn/historyculture/statue-statistics.htm.

4. Gerald Beranek, *Coast Redwood: Tree of Dreams and Fortune* (Fort Bragg, CA: Beranek Publications, 2013), 245, 247. The very first person, at least

a white person, to have climbed a redwood to any height was apparently Richard Vasey, a forestry grad student, in 1965.

5. Jerry Beranek, personal communication with the author, September 3, 2020.

6. Jerry Beranek, personal communication with the author, September 2, 2020.

7. Michael A. Camann, Karen L. Lamoncha, and Clinton B. Jones, "Old-Growth Redwood Forest Canopy Arthropod Prey Base for Arboreal Wandering Salamanders: A Report Prepared for the Save-the-Redwoods League" (Arcata, CA: Humboldt State University, 2000); and Christian E. Brown et al., "Gliding and Parachuting by Arboreal Salamanders," *Current Biology* 32, no. 10 (2022): R453–54, https://doi.org/10.1016/j.cub .2022.04.033.

8. Mika Bendiksby, Rikke Reese Næsborg, and Einar Timdal, "*Xylopsora canopeorum* (Umbilicariaceae), a New Lichen Species from the Canopy of *Sequoia sempervirens*," *MycoKeys* 30 (2018): 1.

9. Scott L. Stephens and Danny L. Fry, "Fire History in Coast Redwood Stands in the Northeastern Santa Cruz Mountains, California," *Fire Ecology* 1, no. 1 (2005): 2–19; Robin Wall Kimmerer and Frank Kanawha Lake, "The Role of Indigenous Burning in Land Management," *Journal of Forestry* 99, no. 11 (2001): 36–41.

10. Humboldt Redwoods Project: https://hsuredwoodsproject.omeka.net /exhibits/show/redwoodobject/native-use-of-redwood, retrieved May 12, 2021.

11. Deborah H. Carver, *Native Stories of Earthquake and Tsunamis, Redwood National Park, California* (Crescent City, CA: National Park Service, Redwood National and State Parks, 1998), 1.

12. Gordon C. Jacoby, Daniel E. Bunker, and Boyd E. Benson, "Tree-Ring Evidence for an AD 1700 Cascadia Earthquake in Washington and Northern Oregon," *Geology* 25, no. 11 (1997): 999–1002. For burl details and photo, see Peter Del Tredici, "Redwood Burls: Immortality Underground," *Arnoldia* 59, no. 3 (1999): 14–22.

13. Mojgan Mahdizadeh and Will Russell, "Initial Floristic Response to High Severity Wildfire in an Old-Growth Coast Redwood (*Sequoia sempervirens* [D. Don] Endl.) Forest," *Forests* 12, no. 8 (2021): 1135, https://doi.org/10 .3390/f12081135.

14. Joe Quirk et al., "Increased Susceptibility to Drought-Induced Mortality in *Sequoia sempervirens* (Cupressaceae) Trees under Cenozoic Atmospheric

Carbon Dioxide Starvation," *American Journal of Botany* 100, no. 3 (2013): 582–91, https://doi.org/10.3732/ajb.1200435.

15. Christa M. Dagley et al., "Adaptation to Climate Change? Moving Coast Redwood Seedlings Northward and Inland," *Proceedings of the Coast Redwood Science Symposium—2016* (US Department of Agriculture, Forest Service, Pacific Southwest Research Station, 2017): 219–27, 258. See also Amanda R. De La Torre et al., "Genome-Wide Association Identifies Candidate Genes for Drought Tolerance in Coast Redwood and Giant Sequoia," *Plant Journal* 109, no. 1 (2022): 7–22, https://doi.org/10.1111/tpj.15592.

16. Richard Preston, "Climbing the Redwoods," *New Yorker*, February 14 and 21, 2005, 222.

17. By far the most evocative and useful book on spore-producing organisms is Merlin Sheldrake's *Entangled Life* (New York: Random House, 2020).

18. Anne Lamott, *Small Victories: Spotting Improbable Moments of Grace* (New York: Riverhead Books, 2014), 3.

19. For a technical but excellent overview of VOCs and plants, see Dušan Materić, Dan Bruhn, Claire Turner, Geraint Morgan, Nigel Mason, and Vincent Gauci, "Methods in Plant Foliar Volatile Organic Compounds Research," *Applications in Plant Sciences* 3, no. 12 (2015): 1500044, https://doi.org/10.3732/apps.1500044.

20. Caroll Hermann, "Report on Self-Management of Mental Wellbeing Using Bonsai as an Ecotherapeutic Art Tool," *Preprints* (2020), https://doi.org/10.20944/preprints202008.0190.v1.

21. Ted Matson, in "What Bonsai Can Teach Us about Patience," May 4, 2021, https://soundcloud.com/thehuntington/what-bonsai-can-teach-us-about-patience.

22. Matson, https://soundcloud.com/thehuntington/what-bonsai-can-teach-us-about-patience.

23. Matson, https://soundcloud.com/thehuntington/what-bonsai-can-teach-us-about-patience.

24. Christopher Stone, "Should Trees Have Standing? Toward Legal Rights for Natural Objects," *Southern California Law Review* 45, no. 2 (Spring 1972): 450–501. Elizabeth Kolbert most recently brought this issue into national public view in a 2022 article, "A Lake in Florida Suing to Protect Itself," *New Yorker*, April 11, 2022.

25. Robin Wall Kimmerer, "Learning the Grammar of Animacy," in *Braiding Sweetgrass* (Minneapolis: Milkweed Editions, 2013), 48–59.

26. Paco Calvo, Monica Gagliano, Gustavo M. Souza, and Anthony Trewavas, "Plants Are Intelligent, Here's How," *Annals of Botany* 125, no. 1 (2020): 11–28.

27. Ricardo Gutiérrez Aguilar, ed., *Empathy: Emotional, Ethical and Epistemological Narratives* (Leiden, Netherlands: Brill, 2019).

CHAPTER 3 · EARTH WORK:
THE NEARLY LOST TREE OF RAPA NUI

1. Mike Maunder has written extensively about the toromiro; see, for instance, Mike Maunder et al., "Conservation of the Toromiro Tree: Case Study in the Management of a Plant Extinct in the Wild," *Conservation Biology* 14, no. 5 (2000): 1341–50.

2. Mauricio Lima, E. M. Gayo, C. Latorre, C. M. Santoro, S. A. Estay, Núria Cañellas-Boltà, Olga Margalef et al., "Ecology of the Collapse of Rapa Nui Society," *Proceedings of the Royal Society B* 287, no. 1929 (May 2020): 20200662, https://dx.doi.org/10.1098/rspb.2020.0662.

3. Z. Zhongming et al., Binghamton University, "Resilience, Not Collapse: What the Easter Island Myth Gets Wrong," *Science Daily*, July 13, 2021, https://phys.org/news/2021-07-resilience-collapse-easter-island-myth.html.

4. V. Rull, N. Cañellas-Boltà, A. Sáez, S. Giralt, S. Pla, and O. Margalef, "Paleoecology of Easter Island: Evidence and Uncertainties," *Earth-Science Reviews* 99, no. 1–2 (2010): 50–60, https://doi.org/10.1016/j.earscirev.2010.02.003.

5. Steven Roger Fischer, *Island at the End of the World: The Turbulent History of Easter Island* (London: Reaktion Books, 2005), 44.

6. Björn Aldén, personal communication with the author, July 3, 2020.

7. Sheldrake, *Entangled Life*, 149.

8. Jaime Espejo, personal communication with the author, July 28, 2020.

9. Robert J. Cabin, *Restoring Paradise: Rethinking and Rebuilding Nature in Hawai'i* (Honolulu: University of Hawai'i Press, 2013).

10. George Pararas-Carayannis and P. J. Calebaugh, *Catalog of Tsunamis in Hawaii, Revised and Updated* (Boulder, CO: World Data Center A for Solid Earth Geophysics, NOAA, March 1977).

11. Olga Margalef et al., "Revisiting the Role of High-Energy Pacific Events in the Environmental and Cultural History of Easter Island (Rapa Nui)," *Geographical Journal* 184, no. 3 (2018): 310–22, https://doi.org/10.1111/geoj.12253.

12. Kathryn A. Hurr, Peter J. Lockhart, Peter B. Heenan, and David Penny, "Evidence for the Recent Dispersal of *Sophora* (Leguminosae) around the Southern Oceans: Molecular Data," *Journal of Biogeography* 26, no. 3 (1999): 565–77.

13. Jaime Espejo, personal communications with the author, numerous dates in 2021 and 2022.

CHAPTER 4 · FINDING TIME: AMBER, INSECTS, AND A FOSSIL TREE

1. As with virtually all fossil trees, *H. protera* has no common name. The lack of a common name isn't really for any precise biological reason. Scientific names are universal and necessary identifiers, but common names vary by language and are essentially vernacular. Common names are friendly. They point to whole organisms we can readily see, or touch, or hold, or get next to. But fossil trees, none of which look how they did when they were alive, occupy different taxonomic territory: worthy of a nomenclatural identifier, but not quite suited to a common name.

2. Bob Goldstein and Mark Blaxter, "Tardigrades," *Current Biology* 12, no. 14 (2002): R475.

3. G. O. Poinar, "*Hymenaea protera* sp.n. (Leguminosae, Caesalpinioideae) from Dominican Amber Has African Affinities," *Experientia* 47 (1991): 1075–82, https://doi.org/10.1007/BF01923347.

4. J. H. Langenheim, "How Is Resin Fossilized and When Is It Amber?," in *Plant Resins: Chemistry, Evolution, Ecology and Ethnobotany* (Portland, OR: Timber Press, 2004), 144–47.

5. There is disagreement about just what constitutes a "fossil" across numerous scientific disciplines. Many scientists speak of amber's contents as fossils. But it's the amber that's fossilized, not the contents of the amber. I'm working with the most regular and traditional definition.

6. H. N. Poinar, R. R. Melzer, and G. O. Poinar, "Ultrastructure of 30–40 Million Year Old Leaflets from Dominican Amber (*Hymenaea protera*, Fabaceae: Angiospermae)," *Experientia* 52 (1996): 387–90, https://doi.org

/10.1007/BF01919546; and David Grimaldi, "Captured in Amber," *Scientific American* 274, no. 4 (April 1996): 84–91.

7. Katharine Gammon, "The Human Cost of Amber," *Atlantic*, August 2, 2019.

8. Langenheim, *Plant Resins*.

9. David Grimaldi, *Amber: Window to the Past* (New York: Abrams, 1996), 87.

10. Claire Thomas, "Saving a Venomous Ghost," *Science* 325, no. 5940 (2009): 531, https://doi.org/10.1126/science.325_531. Forget about your fear of insects; you might be worse off encountering *Solenodon paradoxus*, a critically endangered Hispaniolan solenodon—a shrew-like animal that is, impressively, one of very few venomous mammals in the world, delivering its poison through its saliva, flowing from its salivary glands to grooves in two of its teeth.

11. See, for example, David Peris et al., "DNA from Resin-Embedded Organisms: Past, Present and Future," *PLOS ONE* 15, no. 9 (2020): e0239521, https://doi.org/10.1371/journal.pone.0239521; and Alessandra Modi et al., "Successful Extraction of Insect DNA from Recent Copal Inclusions: Limits and Perspectives," *Scientific Reports* 11, no. 1 (2021), https://doi.org/10.1038/s41598-021-86058-9.

12. Joshua Sokol, "Troubled Treasure," *Science*, May 23, 2019; G. O. Poinar and R. Hess, "Ultrastructure of 40-Million-Year-Old Insect Tissue," *Science* 215, no. 4537 (1982): 1241–42, https://doi.org/10.1126/science.215.4537.1241.

13. G. Poinar Jr., "A New Genus of Fleas with Associated Microorganisms in Dominican Amber," *Journal of Medical Entomology* 52, no. 6 (November 2015): 1234–40.

14. David Penney, ed., "Dominican Amber," chap. 2 in *Biodiversity of Fossils in Amber from the Major World Deposits* (Manchester, UK: Siri Scientific Press, 2010), 22–39.

15. Gammon, "The Human Cost of Amber"; Faya Causey, *Amber and the Ancient World* (Los Angeles: Getty Publications, 2011); Penney, ed., *Biodiversity of Fossils in Amber*.

16. Carl Folke, Steve Carpenter, Brian Walker, Marten Scheffer, Thomas Elmqvist, Lance Gunderson, and C. S. Holling, "Regime Shifts, Resilience, and Biodiversity in Ecosystem Management," *Annual Review of Ecology, Evolution, and Systematics* 35, no. 1 (2004): 557–81, https://doi.org/10.1146/annurev.ecolsys.35.021103.105711; and Craig Moritz and

Rosa Agudo, "The Future of Species under Climate Change: Resilience or Decline?," *Science* 341, no. 6145 (2013): 504–8.

CHAPTER 5 · UNDERSTORY ALLIANCE: THE LONGLEAF PINE AND ITS FIERY PARTNERS

1. David Printiss, TNC North Florida Conservation Manager, in https://www.nature.org/en-us/about-us/where-we-work/united-states/florida/stories-in-florida/longleaf/.

2. "Longleaf Pine: A Tree for Our Time," The Nature Conservancy, October 25, 2022, https://www.nature.org/en-us/what-we-do/our-priorities/protect-water-and-land/land-and-water-stories/longleaf-pine-restoration/

3. Visit to Bowman Road area, Pinehurst, NC, for prescribed burn, with North Carolina Sandhills Prescribed Burn Association, March 6, 2020; also, Jesse Wimberley, personal communication with the author, August 4, 2020.

4. Nicole Barys, "Recovering the Florida Bog Frog," *Longleaf Leader* 13, no. 2 (Summer 2020): 8–9, https://issuu.com/thelongleafleader/docs/longleaf-leader-summer-2020-final/10.

5. Den Latham, *Painting the Landscape with Fire: Longleaf Pines and Fire Ecology* (Columbia: University of South Carolina Press, 2013), 172.

6. Jesse Wimberley, personal communication with the author, June 29 and November 26, 2021.

7. Bill Finch et al., *Longleaf, Far as the Eye Can See* (Chapel Hill: University of North Carolina Press, 2012), 15.

8. Cynthia Fowler and Evelyn Konopik, "The History of Fire in the United States," *Human Ecology Review* 14, no. 2 (Winter 2007): 166, 169.

9. Lawrence S. Earley, *Looking for Longleaf: The Fall and Rise of an American Forest* (Chapel Hill: University of North Carolina Press, 2004), 54–70.

10. David N. Bass, "Woodpecker Stirs Up Brunswick County," *Carolina Journal*, March 6, 2007; Allen G. Breed, "N.C. Landowners' Theory: No Wood, No Woodpeckers," *Washington Post*, September 24, 2006.

11. Associated Press, "Rare Woodpecker Sends a Town Running for Its Chain Saws," *New York Times*, September 24, 2006.

12. Susan Ladd Miller, US Fish & Wildlife Service, personal communication

with the author, September 2, 2020; details on policy: https://www.fws .gov/rcwrecovery/files/RecoveryPlan/private_lands_guidelines.pdf.

13. This is laid out in https://www.fws.gov/raleigh/pdfs/BSL/ltr_to_mayor2 .22.2006.pdf.

14. Jack Kerouac, untitled poem from a letter to Edie Kerouac-Parker, January 28, 1957, in *Jack Kerouac: Selected Letters, 1957–1969* (New York: Viking, 1999).

CHAPTER 6 · MAKING FOLK MEDICINE MODERN: THE ROAD OF THE EAST INDIAN SANDALWOOD TREE

1. Suresh Ramanan, Alex K. George, S. B. Chavan, Sudhir Kumar, and S. Jayasubha, "Progress and Future Research Trends on *Santalum album*: A Bibliometric and Science Mapping Approach," *Industrial Crops and Products* 158 (2020): 112972.

2. Dhanya Bhaskar, Syam Viswanath, and Seema Purushothaman, "Sandal (*Santalum album* L.) Conservation in Southern India: A Review of Policies and Their Impacts," *Journal of Tropical Agriculture* 48, no. 2 (2010): 1–10.

3. Bhaskar et al., 2.

4. Thammineni Pullaiah et al., eds., *Sandalwood: Silviculture, Conservation and Applications* (Singapore: Springer Singapore, 2021). Sandalwood is also mentioned in one of the oldest Indian epics, the *Ramayana*. Also see "Why Sandalwood Is So Expensive," *Insider Business*, 2022, https://www .youtube.com/watch?v=QPRpWg_wU0A.

5. Krishnaraj Iyengar, "Sandalwood in Indian Culture," in A. N. Arunkumar, G. Joshi, R. R. Warrier, and N. N. Karaba, eds., *Indian Sandalwood. Materials Horizons: From Nature to Nanomaterials* (Singapore: Springer Singapore, 2022), 45–58, https://doi.org/10.1007/978-981-16-6565-3_3.

6. For the history of the wood in Hawai'i, see Harold St. John, "The History, Present Distribution, and Abundance of Sandalwood on Oahu, Hawaiian Islands," *Hawaiian Plant Studies* 14 (1947). Also see labeled herbaria samples, such as this one found on the northeast slope of Ko'olau Mountain on Oahu in 1961: https://s.idigbio.org/idigbio-images-prod-webview /2f17e006c5c16e3e8a003a4103033eb8.jpg.

7. Pamela Statham, "The Sandalwood Industry in Australia: A History," in Lawrence Hamilton and C. Eugene Conrad, technical coordinators,

Proceedings of the Symposium on Sandalwood in the Pacific; April 9–11, 1990, Honolulu, Hawaii (Berkeley, CA: USDA Forest Service, Pacific Southwest Research Station, General Technical Report PSW-122, 1990), 26–38. Gandhi funeral pyre details in *North Queensland Register*, September 22, 1979.

8. Sebastian Pole, *Ayurvedic Medicine: The Principles of Traditional Practice* (Edinburgh: Churchill Livingstone Elsevier, 2006), 262–63.

9. V. S. Venkatesha Gowda, K. B. Patil, and D. S. Ashwath, "Manufacturing of Sandalwood Oil, Market Potential Demand and Use," *Journal of Essential Oil Bearing Plants* 7, no. 3 (2004): 293–97.

10. Delphy Rocha and A. V. Santhoshkumar, "Host Plant Influence on Haustorial Growth and Development of Indian Sandalwood (*Santalum album*)," in A. N. Arunkumar et al., eds., *Indian Sandalwood*, 229–44, https://doi.org/10.1007/978-981-16-6565-3_15.

11. S. K. Dash and J. C. R. Hunt, "Variability of Climate Change in India," *Current Science* 93, no. 6 (2007): 782–88.

12. Shaheen Lakhan et al., "The Effectiveness of Aromatherapy in Reducing Pain: A Systematic Review and Meta-Analysis," *Pain Research and Treatment* 2016, https://dx.doi.org/10.1155/2016/8158693.

13. Rachel S. Herz, James Eliassen, Sophia Beland, and Timothy Souza, "Neuroimaging Evidence for the Emotional Potency of Odor-Evoked Memory," *Neuropsychologia* 42, no. 3 (2004): 371–78, https://doi.org/10.1016/j.neuropsychologia.2003.08.009.

14. Mark Plotkin, "Could the Amazon Save Your Life?" *New York Times*, October 2, 2020, https://www.nytimes.com/2020/10/02/opinion/amazon-novel-species-medicine.html.

15. Darrell Posey, "Intellectual Property Rights and Just Compensation for Indigenous Knowledge," *Anthropology Today* 6, no. 4 (1990): 13–16. On pharmacognosy, see Haidan Yuan, Qianqian Ma, Li Ye, and Guangchun Piao, "Traditional Medicine and Modern Medicine from Natural Products," *Molecules* 21, no. 5 (2016): 559, https://doi.org/10.3390/molecules21050559.

16. Mario Molina, interview with the author, October 7, 2020.

17. "Cannabis Strains: How Many Different Kinds Are There?," Medwell Health and Wellness Center, https://www.medwellhealth.net/cannabis-strains-different-kinds/, retrieved May 28, 2021.

18. Sreevidya Santha and Chandradhar Dwivedi, "Anticancer Effects of Sandalwood (*Santalum album*)," *Anticancer Research* 35, no. 6 (2015): 3137–45.

19. P. Balasubramanian, R. Aruna, C. Anbarasu, and E. Santhoshkumar, "Avian Frugivory and Seed Dispersal of Indian Sandalwood *Santalum album* in Tamil Nadu, India," *Journal of Threatened Taxa* 3, no. 5 (2011), https://doi.org/10.11609/jott.o2552.1775-7.

20. Jaime A. Teixeira Da Silva, "Sandalwood Spike Disease: A Brief Synthesis," *Environmental and Experimental Biology* 14, no. 4 (2016): 199–204, https://doi.org/10.22364/eeb.14.26; S. N. Rai and C. R. Sarma, "Depleting Sandalwood and Rising Prices," *Indian Forester* 116, no. 5 (1990): 352.

CHAPTER 7 · A LAWFUL LOT OF WOOD: CENTRAL AFRICAN FOREST EBONY

1. Peter Lowry, an ebony and rosewood expert at the Missouri Botanical Garden, calls the Madagascar ebony wood trade the "equivalent of Africa's blood diamonds": Eric Felten, "Guitar Frets: Environmental Enforcement Leaves Musicians in Fear," *Wall Street Journal*, August 26, 2011.

2. Yoshikazu Yazaki, "Wood Colors and Their Coloring Matters: A Review," *Natural Product Communications* 10, no. 3 (2015): 1934578X1501000332; see also Vincent Deblauwe, "Life History, Uses, Trade and Management of *Diospyros crassiflora* Hiern, the Ebony Tree of the Central African Forests: A State of Knowledge," *Forest Ecology and Management* 481 (2021) 1186551: 1.

3. Much of this chapter is informed by Vincent Deblauwe's comprehensive article "Life History," as well as by numerous personal communications.

4. Deblauwe also cites the text of this law. Regarding Ethiopian tree planting, see also Palko Karasz, "Ethiopia Says It Planted over 350 Million Trees in a Day, a Record," *New York Times*, July 30, 2019. See also "A Future for Ebony in Cameroon," Food and Agriculture Organization of the United Nations, n.d., https://www.fao.org/forestry/47166-0a49139515d4dc5e80fd2154cd20ac7f3.pdf. On DBH, see Yasha A. S. Magarik, Lara A. Roman, and Jason G. Henning, "How Should We Measure the DBH of Multi-Stemmed Urban Trees?," *Urban Forestry & Urban Greening* 47 (2020): 126481.

5. Deblauwe, "Life History," 1.

6. Calvin W. Myint et al., "Fiddler's Neck: A Review," *Ear, Nose & Throat*

Journal, 96, no. 2 (February 2017): 76–79. Pool cue detail from Deblauwe's Supplementary Material, S3; other details from various sources but including William A. Lincoln, *World Woods in Colour* (London: Stobart & Son, 1986), 91. On neck hickeys, see T. Gambichler, S. Boms, and M. Freitag, "Contact Dermatitis and Other Skin Conditions in Instrumental Musicians," *BMC Dermatology* 4, no. 3 (2004), https://doi.org/10.1186/1471-5945-4-3; and Scott C. Rackett and Kathryn A. Zug, "Contact Dermatitis to Multiple Exotic Woods," *American Journal of Contact Dermatitis* 8, no. 2: 114–17, https://doi.org/10.1016/S1046-199X(97)90004-X; along with mentions in a wide range of popular literature.

7. "Persimmon Production in 2018; Crops/World Regions/Production Quantity (from Pick Lists)," Food and Agriculture Organization of the United Nations: Division of Statistics (FAOSTAT), 2019.

8. Preferred by Nature, "Timber Legality Risk Assessment: Cameroon," https://sourcinghub.preferredbynature.org/country-risk-profiles/.

9. Julie C. Aleman, Marta A. Jarzyna, and A. Carla Staver, "Forest Extent and Deforestation in Tropical Africa Since 1900," *Nature Ecology & Evolution* 2, no. 1 (2018): 26–33, https://doi.org/10.1038/s41559-017-0406-1.

10. D. Foundjem-Tita, L. A. Duguma, S. Speelman, and S. M. Piabuo, "Viability of Community Forests as Social Enterprises: A Cameroon Case Study," *Ecology and Society* 23 (2018), https://doi.org/10.5751/es-10651-230450.

11. "International Illegal Logging: Background and Issues," Congressional Research Service, February 26, 2019, https://fas.org/sgp/crs/misc/IF11114.pdf.

12. See, for instance, Glenn Hurowitz, "Guitar Antihero 1: How Gibson Guitars Made Illegal Logging a Cause Célèbre," *Grist*, September 28, 2011, https://grist.org/politics/2011-09-27-guitar-antihero/.

13. Statistics: Bradley C. Bennett, "The Sound of Trees: Wood Selection in Guitars and Other Chordophones," *Economic Botany* 70, no. 1 (2016): 49–63; Scott Paul, Director of Natural Resource Sustainability, Taylor Guitars, personal communication with the author (Zoom interview), December 7, 2020.

14. P. Etoungou, "Decentralization Viewed from Inside: The Implementation of Community Forests in East Cameroon," Environmental Governance in Africa Working Paper Series (WRI), no. 12 (Washington, DC: World Resources Institute, 2003).

15. Li-Wen Lin, "Mandatory Corporate Social Responsibility Legislation around the World: Emergent Varieties and National Experiences," *University of Pennsylvania Journal of Business Law* 23, no. 2 (2020): 429–69.

16. "U.S. Lacey Act," Forest Legality Initiative website, https://forestlegality.org/policy/us-lacey-act; see also Jeffrey P. Prestemon, "The Impacts of the Lacey Act Amendment of 2008 on US Hardwood Lumber and Hardwood Plywood Imports," *Forest Policy and Economics* 50 (2015): 31–44.

17. "Why Ebony Matters: How Taylor Got into the Ebony Business," Chapter 1, https://www.taylorguitars.com/ebonyproject/why-ebony-matters/.

18. Various sources, including Scott Paul, personal communication with the author, December 7, 2020, and Timber Trade Portal industry profile on Cameroon, https://www.timbertradeportal.com/countries/cameroon/.

19. World Bank, "Silent and Lethal: How Quiet Corruption Undermines Africa's Development Efforts," in *Africa Development Indicators 2010* (Washington, DC: World Bank, 2010), 15 (Table 4).

20. Guiseppe Topa et al., *The Rainforests of Cameroon: Experience and Evidence from a Decade of Reform* (Washington, DC: World Bank, 2009).

21. Oral history interview with Vidal de Teresa, February 11, 2020, National Association of Music Merchants (NAMM), https://www.namm.org/library/oral-history/vidal-de-teresa.

22. Cheryl Palm, Stephen A. Vosti, Pedro A. Sanchez, and Polly J. Ericksen, eds., *Slash-and-Burn Agriculture: The Search for Alternatives* (New York: Columbia University Press, 2005).

23. Nadia Rabesahala Horning, *The Politics of Deforestation in Africa: Madagascar, Tanzania, and Uganda* (Cham, Switzerland: Palgrave Macmillan, 2018). See also Mark Omorovie Ikeke, "The Forest in African Traditional Thought and Practice: An Ecophilosophical Discourse," *Open Journal of Philosophy* 3, no. 2 (2013): 345–50, https://doi.org/10.4236/ojpp.2013.32052.

24. Deblauwe, personal communication with the author, January 19, 2023.

25. Yoshikazu Yazaki, "Wood Colors and Their Coloring Matters: A Review," *Natural Product Communications* 10, no. 3 (2015): 1934578X1501000332.

26. W. E. Hillis and P. Soenardi, "Formation of Ebony and Streaked Woods," *IAWA Journal* 15, no. 4 (1994): 425–37.

27. Deblauwe, personal communication with the author, December 20, 2020.

28. G. E. Schatz et al., *Diospyros crassiflora. The IUCN Red List of Threatened*

Species (2019): e.T33048A2831968. https://dx.doi.org/10.2305/IUCN
.UK.2019-1.RLTS.T33048A2831968.en; IUCN *Diospyros* assessments:
E. Beech et al., *Global Survey of Ex situ Ebony Collections* (Richmond,
Surrey, UK: Botanic Gardens Conservation International, 2016).

CHAPTER 8 · BELONGING AND BEYOND: THE BLUE GUM EUCALYPTUS

1. The quote "Californians [. . .] ransack the world . . ." comes from *Garden and Forest*, October 22, 1890, 508–509. And the quote "Anyone who's had to live with blue gum . . ." comes from Peter Coates, *American Perceptions of Immigrant and Invasive Species: Strangers on the Land* (Berkeley: University of California Press, 2007), 136.

2. Alieta Eyles, Elizabeth A. Pinkard, Anthony P. O'Grady, Dale Worledge, and Charles R. Warren, "Role of Corticular Photosynthesis Following Defoliation in *Eucalyptus globulus*," *Plant, Cell & Environment* 32, no. 8 (2009): 1004–14, https://doi.org/10.1111/j.1365-3040.2009.01984.x.

3. Robin W. Doughty, *The Eucalyptus: A Natural and Commercial History of the Gum Tree* (Baltimore: Johns Hopkins University Press, 2000), 4.

4. Coates, *American Perceptions of Immigrant and Invasive Species*, 125.

5. Euc deaths: *Los Angeles Sentinel*, May 15, 1947, 1; and *Los Angeles Times*, "With Beauty Comes Danger," September 26, 1983.

6. Brian Palmer, "7 Billion Carbon Sinks: How Much Does Breathing Contribute to Climate Change?" *Slate*, August 13, 2009.

7. *National Geographic* video, "Human Footprint," 2008, https://youtu.be/B8Iw0TH2czQ.

8. Daniel Quinn, *Ishmael* (New York: Bantam Doubleday Dell, 1995), 37.

9. Alfred James McClatchie, *Eucalypts Cultivated in the United States* (Washington, DC: Government Printing Office, 1902), 14.

10. Erin Blakemore, "This Is What Happened When an Australian City Gave Trees Email Addresses," *Smithsonian*, July 8, 2015.

11. Harry M. Butte and Judith M. Taylor, *Tangible Memories: Californians and Their Gardens 1800–1950* (Xlibris, 2003), 90.

12. Abbott Kinney, *Eucalyptus* (Los Angeles: P. R. Baumgardt, 1895), i.

13. Jared Farmer, *Trees in Paradise: A California History* (New York: W. W. Norton, 2013), 117. Some cities, however, such as Bogotá in Colombia,

forged ahead with extensive, and ultimately disastrous, use of the tree for urban tramway systems.

14. *Los Angeles Evening Citizen News* (Hollywood), April 15, 1970, 24; and *Los Angeles Times*, April 11, 1970.

15. Los Angeles City Directory, 1910, 1743; Gordon Grant, "Eucalyptus: The Beloved Failure," *Los Angeles Times*, October 13, 1974, OC1; on euc as fuel: David Smollar, "Eucalyptus as Cash Crop? Excitement, Caution in California," *Los Angeles Times*, November 24, 1981, SD-CB.

16. *San Francisco Examiner*, October 21, 1991, 12.

17. *Los Angeles Times*, October 22, 1991, A6.

18. *Modesto Bee* (Sacramento, CA), October 24, 1991, 12.

19. Tom Treanor, "The Home Front," *Los Angeles Times*, January 27, 1942, A2.

20. Zach St. George, "The Burning Question in the East Bay Hills: Eucalyptus Is Flammable Compared to What?" *Bay Nature*, October–December 2016, https://baynature.org/article/burning-question-east-bay-hills-eucalyptus-flammable-compared/.

21. *USDA Forest Service Gypsy Moth Digest* (USDA Forest Service Gypsy Moth Digest 2.0.04 released on 11/10/2020), https://www.fs.usda.gov/naspf/programs/forest-health-protection/gypsy-moth-digest.

22. Henry David Thoreau, *Writings of Henry David Thoreau*, vol. 10 (Boston: Houghton Mifflin & Co., 1906), 89.

23. Alieta Eyles, Pierluigi Bonello, Rebecca Ganley, and Caroline Mohammed, "Induced Resistance to Pests and Pathogens in Trees," *New Phytologist* 185, no. 4 (2010): 893–908, https://doi.org/ 10.1111/j.1469-8137.2009.03127.x.

24. J. O'Reilly-Wapstra, Z. Holmes, and B. Potts, "The Genetics of Flammability in the Eucalypt Landscape," *Proceedings of the 2012 Ecological Society of Australia Meeting, 3–6 December 2012* (Melbourne, Australia, 2012), 1.

25. Lawrence Clark Powell, quoting Scottish author Norman Douglas, "Eucalyptus Trees & Lost Manuscripts," *California Librarian* 17, no. 1 (January 1956): 32. Powell was generally a huge fan of the tree.

26. McClatchie, *Eucalypts Cultivated in the United States*.

27. The best overviews of Köppen's work (really, though, the only ones) are J. M. Lewis, "Winds over the World Sea: Maury and Köppen," *Bulletin of the American Meteorological Society* 77, no. 5 (1996): 935–52, https://journals

.ametsoc.org/view/journals/bams/77/5/1520-0477_1996_077_0935 _wotwsm_2_0_co_2.xml; and more recently, R. B. Wille, "Colonizing the Free Atmosphere: Wladimir Köppen's 'Aerology,' the German Maritime Observatory, and the Emergence of a Trans-Imperial Network of Weather Balloons and Kites, 1873–1906," *History of Meteorology* 8 (2017): 95–123.

28. On insects and glyphosate: Daniel F. Q. Smith, Emma Camacho, Raviraj Thakur, Alexander J. Barron, Yuemei Dong, George Dimopoulos, Nichole A. Broderick, and Arturo Casadevall, "Glyphosate Inhibits Melanization and Increases Susceptibility to Infection in Insects," *PLOS Biology* 19, no. 5 (2021): e3001182, https://doi.org/10.1371/journal.pbio.3001182.

29. Travis Longcore, Catherine Rich, and Stuart B. Weiss, "Nearly All California Monarch Overwintering Groves Require Non-Native Trees," *California Fish and Wildlife* 106, no. 3 (2020): 220–25.

30. Bob Taylor, https://woodandsteel.taylorguitars.com/issue/2020-issue-3/ask-bob/ask-bob-eucalyptus-fretboards/.

31. "How a Didgeridoo Is Made—Myths and Facts," https://www.didjshop.com/shop1/HowDidgeridooIsMade-MythAndFacts.html.

32. Christopher B. Boyko, "The Endemic Marine Invertebrates of Easter Island: How Many Species and for How Long?," chap. 9 in J. Loret and J. T. Tanacredi, eds., *Easter Island* (Boston: Springer, 2003), 155–75, https://doi.org/10.1007/978-1-4615-0183-1_10.

33. List of countries to which *E. globulus* was exported: Brad M. Potts, René E. Vaillancourt, G. J. Jordan, G. W. Dutkowski, J. Da Costa e Silva, G. E. McKinnon, Dorothy A. Steane et al., "Exploration of the *Eucalyptus globulus* Gene Pool," in N. Borralho et al., *Eucalyptus in a Changing World* (Proceedings of IUFRO Conference, Aveiro, Portugal, October 11–15, 2004).

CHAPTER 9 · SLIPPERY SLOPES: THE OLIVE TREE AND ITS FRUIT AND OIL

1. This line was penned by Jefferson to his friend and mentor George Wythe, Aug. 13, 1787, discussing his plans to grow olive trees at Monticello.

2. Thomas Senty, Culinary Manager, McMurdo Station, Antarctica, personal communication with the author, January 29, 2021, via Terri Edillon, NSF Office of Polar Communications.

3. *Pacific Commercial Advertiser* (Honolulu, HI), March 6, 1880, 3; Maui trees

fruiting are noted in *Hawaiian Gazette* (Honolulu, HI), December 22, 1896, 3; Ostrich and Egg Farm trees: *Honolulu Advertiser*, November 19, 1891.

4. Fabrizia Lanza, *Olive: A Global History* (London: Reaktion Books, 2012), 18. Half million liters: Tom Mueller, *Extra Virginity: The Sublime and Scandalous World of Olive Oil* (New York: W. W. Norton, 2011), 62.

5. Some of these details are from Nancy Harmon Jenkins, *Virgin Territory: Exploring the World of Olive Oil* (New York: Houghton Mifflin Harcourt, 2015).

6. *Wine Advocate*, July 23, 2020, https://www.wine.com/product/massolino -barolo-2016/638379#.

7. Orietta Gianjorio, interview with the author, March 22, 2022.

8. Claude S. Weiller, "Olive Oil Primer: What is the Koroneiki Olive?," California Olive Ranch, www.californiaoliveranch.com/articles/olive-oil -primer-what-is-the-koroneiki-olive.

9. E. Karkoula, A. Skantzari, E. Melliou, and P. Magiatis, "Direct Measurement of Oleocanthal and Oleacein Levels in Olive Oil by Quantitative 1H NMR. Establishment of a New Index for the Characterization of Extra Virgin Olive Oils," *Journal of Agricultural and Food Chemistry* 60 (2012): 11696–703, https://doi.org/10.1021/jf3032765.

10. See https://calolive.org/our-story/from-the-farm-to-the-table/, as well as https://www.statista.com/statistics/215142/california-olive-production -since-1995/ and also http://www.aoopa.org/assets/uploads/pdfs/Chal lenges-and-Opportunities.pdf.

11. L. P. Da Silva and V. A. Mata, "Olive Harvest at Night Kills Birds," *Nature* 569 (2019): 192, https://doi.org/10.1038/d41586-019-01456-4.

12. Beatriz Gutiérrez-Miranda, Isabel Gallardo, Eleni Melliou, Isabel Cabero, Yolanda Álvarez, Prokopios Magiatis, Marita Hernández, and María Luisa Nieto, "Oleacein Attenuates the Pathogenesis of Experimental Autoimmune Encephalomyelitis through Both Antioxidant and Anti-Inflammatory Effects," *Antioxidants* 9, no. 11 (2020): 1161.

13. Natalie P. Bonvino, Julia Liang, Elizabeth D. Mccord, Elena Zafiris, Natalia Benetti, Nancy B. Ray, Andrew Hung, Dimitrios Boskou, and Tom C. Karagiannis, "Olivenet™: A Comprehensive Library of Compounds from *Olea europaea*," *Database* (2018), https://doi.org/10.1093/database/bay016. The Olivenet database can be found at https://mccordresearch.com.au/.

14. Marco Moriondo et al., "Olive Trees as Bio-indicators of Climate

Evolution in the Mediterranean Basin," *Global Ecology and Biogeography* 22, no. 7 (2013): 818–33; and Helder Fraga et al., "Mediterranean Olive Orchards under Climate Change: A Review of Future Impacts and Adaptation Strategies," *Agronomy* 11, no. 1 (2021): 56.

15. Elena Brunori et al., "The Hidden Land Conservation Benefits of Olive-Based (*Olea europaea* L.) Landscapes: An Agroforestry Investigation in the Southern Mediterranean (Calabria Region, Italy)," *Land Degradation & Development* 31, no. 7 (2020): 801–15. I've converted this article's slope percentages to degrees for more immediately graspable numbers. See also Mauro Agnoletti, ed., *Italian Historical Rural Landscapes* (Dordrecht, Netherlands: Springer, 2013), for broader context and useful details on olive growing.

16. Pierce's disease was named for its discoverer, Newton Pierce, a plant pathologist who lived on Orange Avenue, in the city of Orange in Southern California; grow where you're planted, I say.

17. PIRSA Fact Sheet on *X. fastidiosa*, June 2020, https://www.pir.sa.gov.au /__data/assets/pdf_file/0011/296183/Fact_Sheet_-_Xylella_fastidiosa _-_June_2020.pdf, retrieved February 8, 2021.

18. Erik Stokstad, "Italy's Olives under Siege," *Science* 348, no. 6235 (2015): 620, https://doi.org/10.1126/science.348.6235.620.

19. Ricardo Ayerza and Wayne Coates, "Supplemental Pollination: Increasing Olive (*Olea europaea*) Yields in Hot, Arid Environments," *Experimental Agriculture* 40, no. 4 (2004): 481–91.

20. Kent M. Daane and Marshall W. Johnson, "Olive Fruit Fly: Managing an Ancient Pest in Modern Times," *Annual Review of Entomology* 55 (2010): 151–69.

CHAPTER 10 · ELEPHANTINE: THE AFRICAN BAOBAB

1. Jean-Michel Leong Pock Tsy et al., "Chloroplast DNA Phylogeography Suggests a West African Centre of Origin for the Baobab, *Adansonia digitata* L. (Bombacoideae, Malvaceae)," *Molecular Ecology* 18, no. 8 (2009): 1711.

2. Richard Mabey, *The Cabaret of Plants: Forty Thousand Years of Plant Life and the Human Imagination* (New York: W. W. Norton, 2016).

3. Adrian Patrut et al., "Radiocarbon Dating of the Historic Livingstone Tree at Chiramba, Mozambique," *Studia Universitatis Babeş-bolyai*

Chemia 65, no. 3 (2020): 149–56, https://doi.org/10.24193/subbchem.2020.3.11.

4. David and Charles Livingstone, *Narrative of an Expedition to the Zambesi and Its Tributaries: And of the Discovery of the Lakes Shirwa and Nyassa. 1858–1864* (New York: Harper & Brothers, 1866), various pages.

5. Gerald E. Wickens, "The Baobab: Africa's Upside-Down Tree," *Kew Bulletin* (1982): 173–209.

6. Olga L. Kupika et al., "Impact of African Elephants on Baobab (*Adansonia digitata* L.) Population Structure in Northern Gonarezhou National Park, Zimbabwe," *Tropical Ecology* 55, no. 2 (2014): 159–66; see also Barthelemy Kassa et al., "Survey of *Loxodonta africana* (Elephantidae)–caused bark injury on *Adansonia digitata* (Malavaceae) within Pendjari Biosphere Reserve, Benin," *African Journal of Ecology* 52, no. 4 (2014): 385–94.

7. Gerald E. Wickens, *The Baobabs: Pachycauls of Africa, Madagascar and Australia* (Berlin: Springer Science & Business Media, 2008), 204ff.; see also Duane E. Ullrey, Susan D. Crissey, and Harold F. Hintz, *Elephants: Nutrition and Dietary Husbandry* (East Lansing, MI: Nutrition Advisory Group, 1997).

8. Nicola Jones, "Carbon Dating, the Archaeological Workhorse, Is Getting a Major Reboot," *Nature*, May 19, 2020, https://www.nature.com/articles/d41586-020-01499-y.

9. A. Patrut, D. H. Mayne, K. F. Von Reden, D. A. Lowy, R. V. Pelt, A. P. McNichol, M. L. Roberts, and D. Margineanu, "Fire History of a Giant African Baobab Evinced by Radiocarbon Dating," *Radiocarbon* 52, no. 2 (2010): 717–26, https://doi.org/10.1017/s0033822200045732.

10. A. Patrut et al., "The Demise of the Largest and Oldest African Baobabs," *Nature Plants* 4, no. 7 (2018): 423–26.

11. W. J. Sydeman, M. García-Reyes, David S. Schoeman, R. R. Rykaczewski, S. A. Thompson, B. A. Black, and S. J. Bograd, "Climate Change and Wind Intensification in Coastal Upwelling Ecosystems," *Science* 345, no. 6192 (2014): 77–80.

12. A. Patrut et al., "Fire History of a Giant African Baobab Evinced by Radiocarbon Dating," https://doi.org/10.1017/s0033822200045732. See also Aida Cuni Sanchez, Patrick E. Osborne, and Nazmul Haq, "Climate Change and the African Baobab (*Adansonia digitata* L.): The Need for Better Conservation Strategies," *African Journal of Ecology* 49, no. 2 (2011): 234–45, https://doi.org/10.1016/j.nimb.2012.04.025.

13. M. Fenner, "Some Measurements on the Water Relations of Baobab Trees," *Biotropica* 12 (1980): 207, https://doi.org/10.2307/2387972; Saharah Moon Chapotin, Juvet H. Razanameharizaka, and N. Michele Holbrook, "A Biomechanical Perspective on the Role of Large Stem Volume and High Water Content in Baobab Trees (*Adansonia* spp.; Bombacaceae)," *American Journal of Botany* 93, no. 9 (2006): 1251–64.

14. A. E. Assogbadjo et al., "Patterns of Genetic and Morphometric Diversity in Baobab (*Adansonia digitata*) Populations across Different Climatic Zones of Benin (West Africa)," *Annals of Botany* 97, no. 5 (2006): 819–30, https://doi.org/10.1093/aob/mcl043.

15. Number of flowers opening: Peter J. Taylor, Catherine Vise, Macy A. Krishnamoorthy, Tigga Kingston, and Sarah Venter, "Citizen Science Confirms the Rarity of Fruit Bat Pollination of Baobab (*Adansonia digitata*) Flowers in Southern Africa," *Diversity* 12, no. 3 (2020): 106; and David A. Baum, "The Comparative Pollination and Floral Biology of Baobabs (*Adansonia*-Bombacaceae)," *Annals of the Missouri Botanical Garden* (1995): 322–48.

16. Rupert Watson, *The African Baobab* (Cape Town: Penguin Random House South Africa, 2014).

17. T. A. Vaughan, "Nocturnal Behavior of the African False Vampire Bat (*Cardioderma cor*)," *Journal of Mammalogy* 57, no. 2 (1976): 227–48, https://doi.org/10.2307/1379685. See also M. Sidibe and J. T. Williams, "Pollination," sec. 2.2.2, in *Baobab*, Adansonia digitata *L*. (Southampton, UK: International Centre for Underutilised Crops, 2002).

18. Michael Smotherman, Mirjam Knörnschild, Grace Smarsh, and Kirsten Bohn, "The Origins and Diversity of Bat Songs," *Journal of Comparative Physiology A* 202, no. 8 (2016): 535–54. See also Michael A. Farries, "The Avian Song System in Comparative Perspective," *Annals of the New York Academy of Sciences* 1016, no. 1 (2004): 61–76, https://doi.org/10.1196/annals.1298.007.

19. Peter Matthiessen, *The Tree Where Man Was Born* (New York: E. P. Dutton, 1972), 294.

20. M. Sidibe and J. T. Williams, "Vernacular Names of Baobab," sec. 1.3, in *Baobab*, Adansonia digitata *L*., 11–12.

21. Wickens, "The Baobab: Africa's Upside-Down Tree," 188; this article was later superseded by Wickens's 2008 book on baobabs, which covers the other species in the genus.

22. Jens Gebauer et al., "Africa's Wooden Elephant: The Baobab Tree (*Adansonia*

digitata L.) in Sudan and Kenya: A Review," *Genetic Resources and Crop Evolution* 63, no. 3 (2016): 377–99.

23. "MICAIA Foundation," https://www.devex.com/organizations/micaia-foundation-67411; and "About MICAIA," https://micaia.org/about-us/.

24. Boris Urban, Stephanie Althea Townsend, and Amanda Bowen, "DEV Mozambique: Food Security through Innovative Social Enterprise Development," *Emerald Emerging Markets Case Studies* 10, no. 2 (2020), https://doi.org/10.1108/EEMCS-02-2020-0042.

25. Julian Quan, Lora Forsythe, and June Po, "Advancing Women's Position by Recognizing and Strengthening Customary Land Rights: Lessons from Community-Based Land Interventions in Mozambique," *Land Governance and Gender: The Tenure-Gender Nexus in Land Management and Land Policy* (2022): 65–79; and A. Kingman, "Safeguarding the Livelihoods of Women Baobab Harvesters in Mozambique through Improved Land and Natural Resources Governance," *Land Policy Bulletin*, LEGEND 10 (2018): 2–3.

26. The best scrutiny of the IUCN in the twenty-first century has been via the following works: Martin Holdgate, *The Green Web: A Union for World Conservation* (New York: Routledge, 2014); Medani P. Bhandari, *GREEN WEB-II: Standards and Perspectives from the IUCN* (Gistrup, Denmark: River Publishers, 2018); and a number of articles by the Australian writer and ecologist Lucie Bland. See also the excellent work by A. Rodrigues et al., "The Value of the IUCN Red List for Conservation," *Trends in Ecology & Evolution* 21, no. 2 (2006): 71–76, https://doi.org/10.1016/j.tree.2005.10.010.

27. Bruno R. Ribeiro et al., "Issues with Species Occurrence Data and Their Impact on Extinction Risk Assessments," *Biological Conservation* 273 (2022): 109674.

28. Some of this discussion comes from G. E. Wickens's excellent, synthetic, and authoritative, although dated, article, "The Baobab: Africa's Upside-Down Tree," *Kew Bulletin* 27, no. 2 (1982): 173–209. This was the first work to organize and summarize all of the information then known about *Adansonia digitata*.

29. Lucie M. Bland et al., "Impacts of the IUCN Red List of Ecosystems on Conservation Policy and Practice," *Conservation Letters* 12, no. 5 (2019): https://doi.org/10.1111/conl.12666.

30. Matthiessen, *The Tree Where Man Was Born*, 174.

CHAPTER 11 · WATERLOGGED: THE BALD CYPRESS AND THE WONDERS OF WETLANDS

1. Geoffrey C. Denny and Michael A. Arnold, "Taxonomy and Nomenclature of Baldcypress, Pondcypress, and Montezuma Cypress: One, Two, or Three Species?," *HortTechnology* 17, no. 1 (2007): 125–27.

2. Kristine L. Delong et al., "Late Pleistocene Baldcypress (*Taxodium distichum*) Forest Deposit on the Continental Shelf of the Northern Gulf of Mexico," *Boreas* 50, no. 3 (2021): 871–92.

3. Olivia Barfield, "Inoculation of Baldcypress with Salt-Tolerant Endophytes" (Louisiana Sea Grant College Program, Tulane University, 2021), https://repository.library.noaa.gov/view/noaa/39754; and F. Saadawy, M. Bahnasy, and H. El-Feky, "Improving Tolerability of *Taxodium distichum* Seedlings to Water Salinity and Irrigation Water Deficiency. II: Effect of Salicylic Acid on Salinity Stress," *Scientific Journal of Flowers and Ornamental Plants* 6, no. 1 (2019): 69–80, https://doi.org/10.21608/sjfop.2019.48685.

4. Rutherford Pratt, *The Great American Forest* (Englewood Cliffs, NJ: Prentice-Hall, 1971).

5. New ground in this area has been broken by George K. Rogers, "Bald Cypress Knees, *Taxodium distichum* (Cupressaceae): An Anatomical Study, with Functional Implications," *Flora* 278 (2021): 151788, https://doi.org/10.1016/j.flora.2021.151788.

6. George Brown Goode, *The Fisheries and Fishery Industries of the United States* (Washington, DC: Government Printing Office, 1884), 147.

7. Jonathan Rosen, *The Life of the Skies* (New York: Macmillan, 2008), 25.

8. David Thompson, personal communications with the author, October 28, 2021, and January 9, 2022.

9. Kerry Cawse-Nicholson, personal communications with the author, October 28, 2021, and January 21, 2022.

10. "Mitigating Climate Change through Coastal Conservation," Blue Carbon Initiative, https://www.thebluecarboninitiative.org.

11. "NOAA's Largest Wetlands Restoration Project Underway in Louisiana," April 20, 2022, https://www.fisheries.noaa.gov/feature-story/noaas-largest-wetland-restoration-project-underway-louisiana.

12. Kevin D. Kroeger et al., "Restoring Tides to Reduce Methane Emissions in Impounded Wetlands: A New and Potent Blue Carbon Climate Change

Intervention," *Scientific Reports* 7, no. 1 (2017), https://doi.org/10.1038/s41598-017-12138-4.

13. Henry David Thoreau, "Walking," *Atlantic Monthly*, June 1862, 666.

CHAPTER 12 · TALL STORIES: THE MIGHTY CEIBA TREE

1. A. Chavez Michaelsen, L. Huamani Briceño, H. Vilchez Baldeon et al., "The Effects of Climate Change Variability on Rural Livelihoods in Madre de Dios, Peru," *Regional Environmental Change* 20, no. 70 (2020), https://doi.org/10.1007/s10113-020-01649-y.

2. Paulo Brando, "Tree Height Matters," *Nature Geoscience* 11, no. 6 (June 2018): 390–91.

3. Everton B. P. Miranda et al., "Species Distribution Modeling Reveals Strongholds and Potential Reintroduction Areas for the World's Largest Eagle," *PLOS ONE* 14, no. 5 (2019): e0216323, https://doi.org/10.1371/journal.pone.0216323.

4. Catrin Einhorn, "Alarming Levels of Mercury Are Found in Old Growth Amazon Forest," *New York Times*, January 28, 2022; and Jacqueline Gerson et al., "Amazon Forests Capture High Levels of Atmospheric Mercury Pollution from Artisanal Gold Mining," *Nature Communications* 13, no. 559 (2022), https://doi.org/10.1038/s41467-022-27997-3.

5. A. H. Gentry, "Tree Species Richness of Upper Amazonian Forests," *Proceedings of the National Academy of Sciences* 85, no. 1 (1988): 156–59, https://doi.org/ 10.1073/pnas.85.1.156.

INDEX

ABOUT THE AUTHOR

DANIEL LEWIS is the Dibner Senior Curator for the History of Science and Technology at The Huntington Library, Art Museum, and Botanical Gardens in Southern California. He is also a writer, college professor, and environmental historian.